THE
NEW
WALES

THE
NEW
WALES

EDITED BY DAVID COLE

UNIVERSITY OF WALES PRESS
1990

© The contributors, 1990

British Library Cataloguing in Publication Data
The New Wales
  1. Wales
  I. Cole, David, *1928–*
  942.90858
  ISBN 0–7083–1087–7

Design by Design Principle, Cardiff
Typeset by BP Integraphics, Bath
Printed at Bookcraft, Midsomer Norton, Great Britain

CONTENTS

INTRODUCTION

Nations making history are somewhat like runners in a long-distance race, moving at different paces at different stages. Although our little country has a long history it has only once taken the lead – in the helter-skelter burst of the early Industrial Revolution when we boasted the biggest iron and coal output in the world. That period transformed a beautiful pastoral environment. In the valleys of the south and the slate-quarrying districts of the north the extraction of money-making materials brutalized the country-side. It had the effect of providing most of the population with higher earnings, but a lower quality of life.

The pattern of reliance upon heavy industry affected social conditions, political attitudes, characteristics of fortitude and even culture. Out of all this there also emerged a stereotype of the Welsh personality and environment which people in the rest of Great Britain could recognize instantly. It was ironic that although the caricature was pejorative, even libellous, we Welsh did little to correct it. Indeed, perversely, we even seem sometimes to have added colour to the intellectual clichés.

In the past few decades there has been a variation of tempo in our history-making and this is a propitious time to begin correcting some of the false impressions. Since the War, and particularly in the past twenty-five years, Wales has changed significantly, coping with a fundamental alteration of its industrial and social base in a manner which has not only given it strength but a renewal of self-confidence.

This book is not an attempt to rewrite our modern history and, certainly, it cannot take on the responsibility of erasing all the prevalent misconceptions. It aspires to be no more than a collection of synoptic views about aspects of life in the Principality creating a colourful kaleidoscope rather than a portrait. It covers the main facets of Welsh life with the notable exception of politics, which ebbs and flows so dramatically that it is difficult to give an accurate and sustainable picture that will not be out of date within a short period of time. A country that produced Lloyd George and Aneurin Bevan, nurtured a modern Prime Minister, James Callaghan (now Lord Callaghan of Cardiff) and a Speaker of the House of Commons, George Thomas (now Viscount Tonypandy), and is home to two of the leaders of the Labour party in the 1980s – Michael Foot and Neil Kinnock – deserves, and receives, the coverage of volumes rather than a single chapter.

There is not, either, a special section for the language, but its importance in the whole national ethos emerges clearly through the other commentaries. That the language is thematic to our art, culture and social attitudes is evidence of its intrinsic importance. It also emerges from several of the contributions that much of the strength of Wales lies in its community structure and the sense of loyalty of its people to concepts of place and distinctiveness. In this the language plays a special part which has become important in modern aspects of life such as television, radio, pop music and drama as much as in the traditional written and oratorical traditions. This is encouragement for the future of our native tongue, adding a current relevance to the increased attention which is being applied at all levels of education from primary schools to postgraduate studies.

There are some gloomy forecasts extrapolated from the decline in the use of Welsh in the 'heartlands' and even predictions of the language's demise in twenty years. It can be argued that statistics may be used to prove almost anything and that the growth and expansion of the native tongue in the densely populated urban areas is already significant and will receive a fillip through the national curriculum with Welsh becoming a core subject in many schools and a foundation subject in the remainder. There is a growing sympathy in every stratum of society to the proseletysing of common use of the language. It would be a major disservice if zealots should turn that sympathy to antipathy. Rather should we endorse and acclaim the positive moves which are taking place and endeavour to achieve our unity in accentuating the positive and eliminating all vestige of snobbery about the use of the language. It would not, then, be far-fetched to hope that Wales could become a truly bilingual nation in the next century.

Having said that we wish to rectify some of the stereotyped views it is necessary to emphasize that the new Wales is not an abandonment of the old. It is not a negation of esteem for our heritage but a recognition of progress. What the Principality was a generation ago was not, in most respects, as admirable as it is today, or what it will be at the end of the century. There is, in fact, a benign paradox about Wales as it approaches the millenium. It is a phenomenon which most people would be pleased to experience in their own lives – that as the country ages it gives the appearance of growing younger. Certainly the landscape is becoming greener and many of the vivid scars of the past 200 years have been treated so that they have healed.

There is now an effectiveness about many aspects of life in the Principality that was lacking until the past couple of decades. It is not a matter of assertiveness but, rather, of having the channels to transmit pressure and aspiration and in return receive clear indications of the standards that are required to make the 'powers that be' susceptible to persuasion. Perhaps it is not a coincidence that Wales has had a Secretary of State with a seat in the Cabinet since 1964 – a period of time when it has been able to organize resources to match its resilience in meeting the biggest challenge in its history. To have been capable to confront and overcome the consequences of the near extinction of the coal industry and the substantial diminution of the steel and tin-plate industry and to emerge from such a trial in a healthier state than formerly is an estimable achievement.

The Welsh Office has created, and beneficially used, a series of organizations – the Welsh Development Agency, the Development Board for Rural Wales, Wales Tourist Board, Land Authority for Wales and recently Cardiff Bay Corporation. The Welsh Development Agency was created by a Labour government fifteen years ago, and after an initial period of scepticism, enthusiastically promoted by a Conservative administration.

These 'quangos' have been influential instruments for focusing on special needs in the Principality and for developing plans to implement official policy. By concentrating on specific areas of activity they have also been able to initiate investigations of pertinent issues to a more profound level than otherwise would have been the case. Organizations such as the Welsh Development Agency have a role somewhere between being an arm of government and a commercial operation. Thus the alliance of public funding and a degree of freedom to apply commercial criteria ensure that the application of resources is directed to identified opportunities as well as needs and, therefore, can make measurable progress.

Altogether there has been an advance on a broad front in Wales over the past generation. Apart from its industrial transformation there has been a spread of the utility of skills, a significant improvement in the infrastructure, higher standards of housing, major reclamation of land, a wider provision of recreational amenities, an extension of the access to the performing arts and an elevation of cultural standards. Part of this progress is attributable to the availability of greater resources from government and the growing awareness by industrial and commercial enterprises that they have a social obligation to contribute to the well-being of the communities in which they operate or from which they derive their wealth. The other element is that the public is now much better organized to articulate its desires and the past generation might be termed the era of the pressure group.

Public pressure, however, has not been confined to making demands. There has been a growth of constructive self-help efforts. The voluntary movement in Wales has broadened and deepened to a heartening extent, involving people of all social backgrounds and a wide range of interests. This voluntary activity acts like a yeast in the community and the fermentation process leads to yet greater endeavours and the need for more financial support. So fund-raising has become almost an art form and, fortunately, the public response has been increasingly generous.

As has been remarked frequently a noticeable change has come about in the face of Wales. The mining valleys and villages of the south will recognize the lines from Isaiah, 'every valley shall be exalted and the rough places made plain' if only through singing the words in Handel's *Messiah*. Now in Gwent and the Glamorgans the words are being made fact. The dereliction of the Valleys was not just a scar on the landscape but over a period of two centuries became a psychological incubus that affected the quality of life. The progressive removal of the scars and the reclamation of land for beneficial uses has lightened the gloom and given hope of better things in the future. Much has been achieved already but there are important plans to take the process further forward. Having learnt a terrible lesson there will be an assurance that industry will not be permitted in the future to repeat the despoliation of the past.

If the present level of land reclamation continues the task will be completed before the end of the decade. It is a great achievement that two centuries of topographical desecration should be made good in less than a generation. Not only is this process proving an aesthetic boon but there are great social and economic advantages. In the narrow valleys of the south there is a shortage of building land and the reclamation programme has provided opportunities to erect factories and social amenities as well as the new housing stock which is so urgently needed.

If Wales has made progress on a broad front over the past twenty-five years, the advance has not been uniform and success not unalloyed. There are major problems confronting both the authorities and the people. One of them is to ensure that the inward migration of people with entirely different backgrounds can be integrated into Welsh life and contribute to the intellectual as well as the industrial regeneration of the country.

Certainly management and labour have learned many lessons during the transition from an economy predominantly based upon a few major heavy industries – coal, steel, tin plate – to one which is multi-faceted covering services and cybernetics as well as manufacturing. The process has been a significant contributory factor in achieving a fine record of inward investment while in itself benefiting from the stimulus of the attitudes of foreign companies. The adversarial attitude of 'them and us' has been mitigated substantially and the industrial culture has improved as the attitudes and influences of companies from Japan, Germany and the United States have put down roots in the Principality. Their management approach is different from the British tradition and their expectations are commensurately higher. Two important factors have been the unions' realization of a need for change that would let management help the work-force to improve productivity, earnings and job satisfaction and, on the other hand, management's greater appreciation of the value of the contribution of the work-force. The result has been a more progressive understanding of how to tackle problems and make the most of opportunities. An atmosphere of enterprise and co-operation has been created which is attractive to companies from other countries who are looking for new locations in which to develop.

The ability to react positively to overcome adversity has been demonstrated in the north as much as the south. In the later 1970s and early 1980s the north-east corner of Wales suffered a series of economic blows with the closure of Shotton steel works, costing 8,000 jobs, the run down of the textiles and mining industries and the loss of 650 jobs at the Firestone Tyre plant. This area, however, has now been transformed. Currently there are more than 100 companies located at Deeside Industrial Park, and another 100 at the Wrexham estate between them employing more than 10,000 people. Foreign investment has been attracted from America, the Far East and Europe so that with the development of indigenous companies there is now a wide range of diverse industries from paper making, optical fibres, distribution of frozen foods, aircraft manufacturing and electronics to optical glass, diamond cutting, furniture and aluminium smelting. Furthermore the recent £500 million improvement to the A55 creates better access to north Wales and enhances the attraction of the region for further development.

The good fortune attending the efforts to attract inward investment has had further benefits in stimulating service industries for the big plants and a more entrepreneurial attitude among smaller companies. Indeed, whereas Wales previously had been thought, erroneously, not to produce risk-taking businessmen but rather practitioners in law, medicine, education and religion it now stands at the top of the league of regions in Britain for the development of smaller new enterprises.

There is, of course, a problem in the further success of inward investment. Japanese, German and American companies own an increasing proportion of the capital base of Welsh manufacturing industry. From one point of view it is excellent for creating employment, introducing new skills, raising earning power and import substitution, but might it smother the growth of indigenous companies? The issue is one which requires careful analysis and forecasting of future consequences.

Another problem is how a geographically small nation assimilates people from an alien culture, making them feel welcome and bestowing on them the benefits of the country and its personality as well as deriving from them the obvious advantages which they bring. The last major influx was during the Industrial Revolution. Now there are the executives and workers who are brought by the relocation of their companies and a considerable weight of visitors who come as the result of the development of the tourist industry. Fortunately the population at large eschews insularity and is intent on absorbing the benefits brought by the incomers in a way which will strengthen the indigenous culture and generally improve the quality of life.

The natural advantages of Wales – its topography and coastline – have been used in the past generation for the first time as an asset to enhance the economic circumstances of its people. It is remarkable to recognize that by the beginning of the 1990s tourism has grown so much that it employs more people than any other industry.

So as a result of good performance in commercial inward investment and the development of a leisure and vacation industry the country is having to learn to be on terms with a significant proportion of foreign guests. Because of the nineteenth-century and early twentieth-century influences of religion and liberal/socialist politics Wales has always believed that it embraced 'internationalism' and the 'brotherhood of man'. Applying its internationalism within its own boundaries is a new test. It could be one of the fundamental challenges with which the people of the Principality will have to contend in the next decade.

Concurrent with this dilemma will be the requirement for the institutions of our society – the University, political parties, industrial and cultural organizations – to be outward looking. Not only will Wales's role in Britain be under debate but its relationship with an enlarged democratic Europe will be an issue of profound significance.

It is now a hoary cliché that there has been more change in the condition of man in this century than in the whole period back to the birth of Christ. Wales is participating in that rapid evolution but, as this book shows, it has special elements of transformation which, while stimulating progress, intensify the focus on the inhabitants of a distinctive and small nation. At the core of this problem is the preservation of a Welsh culture and it is gratifying that there are aspects of it which are developing in response to actions taken in the past generation. It will be salutary to observe whether in the next generation there will be a strengthening and expansion of the language – an important aspect of the culture – as a result of steps which have been taken in past years.

Of course, this is only one of the big challenges which have to be confronted as we move toward the millenium. Solutions still need to be found to the problems of housing, low pay, and education. For instance, although more people own their homes and live in better accommodation than hitherto, there remain a large number of houses which date from the last century. Many of them are stone built in terraces in narrow streets and offer little scope for modernization. There is a need to replace them in an aesthetically and socially acceptable way. Domestic architectural standards between 1930 and 1970 were poor but since then they have become more creative, efficient and visually interesting. It is important that if local authority house building is resumed there should be much more concern about environmental and amenity quality.

Wales is currently embarked upon three of the most interesting social enterprises in Europe – the Cardiff Bay Development, the Valleys Initiative and the North Wales Initiative. Apart from the obvious economic implications of these ventures they will have a considerable effect on the future quality of life in Wales. If there is an imaginative and diligent application of high standards these schemes will enrich the lives not only of the people within their areas but of the whole nation by setting examples of excellence.

It is inevitable that the rehousing of so many people – especially within the confines of the Valleys – will use more land than the present buildings. There is a great responsibility imposed on local authorities and domestic and industrial developers to preserve our landscape as an enriching setting for our townscape. The countryside is a finite resource which must not be plundered for factory or housing schemes as it was in the last century. And the land in general needs maintenance; the reclamation and regeneration process which has been so successful in the past decade should continue so that land is 'recycled' and put to ever more beneficial uses. The difference between our former situation and now is that in the 1990s we are both philosophically and technically attuned to achieve the objective.

In recent years the creation of a new industrial structure in Wales, accompanied by an increase in the female work-force, has reduced the average level of earnings relative to other parts of the UK. That should begin to be rectified in the coming years as employment grows in the automotive, electronic and financial services sectors.

An aspect of earning power, whether male or female, is educational attainment. There is a sad irony in the fact that in the Valleys conurbation, where once the grammar schools achieved high educational and behavioural standards, the attainment of school-leavers is now far from impressive.

Yet it is abundantly evident that, in the future, commercial concerns will be competing with each other for the services of the educationally qualified and vocationally trained among the young generation. Those without any scholastic or craft attainment will be the bulk of the unemployed and, increasingly, industry will be seeking ways of substituting mechanical means for unskilled human labour. The employed will earn more while, relatively, the out of work will be worse off. A considerable effort, therefore, has to be made to improve educational and training achievement, especially in areas which previously had long been dependent on heavy manufacturing industry.

Changes have taken place already at the level of higher education and the various institutions of the University of Wales are finding ways of co-operating with industry and commerce. The money that is provided for the colleges for research and development in this way is valuable; in an age of high technology the benefit to business of this intellectual resource will become more and more apparent. Japan is one of the three leading industrial nations in the world and much of its success – especially in innovative enterprise – is due to an extensive and disciplined collaboration between industry and academia. The Welsh economy will advance through emulating the co-operative spirit which motivates this Japanese partnership. Maybe the influx of Japanese firms to the Principality will help encourage the process.

There are tangible and quantitative solutions to most of the challenges facing Wales as it approaches a new century but the one which is pre-eminent is spiritual. Like most Western nations the country is experiencing a sharp decline in religious observance. Here, however, the effects are most striking – so many Nonconformist chapels empty and apparently abandoned, so many churches falling into disrepair. Wales was once called 'the country of the Book' – the Book being the Bible – but today for many people the Book is opened only on the great occasions of weddings, funerals and christenings. The one section of the Christian faith where membership is growing is the Roman Catholic, but the Nonconformist congregations have dwindled alarmingly. This is a problem which is not specifically Welsh, yet it is one of poignant relevance in the history of Wales.

But to return to matters temporal: the glimpses of the Principality today in the various chapters of this volume reveal growing aspirations springing from growing accomplishment. A nation's special identity is labelled most easily in the modern world by its achievements in the media, the arts and sport. In all these spheres there is a new vigour and higher standards. Environmentalism, too, is a universal concern but the practical benefits of reclamation and conservation are more evident in Wales than in any part of the British Isles. Furthermore, there is a determination to meet the remaining challenges and, through imaginative planning and architecture, to create a heritage for the twenty-first century that will be much better than that left us by our forebears. In the past generation the concatenation of advantageous and disadvantageous circumstances has provoked and stimulated endeavours which, in general, have led to the genesis of a new Wales. We are on the threshold of a period of rapid evolution in which the means of communication by land, through new roads and bridges; by air, through an international terminal, and by instantaneous electronic information transfer will make it impossible for a country placed as ours is to stay apart from the European tide of events, even if we wanted to. The only viable option is to take advantage of the current and ensure that we reach the van of the mainstream.

Wales has found a dynamic which, ironically, seems to be more observable to foreign onlookers than to the natives, even though there is a general sense of revival. What has been achieved in the 1970s and 1980s has broadened the horizons of confidence and expectations and presages an exciting future. Consequently, most of the words in this book have an accent of optimism.

INDUSTRY

FROM CRADLE TO REINCARNATION

ALLEN WILLIAMS

IT is impossible to look at the post-War economy of Wales, or indeed the last twenty-five years, without considering briefly what went before. The consequences of industrial decisions made more than 150 years ago still affect the economic considerations of today and it is fitting that we attempt to learn the lessons, if only to make new mistakes not old ones. It is right also, as we enter the last decade of this century of momentous social and economic change, that we review the evolved Welsh industry and consider the future of this economy which, as Professor Glanmor Williams put it, acted as 'The cradle of the world's industrial civilization'.

The child of this cradle was to repay its birth with many years of economic progress and employment, but was ultimately to wreak a callous and cruel industrial havoc. The inheritance proved to be structural instability and environmental despoliation in such a huge and concentrated form that the death throes of this once dynamic economy lasted more than seventy-five years.

The phenomenal growth of the Welsh economy was evident by the mid nineteenth century, and in 1857 Wales was lit by the fires of 173 iron furnaces in full blast at fifty-five different works, a record never again achieved. In that year the combined output of these furnaces was more than a million tons of pig-iron, over a quarter of the United Kingdom's total production, and some 409 collieries were wresting in excess of 13.7 million tons of coal from the earth.

During the next sixty years, with only minor cyclical fluctuations, the industrialization process raced to maturity. Indeed maturity came much quicker than many expected reaching a nineteenth-century peak production of 1.046 million tons of pig-iron in 1871. That record was not to be breached until 1939 with the headlong rush into the Second World War. Indeed, output dropped by 20 per cent between 1871 and 1914.

Coal, however, took much longer to achieve its pinnacle of 60 million tons in 1913. Of this record production more than 3.5 million tons was lifted from north Wales collieries. As an employer coal was supreme. There were more than 250,000 miners in 1914, including a significant 7 per cent (16,257) employed in north Wales pits. There was, however, a cruel price in this search for black energy. In the record-breaking year of 1913, more than 47 per cent of all UK mining fatalities occurred in Welsh pits as 804 miners were killed. Although this was the highest annual number of deaths, the sixty-two years from 1853 to 1914 saw a total of 16,847 miners die, an average of 271 each year.

The primary extractive and manufacturing industries of iron and coal were not the only players in the nineteenth-century industrializ-ation of Wales as lead, copper, zinc, gold, silver and slate were all significant contributors. Slate, concentrated in the north, had reached its peak output of over 500,000 tons and 26,970 employees by 1898. By 1914 output had decreased by 72 per cent and, although produc-tion rallied slightly in the 1930s, the industry had had its day.

Of minor interest to the economic story, but an example of the mineral wealth of Wales, is that 19,655 ounces of gold were mined in 1904, although by 1915 this had fallen to 1,256 ounces and thereafter all but disappeared. The other precious mineral, silver, saw its peak production in 1870 when 160,000 ounces were mined. By 1915 out-put was down to just over 35,000 ounces. After the First World War the industry fell away almost completely.

While the Great War is often cited as the turning-point, after which Britain's industrial growth entered what Professor Pigou euphemis-tically termed the doldrums, the seeds of the inter-war decline were sown as early as 1890. By that year the United States had already outstripped the United Kingdom in the production of steel and pro-duction and consumption of pig-iron. By 1905 Germany also had overtaken the United Kingdom in the iron and steel markets. The United States took the prime position amongst the coal-producing nations by 1900 and by 1913 was mining more than twice the United Kingdom output.

The years immediately following the First World War saw a con-tinuation of the prosperity experienced up until 1913, but it was based unsoundly on reconstruction and rebuilding. By 1922 the first signs of profound recession were evident in Wales with an unemploy-ment rate of more than 7 per cent. Within ten years this figure was to multiply five times to a catastrophic 36.8 per cent.

The inter-war recession exposed the weaknesses of the Welsh economy as cleanly as a surgeon's scalpel. The increasingly peripheral nature of the staple Welsh industries, with their over-specialization and concentration on primary production at the almost total expense of finished products, was a fundamental flaw highlighted by shrink-ing export markets.

In the 1920s foreign demand reduced dramatically. The iron and steel industry had been expanded during the Great War with little reference to cost efficiency and was the first to suffer in the early 1920s as it found itself with too much capacity and uncompetitive prices in both the home and world markets. In 1920 steel production in Wales totalled 1.8 million tons but by 1927 some 30 per cent of the steel used in the Welsh tin-plate industry was imported from Belgium.

While the output of 1920 was slightly exceeded towards the end of the decade, fifteen years later the output matched almost exactly the 1920 figure. Such was this period of stagnation.

Pig-iron production fluctuated considerably throughout the inter-war years and the 1920 south Wales production figure of 692,000 tons had fallen by 60 per cent one year later. This rose to 665,000 tons in 1938 but increased by 90 per cent to more than 1.2 million tons during the 1939 armaments race. While iron and steel suffered the rigours of international competition, the coal industry was devastated, not only by competition but also by new forms of energy as the merchant navy fleets of the world took to the cleaner more efficient oil. In the seventeen years from 1922 to 1939 coal output in Wales plunged by 10 million tons and employment in the industry was reduced by 123,000 miners.

Wales plumbed the depths of recession in 1932 with 244,579 (39.9 per cent) people unemployed in August and an average for the year of 227,000 (36.8 per cent). The unsurprising result was mobility of labour on a massive scale. The decade to 1931 saw a net migration of almost 277,000 people. Glamorgan and Monmouthshire were the major contributors, with most major towns in north Wales holding or increasing their populations. This exodus of biblical proportions continued in the next two decades as a further 181,000 Welsh unemployed sought greener pastures. Not even natural increase could maintain Welsh population levels and there was a decrease in overall population of 169,000 people from 1921 to mid 1939. Even after 1932 unemployment only began to improve at a snail's pace and the unsavoury rush into arms for the Second World War merely reduced unemployment in Wales to 14.3 per cent.

Thus two decades of stagnation, doldrums, recession and depression came to an end on the stage of international politics with Wales, as H. V. Moreton put in his *Search for Wales*, 'hoping against hope that the tide would turn'. The only light on the horizon for Wales was the realization by government that positive management of the regional economies was vital to the future health of the United Kingdom economy as a whole and the subsequent tentative steps taken in the 1930s towards implementing regional policy.

Before 1934 it had been policy to encourage labour mobility, particularly migration from areas of high unemployment to more prosperous regions. In 1934 the Special Areas (Development and Improvement) Act endeavoured to provide employment opportunities in depressed areas. The new approach was 'bringing work to the workers'. As early as 1932 Welsh local authorities, chambers of commerce and other interested bodies were meeting to consider some form of concerted action to bring the 'diversification gospel' of Sir Frederick Rees and Professor Marquand to reality. The first tangible evidence of this new direction in Wales was the formation of the South Wales and Monmouthshire Trading Estates Limited in June 1936. By December 1936 the first scheme for the development of a 272-acre Trading Estate at Treforest was approved with 147 acres to be developed immediately.

Although the end of the Second World War saw Wales with a more modern economy, and no longer totally reliant on staple industries, diversification was still only embryonic. The progress toward a more modern economy in the next forty years, with diversification as its watchword, was to prove a not unsuccessful justification of regional policy. Yet it also proved to be fundamentally flawed and not equal to the final decline of coal and restructuring of the steel industry.

In 1963 a leader in *The Times* stated that: 'The redevelopment of South Wales has been one of the great success stories of the past 30 years.' The progress achieved by 1963 in establishing new industries and, indeed, the almost stable employment scene in Wales seemed almost incontrovertible evidence supporting this view. From the end of 1945, when it stood at 9 per cent, unemployment rose gradually to 12 per cent in March 1947 and to the agony of those who had suffered the 'hungry thirties' it must have been an all too familiar scene. However, the dole queues immediately began to decline month by month until by July 1955 only 1.5 per cent unemployment, more than twenty times less than 1932, existed in Wales. When Harold Macmillan said in July 1957, 'Let's be frank about it most of our people have never had it so good', it was said with some justification. He should have added – 'make the most of it'.

The basis for the prosperity of the 1950s and early 1960s lay not only in the tentative steps to diversification in the 1930s but in the war-time dispersal of strategic industries. Large ordinance factories created at Wrexham, Bridgend and Hirwaun, were later to become major industrial estates providing work-space for many thousands of new manufacturing jobs. Professor Brinley Thomas summed up the effect of the Second World War by saying, 'The war did three things which were to have an enduring effect on the Welsh Economy, it eliminated unemployment, the core of a potentially strong manufacturing sector was established and hitherto unknown employment opportunities for women were created.'

The necessities of war-time had broken down forever the traditional barrier to female employment in manufacturing. By 1966 women accounted for 32.6 per cent of total employment, fourteen years later it was 40 per cent, and in 1989 46 per cent of the work-force was female.

In the five years to 1944, it is estimated that some 65,000 jobs were created in chemical manufacturing in Wales and 37,000 in engineering. This dispersal of industry proved Wales's ability to support new manufacturing business and lent impetus to the policy of diversification.

Table 1
Index of changes in employment 1948–58 (1948 = 100)

		Wales	GB
1958 SIC	Total extractive	41.7	47.3
	Total manufacturing	131.6	108.6
	Total services	117.4	124.2
	TOTAL	105.6	110.9

Source: *Welsh Economic Trends*

Table 1 indicates clearly the continuing decline of the coal industry in the 1950s. More importantly, however, it shows the extraordinary improvement in the level of manufacturing jobs at a rate 23 per cent greater than the rest of Great Britain. The old dependence on staple industries was being broken down, and the profile of employment in Wales was being brought more into line with the rest of Britain.

This reprofiling was a deliberate and concerted act of regional policy with perhaps the major weapon being the Industrial Development Certificate. The IDC effectively forced companies to expand in a development area rather than in a location of their unfettered choice. Wales benefited greatly by being the closest development area to the main centres of natural growth in the UK – the south-east of England and the Midlands. The massive industrial/trading estates in north and south Wales provided the much-needed accommodation for this new industry. During the seventeen years from 1945 to 1962 almost 1,200 projects were approved for factory building, making 16.8 million square feet of space available in south Wales alone. One of the major instruments of regional policy in Wales, the south Wales and Monmouthshire Trading Estates Limited, by 1960 had created, or taken control of, factories employing more than 64,600 people and, regardless of its name, some 4,000 of these jobs were in north Wales.

In 1958–9 the threat of unemployment hit Wales once more. The percentage out of work rose to more than 4 per cent, the highest of the

Table 2

Estimated percentage distribution of employers
(Employed and Unemployed) Wales and GB 1939–1970

	1939	1945	1950	1955	1960	1965	1970
Agriculture, forestry and fishing	3.7	3.8	4.2	3.3	2.5	1.7	1.4
Mining and quarrying	26.3	19.4	14.7	14.2	11.7	9.1	5.9
Manufacturing	23.8	39.5	28.7	32.1	31.1	32.3	36.9
Construction	12.9	3.1	7.0	6.7	7.9	8.0	7.3
Gas, water and electricity	1.2	0.9	1.8	2.1	2.0	2.3	2.2
Services	32.1	33.3	43.5	42.0	44.7	46.4	45.8
TOTAL EMPLOYEES (000s)	696.2	669.2	919.1	945.4	963.6	1003.0	970.4
Male %	86	70	74	72	71	68	66
Female %	14	30	26	28	29	32	34
Unemployment %	18.5	9.0	3.7	1.8	2.7	2.6	4.0

Source: *Digest of Welsh Historical Statistics*

decade. Fortunately the downturn did not deepen, as it had thirty years previously, although by February 1965 unemployment reached 6 per cent, its highest level since June 1947.

It was during this cyclical downturn that many of the industries brought in during the decade after the War failed. Many of the plants were established to provide the much-needed extra capacity of major British companies to meet the post-War reconstruction demands and those of the newly prosperous families who had for so long existed on the poverty line. The new factories had little autonomy in management, being purely production branch plants which were the first and most obvious target for 'belt tightening' by their corporate owners when trade turned down. The critics of regional policy immediately seized on this situation and coined the phrase 'Branch Plant Economy'. This criticism remains with Wales to this day, regardless of the fact that businesses set up in the twenty years to 1965 provided more than 30 per cent of manufacturing jobs. Another twenty years on, in 1984, a further 55,000 jobs had been created and maintained by branch factories and businesses transferred into Wales after 1966.

The year 1966 was crucial in the economic development of the Principality as the Severn Bridge was opened, bringing south Wales into direct contact with the south-west of England and an hour closer to the south-east. The importance of the Severn Bridge and the development of the M4 cannot be overstated in changing Wales from 'a foreign country' to an integral part of the British economy. The second crossing of the Severn is now as vital as the first was nearly a generation ago.

The downturn of the late 1950s again called for regional action by the government. After some years of leniency a more rigorous attitude to the granting of Industrial Development Certificates was brought into operation again to direct the flow of industry to needy areas. In March 1963 the Minister of State for Welsh Affairs estimated that 16,000 jobs would be created in Wales by 1968. Much of this expansion was to lie with the restructuring of the steel industry. That decision was to haunt Wales in the late 1970s and early 80s.

The great strides in diversification and provision of manufacturing jobs seen in the two decades after the War served only to offset the downward spiral of the coal industry. Between 1960 and 1973 coal output in south Wales dropped by more than 40 per cent from 19.4 million tons to 11 million tons. Some sixty-seven pits closed with the loss of 52,000 jobs. Increasing availability of oil, the introduction of nuclear power and a change in consumer taste, demanding a cleaner source of fuel, all served to ensure the continued fall of coal. Although it was expected it was still a painful process. After 1973 the prospects of coal improved with OPEC, the cartel of oil-producing countries, exercising their world-wide power by tripling prices. The coal industry's continued decline was inevitable, however, with further general economic weakness, the steel collapse, reducing coking coal demand, high wage claims and low productivity. By 1980 only thirty-six pits remained in Wales employing 27,000 people.

The fortunes of the steel industry during the 1960s seemed to be maintained with a fairly consistent output just below 9 million tonnes and employment even as late as 1973, was more than 70,000. The stunning collapse of steel between 1973 and 1975 was triggered by the recession which, in itself, seemed a psychological consequence of increased oil prices. The fall of the steel industry was inevitable, however, as the failing competitiveness of the UK steel industry and growing foreign competition caused a loss of demand which wiped out a third of Welsh steel production. It was almost an echo of the 1890s. Although the industry rallied until 1979 the failure to achieve the vital productivity improvements was amply evidenced by a less than 10 per cent cut in the industry's work-force between 1973 and 1975 and only a similar reduction between 1975 and 1979. In 1979/80 steel output again tumbled dramatically to only 3 million tonnes. The attempted corrective action taken earlier in the 1970s can only be described as 'too little too late'. Not until 1979 were major work-force reductions activated, but by 1983 some 38,000 jobs had

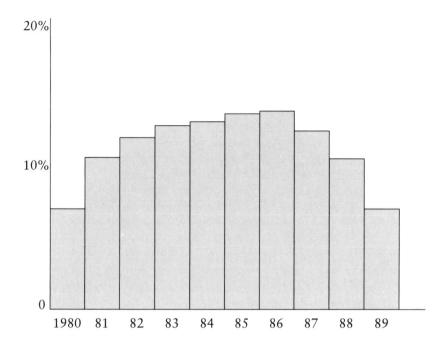

Figure 1
Wales: unemployment 1980–89

been shed in the 'Slimline' programme and only 20,000 steel-workers remained. More than 50,000 jobs had been shed in the process. Finally the recovery and stabilization could begin, with the industry competing on level terms at home and abroad.

Coal in obvious ultimate decline was yet again ravaged by foreign competition, falling world coal prices and a further reduction in home demand. Even guarantees from the Central Electricity Generating Board and British Steel Corporation to buy domestic coal did little to mitigate the plight of the Welsh coal industry. The high level of capital investment at this time served no more than to increase capacity in the face of reduced demand. Five pits were closed in 1983/84 and the National Coal Board expressed its determination to speed other closures and shed some 12 per cent of its 175,000 workforce. Such was the stage for the 1984/85 miners' strike. By 1989 the industry in Wales produced only 5 million tonnes and employed 4,100 miners at a mere seven pits. While the importance of the remaining coal industry should not be underemphasized the ability of 'King Coal' to exert an undue influence on the Welsh economy was no more.

Table 3

Percentage employees in employment 1971–1987
SIC 1980

	1971	1975	1980	1985	1987
Agriculture, forestry and fishing	3.6	2.6	2.3	2.5	2.4
Energy and water supply	7.7	6.6	5.0	5.5	3.8
Manufacturing	33.7	31.8	28.9	23.8	23.9
Construction	6.7	6.1	6.1	5.1	4.9
Services	49.1	52.8	56.8	63.2	65.0
TOTAL EMPLOYEES (000s)	962.0	998.0	1005.0	877.0	863.0
Male %	65.0	61.9	59.5	56.6	55.5
Female %	35.0	38.1	40.5	43.4	44.5
Unemployment[1]	4.7	4.1	6.9	13.8	12.5

Source: *Digest of Welsh Statistics* (1989)

[1] Annual average seasonally adjusted – *Employment Gazette*

By 1985/86 the Welsh economy was in the grips of the worst recession since the Second World War, as unemployment hit 13.8 per cent and 13.9 per cent respectively. Of greatest concern perhaps was the increased rate of decline in the share of employment held by the manufacturing sector. In the five years to 1985 some 81,000 jobs were lost by manufacturing industry reducing its percentage in employment to 23.8 per cent. While it might reasonably be argued that this was merely the continuing process of reprofiling the employment distribution in Wales, relative to the rest of the UK, the future of manufacturing industry in Wales was rightly the subject of increasing concern.

Table 3 indicates clearly the reprofiling process of the recession between 1971 and 1987. Only the service sector increased its percentage of distribution of employees. Nevertheless, behind this exterior of an economy in recession there were already signs that an improvement in prosperity was on its way. As some of the major manufacturing industries suffered, tourism flourished and employed increasing numbers of people.

Between 1981 and 1985 Wales had outperformed the UK as a whole in the growth of per capita Gross Domestic Product. In only one year, 1984, the year of the national coal strike, did Wales fail to better the UK performance. For the four years the compound annual increase in per capita Gross Domestic Product reached 9.81 per cent against a UK figure of 8.6 per cent. Indeed, in 1985, Gross Domestic Product per head in Wales rose by 15 per cent, 5 per cent faster than the overall UK increase.

Against all the odds total Gross Domestic Product for Wales over the period 1981–5 had also outperformed the UK, with an overall increase of 54.6 per cent as against 53.3 per cent for the UK. This was achieved in the face of coal and steel rundowns and without the benefit of oil and gas development seen by the rest of the UK.

The earliest evidence of improving times was in 1985/86 when the British Steel Corporation was able to announce the industry's first net profit for eleven years. The restructuring of the Welsh operations had played a major part along with unheard of increases in productivity. Latterly the Dowlais works was closed in 1987 and Velindre in 1989 bringing the Welsh work-force in steel to 17,000 producing 4.5 million tonnes annually. By the end of 1989 the steel industry had become a profitable and important part of the Welsh economy, but not an overpowering influence.

The invisible improvements became visible in 1986 when in June unemployment began to reduce slowly. In 1987 the annualized unemployment rate was down to 12.5 per cent with the rate of decrease gathering pace. By October 1989 the rate was down to 7.0 per cent with job opportunities being generated at a much faster pace than the UK as a whole.

This improvement in the level of unemployment was achieved in the face of further job losses in coal and steel. Of great importance, too, were the types of industrial activities in which employment was being created. From 1981–4 Wales outperformed the UK in terms of employment growth in many of the more modern industries, for example research and development, rubber and plastics, banking and finance, office machinery and data processing. It is also believed that the aggressive managerial style of Welsh companies, and their work-forces' ready acceptance of new technologies were major factors in this performance. Of particular note was Wales's performance in electronics, where the number employed increased by 15 per cent between 1978 and 1984 while in Great Britain it fell by 15.6 per cent.

In the three years to 1988, Wales proved the most successful region in the UK, in proportion to its population, in attracting inward investment. Consistently it secured 20 per cent of all inward investment into the UK. This was positive proof that industrialists saw Wales as a modern economy and a prime location from which to serve the European market.

A further sign of the reprofiling and modernizing of the economy in the 1980s was the creation of a whole new generation of entrepreneurs. Wales has always been regarded as a nation with an employee culture relying on others to provide jobs, rather than creating its own. The stereotype was of a nation of doctors, poets and preachers.

By 1987, Welsh self-employed already represented almost 6 per cent of that category in Great Britain, a position maintained through to 1989, placing Wales in third place in the UK after the south-east and south-west of England. In Wales the number of self-employed increased by 27 per cent between 1981 and 1985, while the corresponding figure for the UK as a whole was 22 per cent. The importance of this increase in 'home grown' businesses cannot be overestimated in providing an indigenous base to the economy and an enterprise culture to facilitate future economic growth.

Along with this development of an enterprise culture came the realization that if businesses were to grow in Wales an infrastructure was needed to provide the finances and financial services so vital to modern commerce. The traditional sources of business in Wales had been east of Offa's Dyke. In the early days of industrialization they were based on merchant money from prosperous trading towns like Bristol, but later almost totally dependent upon the 'City' in London. Unlike its sister nation Scotland, Wales had never developed its own banking and financial structure to support commercial ventures and in the first half of the twentieth century the preponderance of large and nationalized industries gave no trigger to such a vital development.

While the lack of indigenous sources of corporate finance and advisory services was a major weakness, Wales was also missing out in what was nationally a fast growing employment sector. Indeed, in 1984 of almost two million jobs in banking, finance, insurance, business services and leasing Wales took only 54,000 jobs. Apart from exceptions like Chartered Trust there had been few national organizations based in Wales. In the early 1980s, however, a trickle of these much-needed businesses began with the attraction of the Chemical Bank and AA Insurance Services.

In 1988 positive action was taken with the launch of the Financial Services Initiative sponsored by the Welsh Office and the WDA. Its specific objective of attracting financially oriented businesses quickly achieved notable success with major firms such as TSB, NPI, BNP Mortgages, ECGD, D. C. Gardner Group, N. M. Rothschild and Sons establishing important activities in the Principality. Wales now has a

Amersham International laboratories, Cardiff, uses high precision modern cladding materials to express its advanced products – clinical isotopes.

small but growing nucleus of internationally known companies and organizations to meet the needs of modern commerce for finance and financial expertise. This sector, which provides highly skilled and highly paid employment opportunities, must be given continuing attention in this decade to provide Wales with a vital financial backbone. Already there is one Welsh Venture Capital Fund and a second is planned.

Obviously Wales is set fair to take a greater proportion of important service jobs, but Welsh industry has always maintained a high percentage of manufacturing jobs. Nowhere is this more obvious than in the automotive components industry.

During the last twenty-five years Wales has evolved a significant automotive components sector with now more than a hundred units providing employment for over 19,000 people. Indeed, Wales has a greater percentage of vehicle and vehicle component manufacturing employment, 8.4 per cent of all manufacturing, than the average for the UK, 5.2 per cent. Competitive wage rates and, more importantly, the availability of skilled labour has attracted internationally known companies like Ford, Lucas, Borg Warner, Ferodo, Fram to set up and expand in Wales. At the forefront of automotive technology is AB Electronics providing the most advanced electronic systems.

The most recent additions to this growing sector were the Bosch expansion to Llantrisant – a £110m investment which will ultimately provide 1,200 quality jobs in south Wales – and Toyota's development at Deeside with an investment of £100 million providing 300 skilled jobs in north Wales. The importance of this sector providing skilled, well-paid employment cannot be overestimated and will be a strength to build upon through into the next century.

In summary, it is useful to consider a series of enterprise indicators to present a picture of the new Welsh economy and its relative performance.

Unemployment Feb. 1990 (seasonally adjusted figures supplied by Department of Employment)	UK: 5.6%	Wales: 6.4%
Rate of growth of new companies registered 1987 (Jordans)	England & Wales: 16%	Wales: 53%
Percentage of work-force self-employed (*Regional Trends*)	UK: 11.6%	Wales: 14.6%
Business survival rate 1980–6 (DTI)	UK: 20%	Wales: 35%
Growth in net manufacturing output (Business Monitor PA1002)	UK: 24%	Wales: 35%
Growth in net output per employee in manufacturing 1983/6	UK: 29%	Wales: 37%

As a statement of affairs the above indicators present a healthy picture with potential for development.

The 1980s saw a transition in the Welsh economy of unparalleled magnitude in the UK, although it is the culmination of almost sixty years of change. To ensure continuation of the transformation, it is important that the key factors in the process are considered.

Environment: The industrial areas of Wales have seen massive improvements in their environment after a century and a half of commercial despoliation. Since 1966 more than 15,000 acres of derelict land have been reclaimed for new economic and amenity purposes. This has not only given Wales 'room' to accommodate new and expanding industries, but also it has created a new image so vital to the country's need to 'market it itself'. The Ebbw Vale Garden Festival in 1992 will provide a suitable platform to demonstrate the new Welsh environment. In the image-conscious 1990s the ability to project congenial modern conditions will be paramount in attracting new industry to Wales and in retaining a skilled and qualified work-force. At current levels of expenditure it is forecast that all major dereliction in Wales will be reclaimed by the end of the decade.

Communications: The Severn Bridge, the M4, the Heads of the Valleys road and improvements to the A5 in north Wales have all demonstrated clearly how crucial modern communications are to commercial success. More recently the westward extensions to the M4, the A470 to Merthyr, the A467 north of Newport and the Rhondda Valley link have proved how the commercial potential of previously depressed areas can be revitalized in a short space of time. The continued development of new roads, particularly the A55, Valley town bypasses and the dualling of the Heads of the Valleys road are vital to maintain the current momentum of improvement in the economy. Perhaps the most crucial of all is the need for a second Severn crossing to ensure Wales can take its rightful role in Europe.

Labour Force: The availability of an adaptable, reliable and skilled work-force has allowed the economic change to take place. In the 1990s the presence of skilled labour able to meet new demands of productivity will be the 'unique selling proposition' which will attract commercial enterprises to Wales and maintain the present levels of business formation and expansion. The availability of a modern trained work-force must be a key objective for the New Wales.

Regional Policy: The positive discrimination afforded to Wales in varying degrees since the 1930s has proved a key factor in diversifying the economy. While this has tended to be a 'shotgun' approach to the reprofiling of the economic base of Wales it is, to a great degree, accomplished. A policy of fine tuning is now called for and has been implemented, in part, through project management in recent years. This project management has taken the form of various initiatives.

The Rural Initiative – appropriate commercial activity in rural areas.
The Financial Services Initiative – creating a financial base in south-east Wales.
The Valleys 'A Programme for the People' – focusing commercial investment in a traditional but depressed industrial area.
The A55 Initiative – to extend the commercial success of north-east Wales westwards.

It is this type of finely targeted activity which will now bring the various elements of the economy to the balanced profile allowing even greater strides during the 1990s.

It is appropriate that this review, should be carried out as Wales enters a new decade. The economy of Wales is now leaner and fitter than at any time this century. The old dependence on traditional industries has all but gone and a sound economic base of modern manufacturing industry has been created. Less vulnerable the Welsh economy may be, but vulnerable it still is, as is any regional economy outside the south-east of England. Continued co-operative effort between government, its agencies and industry is vital to maintain the increasing prosperity of this new Wales.

Select Bibliography

K. D. George and Lynn Mainwaring, *The Welsh Economy*
R. Brinley Jones, *Anatomy of Wales*
Gerald Manners, *South Wales in the Sixties*
Bowles Research, *Wales the Modernising of an Economy*

AGRICULTURE

COMPLEXITIES OF MODERN FARMING

ROLAND BROOKS

A N industry tottering on the brink of recession or a fitter, slimmer agriculture better able to meet the challenges of the free European market at the end of 1992. Both these seemingly contradictory assessments of Welsh agriculture as it enters the last decade of the twentieth century are basically true.

The industry is employing fewer people than it did a quarter of a century ago with no loss of production. But also true is the fact that farmers are suffering from inflation. At the end of 1989 more than 40 per cent of farmers' average income was spent on repaying loan interests, and their competitive edge in Europe was being blunted by the increasing Green Pound gap. Indeed, farmers' unions said that the gulf between sterling and the Green Pound (the Common Market device to equate European farm prices and the real pound) was as high as 19 per cent for some products.

In his 1990 New Year message, Geraint Davies, chairman of the National Farmers' Union Welsh Council said that it was a matter of great concern that Welsh farmers had to reduce investment to a trickle at a time when the industry should be gearing up to face the increased competitive pressures which could be expected after 1992. 'The immediate priority of the United Kingdom Government at the start of 1990 must be to put the brakes on urgently to halt the agricultural industry's drift into recession,' he stated.

The slimming down of the farming industry in Wales is not a recent happening. Farm amalgamations during the past twenty-five years have reduced the number of holdings in the Principality from around 48,000 to 30,000. Over the years, there has been a reduction in the number of holdings of all sizes but most significant – and not unexpected – is the drop in the number of farms of less than twenty hectares (about fifty acres). A quarter of a century ago there were 28,434 farms of this size in Wales, now there are fewer than 12,000. This is a sure indication not that big is beautiful but that for many a year size has been the key to economy of production.

This agricultural change is not confined to acreage. In practically every sector of the industry the basis of production, whether it be livestock or crops, has grown or decreased to meet economic circumstances, often dictated by the government in London or by the EEC in Brussels.

An example of this is milk production. The number of people involved in this agricultural sector has decreased steadily since the mid 1960s, but there has been a marked acceleration in this decline since the introduction of quotas. The quota system led many dairy farmers to quit milk for sheep or beef. Between 1965 and the intro-

Sheep-farming territory in Snowdonia.

duction of quotas in 1984 the number of dairy farmers in Wales fell from 19,800 to 7,300. During the same period, however, the amount of milk produced went up from 1,170 million litres to 1,780 million. Between 1984 and 1989 the number of producers fell from 7,300 to 5,482 and production dropped from 1,780 million litres to 1,378.5 million.

That was the EEC intention of course. But one of the criticisms of such a policy is its social severity. The most able producers remain while the poorer are forced out of business. This might be sound economics on paper but on the ground it makes for severe hardship. This was the situation in Wales, particularly in the south-west where small newcomers to the industry left because the sledgehammer-like impact made their holdings unviable when they were not given enough quota to allow for expansion, a necessity for most entrants.

In the past quarter of a century the changes in other sectors of Welsh agriculture have been notable, if not quite as dramatic. During those years the number of cattle in Wales rose from 1,236,453 to 1,361,800. Within these figures – excluding bulls and young cattle – there was a fall in dairy-breeding cows and heifers from around 408,000 in 1965 to about 330,000 in 1989 and a rise in the beef herd from 138,000 to 194,000. Over the same period the number of sheep and lambs rose from a little over 6 million to more than 10 million. The improvement has been substantially encouraged in recent years by grants from the Common Market Sheep Regime, which is now being revised with the obvious intention of halting the recent rapid increase. Conversely pig numbers have fallen from 304,000 in 1965 to 120,000 in 1989 as that sector came increasingly under economic pressure and became highly specialized. Cropping in Wales has also changed appreciably over the same period due in no small degree to the dictates of government and European Community policies.

As cattle and sheep numbers have increased so has the area of grassland on which to keep them. Arable crops too have changed with a huge swing away from oats – 27,600 hectares in 1965 down to 4,700 in 1989. One of the most significant crop changes in Wales is the potato, which has fallen from 8,347 hectares in 1965 to almost less than half – 4,200 hectares – in 1989. By far the largest area of potato production in Wales is in the old county of Pembrokeshire. A quarter of a century ago almost half of the Welsh crop (3,889 hectares) was grown in the county. Now the three old counties of Dyfed – Carmarthenshire, Cardiganshire and Pembrokeshire – together produce more than half of the Welsh crop, but the area is down to just 2,698 hectares.

There are two main reasons for the reduction. The improved facility to store potatoes has meant less demand for the early summer varieties, which are a west Wales speciality, and the area has still not made up the decline in production which followed greater imports from Cyprus, Egypt and France some years ago. Improved production methods in west Wales are now beating off the import competition. One producer recently said that 'we can now produce potatoes as cheaply and without their higher transport costs'. So there is a more than fair chance that the near future could see a swing to greater output from the west Wales area, providing there is demand for the crop. Although the production area has dropped by about 50 per cent the yield has increased from about seven tons per acre in the early 1960s to something like seventeen tons nowadays, largely because of the introduction of crop irrigation and the use of improved weed killers.

Another west Wales, notably Pembrokeshire, enterprise that has seen a great change in the last quarter of a century is turkey production. This developed in the county because the timing – potatoes in the early summer and turkeys for Christmas – dovetailed well. But few Pembrokeshire producers developed the large-scale production units of farmers in other parts of the country, to cater for the demand for the frozen birds.

But it is not just the land area or the production of crops and livestock that has changed. Many farmers' attitudes, prompted by growing urban pressures, either directly or through government, have also altered. As the economics of production have tightened there has been an increasing call for farmers to diversify into different on-farm ventures such as providing tourist, sporting and other facilities. Such a move would have been unthinkable twenty-five years ago. At that time the general attitude when anyone dared suggest farmers could provide bed and breakfast for tourists was that the farmers' job was to produce food. Anything else was regarded as indicating a failure to 'make a go' of farming.

But since those times practically anyone on a tourist route, and many off it, have started to provide B and B facilities. Some go much further and have developed farm food and craft shops in converted barns, while others have developed totally different ventures such as ski slopes, golf courses, rare breed parks and country leisure activities such as fishing and shooting. By 1990 the National Farmers' Union in Wales was receiving such numbers of inquiries from farmers for help with the development of new enterprises, that it produced a 'Farmers' Fact File' to provide business opportunity information for its members. The range of advice offered includes information on fish farming, goat keeping, snail and quail rearing, the production of rabbits, mushrooms and Christmas trees and the provision of watersports and motorsports.

The growing consumer demand for health food products is being met by a move to organic food production. This is particularly so in Dyfed where, apart from individual farmers producing a variety of vegetables, cheeses and other products, Britain's largest organic farm co-operative is based. Organic Farm Foods Ltd, which began producing organically grown vegetables in the corner of a shed with a staff of four, employed more than 100 workers and had 40,000 square feet of factory space on Lampeter's industrial estate by the end of 1989.

The other major indications of the changing attitude of the industry is the attention now paid to co-operation and conservation. The call for improved marketing through co-operation is not new. Many, including the former Secretary of State for Wales, Peter Walker, have urged this for some years, but there is now an increasing momentum as farmers become aware of the necessity for the move.

One of the most successful co-operative ventures is Welsh Lamb Enterprise, a lamb promotional body which is financed by a small levy on members based on their numbers of sheep. This body has done much to improve lamb consumption at home, by developing new

Organic Guernsey cattle on Brynllys farm, Borth, Dyfed.

cuts, and abroad, by researching the precise needs of the meat trade in European and Middle East countries.

Finally, conservation. More and more farmers, smarting under public criticism of intensive production methods, are trying to prove, or improve, their status as 'guardians of the countryside' – in some cases aided by government grants – by deliberately letting their hedges grow as habitats for bird and insect life, or by planting more trees or by developing ponds on their farms. There is now a debate as to whether farmers should spend more of their time as country caretakers and the extent to which this should be financed as a public service by government.

Could we see, at the end of the new decade, two types of farmers – the straightforward food producer, whose output is controlled to avoid large surpluses, and a 'caretaker' farmer who provides facilities for a more leisured public and who grows food strictly in accordance with public conservation demands?

TOURISM

LEISURE AND PLEASURE FOR PROFIT

GWYNFOR O. DAVIES

'It is not surprising that to travellers of almost
every diversity of taste and pursuit, the
Principality of Wales presents objects of peculiar
and varied interest.'

THE quaint wording is the clue to the fact that this was written
some 150 years ago in *Black's Guide to Wales*, but the sentiment is equally relevant to tourism and leisure pursuits in
Wales at the beginning of the 1990s.

Topographically the country is well blessed with a coastline that
covers three sides of its terrain, and mountains and rivers that com-
bine in such a pleasant aspect that the small Principality has five
officially designated Areas of Outstanding Natural Beauty and three
National Parks. These physical attractions are complemented by a
strong Welsh cultural, linguistic and historical heritage, all of which
provide the stimulus of something different for the holiday-maker.
Welsh culture has its twin roots in the rural agricultural and the
urban industrial scenes. Tourism occurs in both contexts and, in a
difficult economic period, it is one of the few buoyant industries
forming part of the process of the modernization and change in
Wales.

Apart from a strip along the north Wales coast and two or three
resorts in the south, the physical attractions of Wales were not com-
mercialized until the 1950s. Until then there had been little investment in tourism and there was no co-ordinated approach to com-
municating the attractions to potential holiday-makers. Then a
voluntary body, mainly funded by local authorities, came into being
and did much to educate the people of Wales to the economic
potential of their assets.

The dynamic growth of tourism in Wales began at the time of the
investiture of Prince Charles as the Prince of Wales. World attention
focused on Caernarfon Castle and Wales for that event in 1969.
Fortuitously that year, too, saw the establishment of the Wales
Tourist Board as a result of the Development of Tourism Act. Since
that time the energetic advance of the tourist industry has produced
the practical benefit of more than 95,000 jobs, representing 9 per cent
of total employment in Wales and a total annual income of £1,000
million – more earning capacity than any other single industry in the
Principality.

One measure of progress is the comparison between the number of

Marloes Sands, Preseli, Dyfed.

tourist attractions available in the 1950s – just fifty – and the present-day figure of more than 300. The pace of progress can be gauged by the fact that half of today's tourist attractions have been opened since 1970. These modern schemes are backed by castles, country houses, cathedrals, archaeological sites, museums, galleries, wildlife parks and steam railways. In the past, many of the popular attractions have been located in areas of low-population density in the west of the country in Gwynedd and Dyfed and, while this remains true, the so-called 'gateway counties' of Clwyd and Gwent are making much progress in developing tourism.

An imaginative development in the past decade has been to turn relics of our industrial past into commercial attractions for today's visitor. As a result the names Blaenafon, Blaenau Ffestiniog, and Dinorwig are now written large on tourist maps They are known respectively for visits down the coal mine called Big Pit and the ironworks, slate quarries, and a modern working pumped storage power station. Former docks are now transformed into attractive leisure harbours. Marinas at Swansea and Neyland have received EEC Blue Flag Awards for good design, cleanliness and freedom from pollution. The thirteen narrow gauge railways are marketed as 'The Great Little Trains of Wales'. The most popular is the Ffestiniog

Snowdon Mountain Railway.

Railway at Porthmadog which carries some 250,000 passengers a year. In the late 1980s, two railways were reopened to meet tourist demand: the Aberystwyth Cliff Railway climbing steeply to the camera obscura high above the town, and the Brecon Mountain Railway from Merthyr Tydfil. These two together already carry more than 150,000 passengers a year.

Just as the nation's industrial heritage is of interest so, too, is modern industrial tourism. Visitors are intrigued to watch glass being blown or engraved, wood being turned, toy soldiers being cast, cheese or candles being made. Whatever the industry or craft, people are fascinated to see the skills and expertise of others at work.

Long before our industrial past was considered of interest to visitors, natural attractions such as the Swallow Falls, Bodnant Gardens and Dan-yr-Ogof Caves, the largest show caves in western Europe, were developed. The three Welsh National Parks – Snowdonia, the Pembrokeshire Coast and the Brecon Beacons – are long established. Additionally five Areas of Outstanding Natural Beauty (AONB) were designated over a period of thirty years. Two peninsulas, Gower and Llŷn were the first in 1956, with Anglesey ten years later, the Wye Valley in 1971 and the Clwydian Range in 1985.

The main aims of these AONBs is to keep development harmonious with the landscape, and to encourage the use of underground power lines and high standards of building. There are rules to resist new mineral workings and limit conifer woodlands so as to protect heather moorlands and archaeological sites. Countryside visitor centres, such as the Brecon Beacons Mountain Centre and those at Pembrey and the newest one at Loggerheads in the Clwydian Range, have been developed to meet a demand for a rural experience from people who are becoming increasingly aware of 'green' issues.

The 1970s saw the establishment of two long-distance walking routes, the Pembrokeshire Coast Path and the Offa's Dyke Path both 250km. long. Demand has also grown for a network of less rigorous way-marked footpaths giving further controlled access to the countryside. In the same spirit fourteen heritage coasts were designated for the better conservation and management of particular stretches of coastline.

A visitor can take a romantic trip through Welsh history by visiting the many sites which have projected themselves creatively by illustrating their links the past. At Beaumaris visitors can enter the Timelock for an audio-visual show bringing to life the exciting and

The 70-acre Bodnant Gardens, Clwyd laid out in the nineteenth century are a celebrated piece of landscape gardening and judged among the finest in Europe.

Llechwedd Slate Caverns, Gwynedd, where visitors may take a guided tour through the nineteenth-century mines.

A glimpse of living conditions during the Industrial Revolution. This terrace of cottages from Rhyd-y-car, Merthyr, has been reconstructed at the Welsh Folk Museum at St Fagans, near Cardiff.

often cruel history of Anglesey from the days of the Druids onwards. They can take a guided walk from Twm Barlwm, the Iron Age fort near Newport in Gwent; attend a Roman Day at Caerleon; spend time at the medieval village at Cosmeston near Barry, or the Tudor Festival at Llangedwyn near Maesteg; watch a Civil War re-enactment in Chepstow Castle, or dress as a Victorian for a day at Tredegar House in Newport, or at Llandudno. It is even possible to live as a Victorian for a week at Llandrindod Wells each September. Increasingly, too, particularly in south Wales, one can step back into the era of the Industrial Revolution.

Recent statistics show that Wales's fifteen most popular tourist destinations are the castles at Caernarfon, Harlech and Pembroke, the National Museum in Cardiff, the Welsh Folk Museum at St Fagans, Big Pit Mining Museum at Blaenafon, Swansea Maritime and Industrial Museum, the Snowdon Mountain Railway, the Ffestiniog Railway, Dan-yr-Ogof Caves, Penscynor Wildlife Park, Llechwedd Slate Caverns, the Rhyl Sun Centre, the Welsh Mountain Zoo at Colwyn Bay and Bodnant Gardens. Not far behind in popularity is Portmeirion, the italianate village created on the coast near Harlech by the architect Clough Williams-Ellis. It regularly attracts more than 250,000 visitors each year. And 1990 sees the opening of Llangoed Castle, also designed by Clough Williams-Ellis, as a country-house hotel near Brecon. The house has been developed by Sir Bernard

The italianate village at Portmeirion, Gwynedd designed by Sir Clough Williams-Ellis.

Ashley, chairman of the Laura Ashley organization, which has done so much to boost the economy of mid Wales. Though mid Wales enjoys only 20 per cent of the tourism business of Wales (40 per cent going to north and south equally), it is a critical element of the region's economy, supplying one fifth of its employment.

The 1969 Tourism Act empowered the Wales Tourist Board to give financial help towards the capital cost of projects to improve or provide tourist amenities such as, for instance, developments at Butlin's holiday camp in Pwllheli or the station at Llanfair P.G. (the village on Anglesey with one of the longest names in the world). Until recently, however, the amount of financial aid has been very small in comparison with the assistance given to manufacturing industry. But as we enter the 1990s tourism is accepted as being a major element within the Welsh economy. Other government agencies such as the Welsh Development Agency, Development Board for Rural Wales, Welsh Water, and the Countryside Commission now work closely with the Tourist Board. Some of the local enterprise boards, the Prince of Wales Committee and the Civic Trust for Wales have also played a prominent part in improving the environment and ambiance of communities throughout the Principality.

In 1984 a new government agency, CADW (the Welsh word for 'keep') was created. CADW's responsibility is to conserve the ancient monuments and historic buildings of Wales and bring a fresh impetus to their presentation. A quick glance through a tourist calendar shows major exhibitions such as 'Gerald of Wales' or the 'Life in the Palace of a Prince of the Church' at the Bishop's Palace, St Davids. As well as such well-researched interpretive exhibitions, CADW has also brought life and entertainment within the walls of our historic ruins by promoting 'fun-days' such as an Easter 'Eggstravaganza' in Raglan Castle, Viking raiders at Caernarfon, a May Day dance in the Roman amphitheatre at Caerleon, and a medieval and cheese fair aptly held at Caerphilly Castle.

As would be expected music of all types is an important element of the Welsh cultural scene. Events fill the year's calendar and range from the Welsh Proms and the prestigious 'Cardiff Singer of the World' competition, held in the acoustically superb new St David's Hall in Cardiff, to the Llangollen International Eisteddfod and vast pop concerts. The Welsh National Opera Company, based at Cardiff, performs throughout Wales, and indeed world-wide, and at the other end of the scale the annual Brecon Jazz Festival which received the 'Best Music Festival Award' in 1987 has been acclaimed as one of the Principality's great musical successes.

Sicilian folk group at the Llangollen International Eisteddfod.

The 1980s witnessed significant growth in short breaks as opposed to long holidays, and this business has become more and more important for the Welsh tourism industry. The increase in the numbers of early retired or part-time employed people, the increase in leisure time and disposable income, more flexible holiday arrangements and better communications (particularly by road) have all contributed to the growth in day trips and short holidays.

The improvement in communications has been recognized as vital

Mountain-biking at Llanwrtyd Wells in mid Wales.

to a modern industrial and tourist economy. International flights arrive at Rhoose airport from Canada, the United States, and Europe; high speed trains take only 1 hour 40 minutes from London to Cardiff; modern ferries bring travellers from Ireland into Swansea, Fishguard and Holyhead. The M4 crosses the Severn Bridge and a fast modern road takes traffic now far to the west of Swansea. Mid and north Wales are served by the M74 which branches off from the M6, and the modern Conway bypass speeds traffic along the north Wales coast on the A55. This road has opened up north Wales to the people of the north-west of England. Other improved roads, such as the A470 between Cardiff and Merthyr Tydfil, are easing the still tortuous but rewardingly scenic north–south journey.

Traditionally the months from June to the end of September were the high point of the tourist year, but in the past decade much effort has gone into extending the tourist season. Now, many tourist attractions and accommodation facilities remain open throughout the year. The Wales Tourist Board entices visitors out of season with their hundreds of 'Great Little Breaks' packages, sometimes focusing on special interests such as photography, golf, canoeing or microwave cookery.

There are various types of tourism; mass market at coastal resorts such as Barry, Porthcawl, Pwllheli and Rhyl; hotel-based as at the long-established resorts of elegant Llandudno and charming Tenby; self-catering, activity and adventure based, and farm tourism, all of which have expanded rapidly and become critically important to the rural economy.

The efforts made to improve communications and holiday facilities have brought their reward. In recent years tourism in Wales is estimated to have brought in well over £1,000m each year. This figure includes £600m from domestic holidaymakers, £375m from day visitors and over £100m from overseas visitors. Eleven million tourist trips and 50 million bed-nights were spent in Wales by British people. The latest available statistics show that two and a quarter million overseas tourists visited Wales in 1988. In order of magnitude they came from the USA, then from Australasia, West Germany, France, Canada, Holland and Scandinavia. But so far Wales attracts only 5 per cent of all foreign visitors to the United Kingdom, whereas double that number go to Scotland. High-spenders, the Americans in particular, demand top quality facilities, especially hotels. In the last few years there has been substantial investment in these. The Wales Tourist Board has made considerable progress in raising standards of accommodation and other facilities. The Board's verification, and other quality control schemes are now being studied by other countries, particularly Iceland and Ireland.

Accommodation goes the full range, of course, from camping and caravanning, simple barn or climbing accommodation, bed and breakfast, farmhouse, inn, traditional seaside, coaching and country house hotels, as well as in modern international hotels such as the Holiday Inns at Cardiff and Swansea, Ladbrokes at Swansea and Newport, and a Campanile (a French group) at Cardiff. New buildings are not the only answer. There are fine old hotels throughout Wales which retain the link with their history but are being upgraded to meet the modern standards required by sophisticated visitors. In 1975 a mere 12 per cent of hotel bedrooms had *en suite* bathrooms, five years on that percentage had risen to 55 per cent. Prime examples of upgraded fine old hotels would be two in mid Wales, the Lake Vyrnwy Hotel, deep in the countryside, and the Metropole Hotel at Llandrindod Wells. This solid Victorian Spa hotel now has a fine indoor pool and bathrooms in all 125 bedrooms. Timeshare accommodation is a relatively new development in Wales and the signs are that this will become increasingly popular.

Caravan holidays are also big business. In 1988, 15 per cent of all tourism 'bed-nights' were spent in the Principality in static caravans. Trecco Bay Caravan Resort at Porthcawl is known to be the largest caravan park in Europe. Attention has been paid to upgrading and landscaping caravan sites of all sizes.

Tintern Abbey, founded by the Cistercians in 1131, in the beautiful Wye Valley in the old county of Monmouthshire (now Gwent).

Youth hostels have a new image and now cater for a rather different clientele, with family-rooms often available. Llangollen Youth Hostel is the first of this new style aiming to project the organization's fresh approach with a range of outdoor activities under the guidance of qualified instructors. Choice of specialist activities at Llangollen includes archery, abseiling, climbing, canoeing, mountain biking, orienteering, sailing and pony trekking. Outside the Youth Hostel Movement, there is a range of health and fitness activity and outdoor leisure holidays which are growing in popularity. These also include special provision in general facilities and accommodation for the disabled.

In the period following the Second World War, Wales had a poor reputation for cuisine but eating out has changed markedly. An enterprising initiative called 'Taste of Wales' has been launched to encourage the use of local ingredients, their fresh preparation and to stimulate the pursuit of excellence by chefs in Wales. Over the past decade more and more restaurants have earned recognition for their cuisine on a national scale.

Perhaps the centre of the burgeoning tourist area is south Wales. Cardiff is fast becoming a most lively capital city. Though it is Europe's youngest (created a capital in 1958) and one of the smallest

(300,000 population) it has a superb post-Victorian Civic Centre near its castle which dates from three eras, Roman, Norman and Victorian. The Marquis of Bute and his architect, William Burges, created a unique extravaganza within the castle, and a 'folly', the fairy-tale Castell Coch, perched high on a hillside at the entrance to the famous south Wales Valleys. Cardiff in those days was the world's greatest coal-exporting port. The dockland area, known to the world as Tiger Bay, is now being transformed and there are plans to convert the bay into a vast lake by a barrage linking Cardiff Docks to Penarth, where already there is a fine new marina.

The Victorians endowed Cardiff with a multiplicity of parks and gardens, and in 1988 the city won the coveted Britain in Bloom prize. With modern shopping centres alongside seven Victorian and Edwardian arcades, it is becoming a magnet for customers in busloads even from the Midlands and across the Severn Bridge. Pedestrianized thoroughfares become the stage for imaginative street festivals

Cardiff Castle from Bute Park.

during the summer months. In 1989 these events included the Festival of Street Entertainment and FIFI, the First International Festival of Iron.

A survey in midsummer 1989 showed Cardiff beaten only by Madrid as a value-for-money tourist city. Facilities opening up within the last few years include St David's Concert Hall, a top-class ice-rink where the Cardiff Devils ice-hockey team play, a huge Super-Bowl ten-pin bowling venue, the 'hands-on' Techniquest Science Centre and an international athletics stadium. Surveys have shown Cardiff to have the most live entertainment per head of the population anywhere in Britain. The Welsh capital is fast building a reputation among visitors as a city of culture and convenience.

Leisure and tourism together are set fair to be the boom industry of the 1990s. Levels of consumer spending have increased annually throughout the 1980s and are forecast to rise even more strongly by 1993. Against this background of dramatic spending on leisure activities there seem to be significant changes in the public's tastes and interests, with a growing desire to do rather than view things. This shift in preference is matched by the increase in such facilities as leisure centres, theme parks and activity holidays.

Just forty years ago the first package charter holidays were initiated, making foreign holidays easily available. During the late 1970s the combination of relatively cheap flights and rising levels of disposable income made overseas package holidays extremely popular. By the late 1980s, however, demand for such holidays began to fall for a variety of reasons – disenchantment caused by aircraft delays, poor standards of accommodation, polluted beaches and rowdyism, extreme heat, and the risk of ill health. The 1990s are likely to see fundamental changes in what Britons seek from their holidays. The extensive experience of foreign holidays across the range of British socio-economic groups has created more sophisticated, value-conscious visitors able to make international comparisons of standards and facilities. For the same reason overseas visitors, arriving in even greater numbers, are also demanding from their holidays more freedom and independence than that allowed by a package tour. Product development is a key area. Changes in the expectations of tourists require fresh approaches. Resources need to be matched constantly to varying demand patterns and emphasis placed on improving standards and upgrading facilities.

Much is planned for tourism and leisure in the early 1990s. The first year of the decade has been designated European Tourism Year. Wales's contribution will concentrate on our Celtic heritage, and a

Llansteffan Castle overlooking the beach. The castle was probably refortified in the twelfth century. The site was occupied by an Iron Age promontory fort as early as the sixth century BC.

'Trail of the Celts' will link sites of Celtic interest and Celtic festivals throughout Europe.

With the advent in 1992 of the single European Market there will be, inevitably, an advance in continental trade and travel. The following year should contribute even more to the accessibility of Wales when the Channel Tunnel is due to open. In Wales the Tourist Board aims to generate £1.3 billion annually by 1992 when Europe becomes part of our 'home market'. In that year the Ebbw Vale Garden Festival is expected to attract some 2 million visitors to south Wales and to be the single biggest event in the United Kingdom. It will be the demonstration par excellence of the greening of the Valleys.

From its solid base the Welsh tourist industry must now respond effectively to the demands of ever increasing international competition and the problem of rapidly changing economic conditions. The challenge is obvious and development opportunities exist – identified but not yet exploited. Success has already been achieved with the county and district local authorities creating new attractions and improving the infrastructure. It is clear that urban areas have an unexploited potential. Fortunately there is a growing creative input from local sources in identifying potential tourism and leisure facilities. This grassroots interest is vital to the progress and sensitive development of the tourist industry.

There is much greater general awareness now than, say, ten years ago, of the importance of general tourism to the Welsh economy. The run-down in the extractive and manufacturing sectors in recent years has brought about a fundamental shift in attitudes towards employment in tourism. Now more attention needs to be paid to the 'quality' of jobs created, rather than the quantity. Successful employment in tourism is skilled, and so more and more educational institutions offer training in the industry. Several full and part-time educational courses have been introduced. For instance, the University College of Swansea recently has established a Chair in Tourism. And already Leisure and Tourism feature as subjects in the school. Curriculum and Travel and Tourism GCSE options exist, reinforcing to schoolchildren the importance and status of this fastest-growing service industry.

Within the British context Wales has the advantage of being both familiar and different, having its own unique culture and the Welsh language (spoken by about one-fifth of the population). The word for welcome, *Croeso*, is being stressed more and more as the watchword for the tourist industry in Wales. Occupying people's ever-increasing leisure time requires a professional approach, and a caring philosophy is as important as enhancing the environment. No matter how much investment goes into developing and marketing tourism the success of the industry depends, in the long run, on the attitude of the people providing the services to the holiday-makers. Wales can claim to have made considerable progress in moving up-market over the last two decades. It can look forward with confidence to the challenges and opportunities of the 1990s.

A HERITAGE OF BEAUTY

GEOFFREY INKIN

Two thousand years ago the advanced guard of the first Roman column, tentatively moving westward along the coastal plain towards Caerleon, would have breasted the shoulder of land above the Coldra at Newport and peered, perhaps somewhat anxiously, through the verdant cover up the Usk Valley. He would have seen that beautiful valley, with rich river meadows leading up towards the plain where the town of Usk now stands, towards the gradually increasing hills to the brooding Black mountains, the Skirrid and the Brecon Beacons beyond to the north. It is a view which is shared almost identically today by the northerly traveller on the modern A449 as he climbs up from the M4 at Newport. Although it lacks the dramatic abruptness and domination of Snowdonia, it typifies the unchanging character and style of Wales and emphasizes that whatever infrastructure intrusion there may have been, or is, the

The Brecon Beacons – Corn ddu from Pen-y-fan.

The Usk Valley from Allt yr esgair.

change is superficial, often reversible and rarely diminishes the fundamental influence of the country and its history on the lives of the Welsh.

Compressed within its limited area, no more than the state of Massachusetts, Wales has one of the richest historical and cultural heritages and astonishingly mixed variations of landscape in Europe. On any arbitrary line drawn from any extreme of the country the variation from rugged mountain, through green upland to soft, rich grazing valley is consistent only in its contrasts. The long and sometimes troubled history of the country is interwoven with the physical characteristics. More than 600 castles in 8,000 square miles make it the most densely fortified in Europe. They reflect the difficulties which the early rulers of England faced in attempting to control the turbulent princes and their tribes in this remote western area.

Industrial despoliation recalls the Klondike-like developments following the Industrial Revolution and reflects the extraordinary economic and social change in housing and industrial architectural heritage especially in the Valleys in the south. The coastal cities and towns of the South Wales Coastal Plain remind the visitor of the great wealth that was created by coal, iron and steel and the indigenous skills and cynical deprivation that provided that wealth.

Although the aim of this review is contemporary, this rich inheritance provides the backcloth for the continuance of change. The two hundred years since the beginning of the Industrial Revolution saw the development of Cardiff from the twenty-ninth ranking town in Wales with a population of barely 2,000 at the beginning of the nineteenth century into a bustling vigorous city of nearly 300,000 today; it saw the transformation of the Valleys from steeply-wooded clefts, running from the sea to the moorland of the Beacons, into densely populated ribbon, valley floor developments with inadequate roads, and a plethora of railways and canals, which at that time led the world in the development of infrastructure and technology; of mountain top and river used for dumping the detritus of the extractive industries; and in consequence of demanding and dangerous occupations, close communities and relative isolation developed the strong community identity that characterizes the Valleys. Despite the rape of these valleys, the beauty of the open country above and around the villages and towns and the dramatic changing colour of the seasons, in conjunction with the strong sporting instincts of those who live there, make a remarkable contrast for what most outsiders perceive as an essentially urban environment. The intrinsic beauty is undefiled.

Sixty years of structural decline, illustrated most dramatically by the drop in employment in the coal industry from 250,000 in 1945 to less than 10,000 in 1989, have led to the beginning of a series of profound changes in the Valleys. Improved communications to meet the demands of road transport have produced not only the obvious result of improved transit time, but have given a new perspective of the Valleys and their communities, limited before by the visual restrictions of the old tortuous, traditional trunk roads. Where coal tips once stood in valley and on peak, the land reclamation schemes of the last ten years, expertly and jointly implemented by the Welsh Development Agency and the local authorities, are beginning to mature with contoured grass, waterfall and tree-planting. The extraordinary effect of this continuing scheme will rapidly become more and more impressive as the areas covered increase and maturity develops. Rivers, like the Taff and the Rhymney, were used for coal washing without restriction. For more than a century they ran black. Coal dust mixed with the natural sand formed the banks and island beaches of these and most Valleys' rivers. Now they run clean. Salmon, sea trout and trout pay incontrovertible tribute to this recovery.

Little commercial or new housing investment had taken place in the Valleys since the Depression. However, stimulated by central government investment, new industrial estates have grown and expanded, major inward investment momentum has increased and the external perception of the market for more specialized investment in housing and in the regeneration of town centres has changed dramatically. In 1989 the Land Authority for Wales had more than fifteen such schemes in hand at different stages from tentative conceptual interest to land assembly, with a total capital investment potential of more than £200 million pounds. The demand for private housing has been stimulated similarly. For the first time for many years, schemes to meet all sectors of the market from executive housing to starter homes and new rented accommodation are in hand throughout the Valleys areas of south Wales.

The combination of all these changes is improving the aspect of the Valleys, their accessibility and the consequent ease with which people can travel to other areas for work, while maintaining the unique and irreplaceable community spirit that is so dearly bought and so easily lost.

The preparation for the National Garden Festival in 1992 in Ebbw Vale is the most dramatic and sweeping illustration of this change. The site of what was once the largest steelworks in Europe has been reduced to about a sixth of its original size, where a specialized and modernized steel plant still operates. The remainder of the site, which previously had the gargantuan sheds of the heavy foundry end and the extensive tip and railway sidings that serviced the plant, is now being prepared for the Festival. It is an ambitious and enterprising scheme, which illustrates more dramatically than any other development the profound nature of the change in the Valleys. It was a brave political decision to initiate the Festival in Ebbw Vale. But it was a clear indication of the political determination to launch a programme for the environmental improvement of the Valleys by the removal of the residual dereliction of the Industrial Revolution, coupled with the sequential opportunities for modern investment on the site created for the Festival. It is, of course, also the most dramatic example of the widespread land reclamation programme.

The remarkable improvement in communications is not limited to the south, though sadly the traffic justification for a major, uprated direct route connecting north with south lacks authority or optimism. The new A55, running east from Chester and destined eventually to link up with the A5 at Bangor, has already had a profound effect on the north Wales coast as far west as Llandudno. The vast and

Conway Castle, erected by Edward I, is regarded as one of the great fortresses of Europe.

environmentally sensitive scheme at Conway to sink the tunnels for the A55 beneath the estuary, thus avoiding despoiling its beauty, is well advanced. Despite its disproportionate cost, the environmental benefit will justify the investment. The innovative technology is also a matter for quiet pride. Westward of Conway awaits a series of complex and challenging road engineering projects along the coast which will enhance the economic opportunity of the more westerly areas and relieve overcrowded and unsuitable roads.

But political and social difficulties lie ahead as a consequence of these dramatic infrastructure improvements. In the north-west of the country lies the heartland of the indigenous culture and language. The improvement in accessibility may bring material economic opportunities to enrich the population, to reduce unemployment, to improve leisure and entertainment facilities and to encourage the development that is necessary to meet those beneficial changes. But, unless the change is sensitively managed by new arrivals and, equally importantly, sensitively responded to by the existing communities, less worthy tensions and resentment will be generated that are too often a consequence of change. Our language and culture, which are indivisible, must be protected and encouraged as they are a living and visible characteristic of European uniqueness. It is a potential dichotomy that will have to be extremely carefully handled to maximize the conjunction of the historic and contemporary benefits.

Wales is fortunate to have one of the most varied and beautiful coastlines. The high and forbidding cliffs of south Pembrokeshire, the coastal forts and castles of the north-west, the varied river mouths of great beauty and rich wildlife, the sandy bays and tree-lined slopes of the precious and curiously isolated Gower, the estuarial interface of industrial dereliction and natural beauty of Llanelli and Burry Port, have an extraordinary quality and variety. Much of that which is unspoilt is owned and protected in perpetuity by the National Trust and the National Parks of Pembrokeshire and Snowdonia. But with improved westerly road access there are the dangers of insensitive and concentrated development diminishing the asset which attracts them.

The long-standing encroachments of vast and profitable caravan sites, especially along the Clwyd coast and in parts of south-east Wales, sited without sympathy for their surroundings and almost always interposed in the most sensitive area between the coastal road and shore, despoil the landscape. We have much to learn from our European neighbours, who provide facilities on at least the scale we

Three Cliffs Bay, Gower Peninsula, West Glamorgan.

have and with a higher standard of integral services but with minimal, if any, environmental intrusion. That great Welshman and recorder of our national life and heritage, Wynford Vaughan Thomas, wrote in this context '... for many Welshmen themselves treat the legacy of beauty we have received from the past as if it can be easily exploited for the profit of the present. They ignore the condemnation of the future'. The future and exciting opportunities for the improvement of harbours to meet the increasing water leisure demands, for homes and for essential public facilities, must be reconciled to the demands of our environment. The factors are not mutually exclusive; they should be constructive and complementary and the implicit change must be beneficially managed in the general interest. It is a formidable challenge, but not impossible to meet provided there is a firm but effective planning background with enlightened regional co-ordination.

Agriculture is a primary industry in Wales. As a result of the soil type and high rainfall of the west, it is dominated by a grassland economy. Its presence pervades the countryside of Wales. It is a rich and living thread interwoven into the complex fabric of rural life. The carefully bred dairy cow, probably the product of generations of careful selection, the beef suckling cow often now of exotic European breed, the hardier upland breeds like the striking Welsh Black and the ubiquitous sheep give an appearance of life, movement and depth to the countryside throughout Wales. The profound changes in the industry elsewhere in England through intensive crop production, mechanization, chemical control and the removal of hedgerows has not affected the scale or beauty of the Welsh countryside. Productivity has increased, but the practical and mechanical means of this are concealed within the cow shed and dairy although the latter too often are sited and built insensitively. The extensive reclamation for grazing of large areas of hillside shows in new enclosures and the bright contrast between new grassland and bracken and heather. The maturing conifer plantations, which attract the criticism of some, contour the hills in increasing maturity; the Forestry Commission and other forestry interests have increased the proportion of broad-leaf varieties. After the life of the conifer, the residual trees will complement the ancient primeval oak forests which abound on the valley hillsides.

It is in mid Wales that the full variety of the landscape, the agricultural and the rural heritage, is best seen in a rich interwoven tapestry. It is not without significance that in the twelfth century the English established administrative control of Wales from the Shropshire town of Ludlow. Situated ten miles east of the Welsh border, centrally between north and south, the town provided direct access into the heartland of Wales. Travelling westward from Ludlow into the old counties of Montgomeryshire, Radnorshire, Breconshire, Merioneth and Cardiganshire, lush grassland areas carry some of the finest dairy herds in the country. The hills are always near. At first gentle with bracken tops and small hill farms nestling in the valleys with black cattle and ever present sheep – harboured on low ground below the farmsteads through the winter. Further to the west the hills increase in size and steepness with fewer homesteads and less intensive farming.

The Elan Valley and other reservoir systems reflect the Victorian prudence of the Liverpool and Birmingham corporations, who acquired a pure water supply in perpetuity, displayed the engineering excellence of those who designed and built the supply systems and provided, apparently also in perpetuity, a rich source of argument over the equalization of water charges! To the layperson this is an arcane disagreement which means that the English cities obtain water at lower cost than those who live in the country from which it is drawn! Despite artificiality, the lakes add a dramatic dimension to the country, and provide both a major tourist attraction and important leisure facility for fishermen, dinghy sailors and those who enjoy the innocent and peaceful pleasure of looking at water.

The depopulation of central Wales and an unacceptably high level of unemployment in the residual population led to the establishment in 1977 of the Development Board for Rural Wales. The Board, equipped with analogous powers of New Town and Urban Development Corporations, is charged with the economic and social regeneration of mid Wales. It has had remarkable success in promoting indigenous growth and attracting inward investment, increasing the housing stock and initiating leisure and tourist facilities, without damaging the underlying asset of sensitive environment and community.

The ancient town of Newtown is both the focus for this success and the location of the offices of the Corporation. The bustling town centre, redeveloped in harmony with the old, and the new factories lying under the hill to the south are living tributes to the determination and imaginative vision of those who have served the Development Board and the community of this large and diffuse area. Some ten miles to the north-west lies the headquarters and principal manufacturing facility of the internationally known Laura Ashley. The casual visitor might think it incongruous to see the large dark green lorries of the firm with the Paris, Rome, New York and London livery

Greenbridge of Wales, near Pembroke.

on their sides rolling out of a remote Welsh village. But it is a reflection of the potential that exists in the most improbable places given
the vision of the entrepreneur and the politician who is prepared, and
able, to assist in the transformation of opportunity into economic
reality.

Eventually the westward traveller breaks out from the valley and
hill on to the expanse of Cardigan Bay. Stretching in a great sweep
from the Llŷn peninsula in the north to the complementary Pembrokeshire peninsula in the south, it is an incomparable stretch of
coast and sea. Aberystwyth, a seaside town with a thriving college of
the University of Wales, which includes one of the leading agricultural institutions of the United Kingdom and the National Library of
Wales, lies at almost the central point of the bay. It has a robust and
independent character which, despite its relative isolation welcomes
the visitor who is refreshed by its attractive Victorian innocence and
the bracing, clear westerly wind. To the north lies the beautiful,
unspoilt and mysterious Dyfi estuary with ancient trees and small
white cottages running right down to the water and the salt marshes

which frame it. It is a place of peace and stimulates the romantic image of the history of Wales.

There is evidence of growing tourist interest in this lesser known region. The inadequacy of north–south and lateral communication conveys obvious disadvantage, but similarly in maintaining the relative remoteness the same inadequacy serves a useful purpose. It is a complex economic and environmental benefit-and-disbenefit situation. For those who have the good sense to visit this beautiful area the essential tourist facilities at all levels of demand are improving and becoming more widespread.

But the urban vista is at least as important a topographical component as the rural, even if the latter is bigger and more dramatic in natural phenomena. The major towns of the south, Cardiff, Newport and Swansea, and Wrexham in the north-east are witnessing change and improvement through investment and enterprise on a scale undreamt of even five years ago. Swansea led the way through municipal initiative in 1979 by refusing to fill in the town dock for development, restoring it as a yacht harbour and initiating an ambitious development programme which is now almost completed. A barrage dam across the River Tawe will open up further development opportunities to complement that which has already been achieved and reclaim more derelict dock and redundant industrial land. Despite its more westerly position, the city is bustling and confident and significant growth is imminent.

Cardiff, as the youngest capital city in Europe, has seen a remarkable recovery. Property investment in major office and conference centre developments and the creation of one of the finest shopping centres have transformed the city. The development of major peripheral road systems, without damaging or intruding into the mature city centre, has been a very important component of change. The establishment of an Urban Development Corporation in 1987 to regenerate 2,700 acres of derelict and rundown land in south Cardiff, with a 500-acre lake in Cardiff Bay as a focus for that opportunity, will complement in dramatic style the earlier and contemporary improvements north of the divisive railway tracks. It is already a city of which Wales is proud. It is recognized as one of the major cities in the political, administrative, cultural and commercial sense and it will have its reputation enhanced in both the national and international context. Newport, too, with its advantageous easterly position on the motorway, has achieved considerable success in attracting major office relocations from London and south-east England. The town centre has been transformed from a rather gloomy

Cardiff Civic Centre. The earliest buildings – the Law Courts, City Hall and the National Museum of Wales – are in the foreground, and the most recent buildings from the north, including from left to right the University of Wales, College Cardiff Redwood Building, the Welsh Office, and the University College's departments of anatomy, physiology and biochemistry. The Students' Union and the Sherman Theatre are on the extreme right.

Victorian scene to an attractive, modern and bustling context, which complements the major developments on the periphery and the existing and imaginative dock and riverside proposals which are now in hand.

All these coastal plain developments are in areas linked by excellent new road systems and renovated railway feeder services to the valley communities lying to the north. The improvements reinforce the symbiotic relationship between city and the Valleys. The landscape, reclamation, planting, building improvement and investment, within the rich historical and industrial archaeology context play a critical role in the remarkable economic renaissance after sixty years of structural decline.

We must take care that our stewardship of this powerful change serve the best interests of the future, to which the unique and varied landscape of this beautiful country provides an extraordinary backdrop.

REGAINING THE WASTELANDS

GWYN GRIFFITHS

BEFORE the Industrial Revolution, most mineral extraction sites and obsolete industrial structures in Wales tended to succumb to a gradual recycling process of decay and recolonization by nature. For example, the early ironworks located in Pontypool Park had been abandoned and returned to formal parkland by the early nineteenth century, and nature had smoothed and blanketed the extensive Roman gold-mining and processing works at Dolaucothi in Dyfed. Almost the only exceptions were military structures such as castles and hill-forts built specifically to resist destruction.

The Industrial Revolution brought with it a scale, intensity and complexity of development and despoliation which totally exceeded the ability of man and nature to obliterate or mask it. A significant number of factories and industrial plants were modernized, adapted for reuse or replaced, and a number of sites such as the Rio Tinto Zinc location in Llansamlet have been found to contain three generations of works built one on top of the other. However, the scale of colliery and slate spoil heaps and mounds of metaliferous mine wastes and slags was such that they were accepted as permanent features of the landscape and an inevitable consequence of mineral extraction. Even the planning controls brought in since 1948 have tended to be limited to regulating new mineral activities, so implying acceptance of the permanence of past dereliction, particularly tips.

Historically, the dominant impression of dereliction in Wales tended to be that of tips associated with disused collieries and steelworks. This image was false because a similar acreage of despoliation arose from other causes. Lead, copper, zinc and gold have been mined at approximately 700 sites in Wales, and slate quarrying has devastated thousands of acres of land. Other dereliction has included railways, docks, power stations, gas works, military installations, chemical works, factories and industrial waste tips.

Prior to the Aberfan tip disaster in October 1966, only three reclamation schemes had been grant-aided in Wales. They covered a total of one hundred acres, at a cost of £33,000. Aberfan brought with it a realization that it was essential for tips to be rendered harmless and stable. This resulted in the almost immediate creation and funding of the Welsh Office Derelict Land Unit, charged with implementing a major programme of land reclamation in Wales.

It is true to say that initially reclamation was seen as the last step in eliminating the remnants of the Industrial Revolution, but it is now recognized as the key first step in the regenerative process. The first objectives in reclaiming land were removal of hazards and the improvement of the environment. Slowly, the importance of reclaiming land for new employment opportunities has grown until it is now generally accepted that land reclamation is the key first stage in the comprehensive regeneration of run-down industrial communities. The story of reclaiming derelict land in Wales is one of concerted co-operation between central and local government and, since 1976, the Welsh Development Agency (WDA), supported by designers and contractors. Grant aid has been made available to local authorities to enable them to acquire and reclaim land. The role of the WDA is to determine all-Wales priorities and programmes, while the local authorities implement individual projects.

Although the reclamation of derelict land uses conventional civil engineering equipment and techniques, the scale and nature of their application is greater, and the works have to have a permanence not usually demanded of civil engineering structures. The particular problems and challenges to be overcome in Wales include natural underlying instability, unpredictable groundwater regimes, steep over-glaciated valleys, high rainfall and heavy sheep trespass. These particular Welsh problems are additional to contamination, derelict and buried structures, mine workings and shafts, difficult materials such as slurries and tailings, and an absence of topsoil. There has now developed a specialist branch of civil engineering dealing with derelict land. In collaboration with experts in the botanical sphere it has refined techniques to reclaim, manage and develop land and to monitor the effectiveness and durability of work done.

Between 1966 and 1990, approximately £170m has been spent on reclaiming 800 sites covering 17,000 acres of derelict land. That equates to the area of a full-sized football or rugby pitch being reclaimed every day of every year for the past twenty-four years. In recent years, there has been a marked increase in the level of funding in Wales to a peak for 1989/90 of £25m. This will result in the clearance of a record 1,800 acres in a financial year, equivalent to three pitches being cleared every day.

In addition to land cleared with grant aid, commercial ventures by developers, safety works by British Coal and reclamation by the extraction of coal from tips and by opencasting have removed perhaps a further 5,000 acres of dereliction. The net effect, therefore, has been the halving of the dereliction which existed in 1966 and has arisen since. The concentration of resources on the most obtrusive despoliation with greatest potential, has brought benefit far greater than that suggested by the statistic of 50 per cent completion of the task. At the current rate, most significant dereliction near communities or along main routes of communication should have been eliminated by the

Clydcch Vale, Rhondda,
looking towards the site of
the Cambrian Colliery in
1974.

turn of the century. The inevitable obsolescence which arises from industry will continue to produce challenges but the massive accumulated legacy from the Industrial Revolution will have been eliminated, and the continuing problem will have been reduced to a manageable component of a steady ongoing process of renewal and regeneration.

Measurement of the effects of land reclamation falls under two main headings – environmental and economic. The environmental benefits can be classified as visual, recreational and ecological. The visual benefits should.not be judged as the comparison, on a site-by-site basis, of the scenery before and the scenery afterwards. They must be the cumulative effects of reclamation schemes on a locality. I believe it is of greater importance to tell the world that the Welsh environment is being rapidly restored than to agonize over attempts to quantify the degree of reclamation. The recreational value of the work is not restricted to the creation of space for playing fields, squash-courts and sports centres, important though they are. Reclamation has created many country parks, lakes, footpaths and informal amenity areas offering scope for a wide range of woodlands, wildlife habitats, fisheries and water recreation areas. The ecological benefits include the control or elimination of contamination from air, land and water, and the reintroduction of flora and fauna. Encouraging signs of at least some success beyond the basic greening of sites have been the sighting of herons taking off from the Lower Swansea Valley

The reclaimed site of the Cambrian Colliery in 1987.

and the former Oglivie Colliery at Deri, and a woodcock being disturbed off the former lead-waste tip at Parc Mine in the Gwydyr forest.

The financial benefits of land reclamation are not those of a conventional balance sheet. In narrow terms of cost and value, the books would show an outlay of £170m to achieve a total land value of perhaps only a quarter of that figure – and even that value only realizable over a long period. But reviewed another way, the £2.8m spent to reclaim the 280-acre Clydach Vale site compares well with the £1,000m present-day value of coal that has been extracted from that site in its working life. Perhaps the £2.8m should be seen as a minor adjustment to the historic Clydach Vale balance sheet rather than a major current deficit.

In terms of financial leverage, land reclamation expenditure becomes more justifiable. One £750,000 project has brought forward £120m of private sector investment. If a fifth of all reclaimed land is ultimately developed, the expenditure of £170m to date could finally generate investment in development amounting to five or ten times that figure. Calculating the likely investment upon reclaimed land is a difficult task, but it becomes almost impossible to assess the scale of other investment which has occurred as a result of the improved environment. This investment can be in tourist ventures served by routes which have been upgraded or visually enhanced, development of greenfield sites previously blighted by adjacent dereliction, and the upgrading of existing commercial, industrial and residential property previously depressingly affected. Over the years the WDA has photographed the derelict sites before and after reclamation but, unfortunately, not the urban surroundings of derelict sites. It would have been enlightening to monitor peoples' responses to an improved environment. There is a strong impression, however, that residents respond to such improvements by investing substantially in house improvements to capitalize on their improved environment. In this way they show a willingness to make a new and lasting commitment to their community.

Already, 120 reclaimed sites accommodate industry. These range from small blocks of workshops to major Enterprise Zones. Over seventy housing developments stand on reclaimed sites, as do a range of commercial and service developments such as banks, hotels, hospitals, schools, police stations, ambulance stations, marinas and sports centres. In addition to these bricks and mortar developments reclamation has created a wide range of amenities and assets, including twelve country parks, eleven lakes, over fifty sports grounds and thirty road improvements. Reclamation is almost the only source of land for industry, particularly in the Valleys of south Wales. Without this work the viability of their communities would be seriously threatened, as would the basis for any significant investment in housing commerce or industry.

A key to the future success of the old single industry communities must be diversification. That is occurring with the development of a broad spread of types of industry, and can also be bolstered by the exploitation of a fascinating industrial heritage. Preservation and interpretation of this heritage is important to the communities themselves, but can also bring leisure and tourism business to these areas. Major sites which have been the subject of land reclamation support include Trevithick's tunnel, the Dowlais Stables and the blast-engine house in Merthyr, the Melingriffith pump in Cardiff, the Bronze Age lead mines on the Great Orme Llandudno, the Rhondda Heritage Park, and Big Pit Mining Museum, Blaenafon.

Finally in assessing the financial impact of reclamation in Wales the question has to be posed: 'What would the economic position of Wales be now, if no reclamation had taken place since 1966?' The answer would reveal a depressing picture of dereliction without space for redevelopment or the quality of environment necessary to encourage local or inward investment.

We are within a decade of completing the removal of the signs of despoliation from Welsh communities, but because outside perceptions tend to lag at least ten years behind the reality, we must now tell the world that the objective will be attained. The record to date should convince people that it will be achieved.

It is becoming ever more evident, however, that even when all dereliction is removed, many areas, particularly in the Valleys, will have less land than is ideally necessary. It is essential, therefore, to ensure that the allocation of uses for that land and the development upon it are of the highest quality. If we do not we will be accused by future generations of wasting one of the key assets necessary for regeneration and an enhanced quality of life.

The ultimate test for the land reclaimer will be that of time. Well-designed sites should, given ten or fifteen years to lose their newness, merge back into the landscape to be unidentifiable as reclaimed land. The only exceptions should be those elements retained as reminders of our industrial heritage. Again, quality must be the key. We must retain the best examples and interpret them well.

The greatest quandary relates to the retention of a typical coal tip. I sympathize with those who adopt a NIMBY stance, or regard any tip as an unacceptable reminder of hard times and deprivation, but if given a choice, while begging forgiveness of the good people of Rhondda Fach, I would opt to retain Tylorstown Top Tip albeit in a slightly repaired form. It is a magnificent monument set away from development and visible from many high points throughout the coalfield and in the west of England.

Land reclamation and the construction of new roads and bypasses have brought about many of the most striking changes in the Welsh environment. Hazardous and unsightly eroding tips are becoming a thing of the past. Rivers are becoming cleaner. Heavy main road traffic is being channelled out of congested built-up areas, and these new roads are improving communications and opening up superb new vistas. Simultaneously there is a rapidly growing awareness of the importance of our environment. Public recognition of the need to plant trees received a major boost from the 'Plant a tree in '73' campaign. The fruits of that venture are now reaching early maturity, as are the many trees planted in the early road improvement and reclamation schemes. We have yet to reap the full rewards of the later planting, such as that along the Heads of the Valleys corridor and on the side slopes of the A470 between Abercynon and Merthyr, but Wales is steadily becoming a greener land. This broadleaved afforestation will not only bring with it a softer and more beautiful landscape, it will provide habitat for birds and animals. To capitalize fully on the achievements to date, we must ensure that the process of environmental enhancement is maintained. Greater awareness will enable people to enjoy their surroundings and contribute more effectively to their protection and improvement. It will also reduce the likelihood of deliberate or accidental damage to the environment.

We must, however, avoid complacency. We must ensure that man's current and future activities create fewer and fewer burdens on the environment so that damage caused is limited in extent and is of a type which can be reversed at acceptable cost. The techniques are available to deal effectively with the major items of physical damage which have occurred. We must now ensure that we can adequately control chemical and radioactive pollution. Their greater ability to spread, and the greater difficulty and cost of dealing with them demand that we have to prevent rather than cure such problems. This is a particular challenge for the newly created National Rivers Authority.

Lastly, we must achieve quality in our built environment since it is this environment which impinges on people for most of the time. A beautifully landscaped background does little to counter an ill-designed urban foreground. We must strive for excellence in layout, construction and amenities. These are of paramount importance in enhancing quality of life.

GETTING BETTER BY DESIGN

DALE OWEN

WALES, as an ancient land of myth and magic, still exerts a fascination for visitors looking to experience the mysterious Celtic quality of this unique and attractive part of Britain. Few seem disappointed but there is little doubt that those who live here have come to believe some of the more popular myths themselves. For instance, many otherwise well-informed people accept that although a literate and music-loving nation we have little appreciation of the visual arts and no architecture worth mentioning. Remarkably, this misconception is held even by some architects, notwithstanding substantial evidence to the contrary.

Wales is, of course, a small country, largely mountainous, but with a population of under three million, it supports an important section of the British economy. It also has a long history and a clearly established cultural identity, evident in its architecture. From pre-Roman times to the Industrial Revolution there is a heritage of buildings which, although fewer in number and sometimes less elaborate than their counterparts beyond Offa's Dyke, are no less significant architecturally. Because of its position on the western side of Britain, changes in architectural style were slower to take effect in Wales. Nevertheless cathedrals, abbeys and churches, castles and houses great and small, illustrate the richness and variety of our historic heritage.

Visitors to Wales became far more significant in the late eighteenth century when the Romantic movement, coupled with the difficulties of continental travel during the Napoleonic wars, meant that tours of Wales helped to replace the Grand Tour in fashionable society. Hence the many accounts of travels in Wales from Thomas Pennant in 1778 to George Borrow in 1862. Interest in 'Romantic Wales' coincided with the effect of the Industrial Revolution on the building industry. Exciting new constructional techniques using Welsh iron for bridges helped to improve travel, including the beautiful Waterloo Bridge, at Betws-y-coed and the suspension bridges at Conwy and the Menai Strait, all by Thomas Telford. That these and the many earlier buildings of interest are geographically widespread may have been inconvenient for visitors in the past. Today, the Wales Tourist Board finds this an advantage in stimulating travel throughout the Principality.

The Industrial Revolution brought Wales increased population and wealth, new housing, chapels and industrial buildings. At the same time there was also an increase in the number of good country houses. Sadly, as in England and Scotland, large numbers of these have been demolished or lost through neglect. Nevertheless, as Thomas Lloyd pointed out in his recently revised survey *The Lost*

Houses of Wales, the Welsh country house, while usually less grand than its English counterpart, was of comparable quality and considerable charm and well adapted to its rural setting. In 1803 Pinkerton stated that 'Wales abounds in elegant edifices'. He and many other visitors shared a high opinion of their delightful picturesque quality. Fortunately many still survive, though as Thomas Lloyd says 'untroubled by publicity and scholars of architecture'.

In addition to grand country houses, the range of building types from the late eighteenth century to the First World War was comprehensive and included work by many of the leading British architects of the time. This was well illustrated in the exhibition and catalogue on architecture in Wales, 1780–1914, prepared by John Hilling for the Welsh Arts Council in 1975 – Architectural Heritage Year.

In the late twentieth century Wales has been strongly influenced by the modern movement in architecture. Its importance has been international in scope and fundamental to architectural teaching and design. The modern movement began as a reaction against the Victorian and art nouveau style of the turn of the century. Its early years were dominated by the great masters – Walter Gropius, Mies Van der Rohe and Charles Eduoard Jeanneret or Le Corbusier. The publication in the 1920s of Le Corbusier's seminal book *Vers Une Architecture* showed him as an exceptional writer and publicist, as well as a brilliant architect. He argued that architecture should match the technology of its age and that as the Parthenon expressed the technological level of Hellenic Greece, so our buildings should equal the contemporary motor car, ship or aeroplane in their technological and machine aesthetic.

Walter Gropius presented the modern movement not as a style but

A 1930s house at Penarth, South Glamorgan, typical of the modern movement in architecture, designed by Gordon Griffiths.

Continuity of the modern movement in post-War architecture clearly expressed at BBC Wales Broadcasting House, Llandaff, Cardiff, by Sir Percy Thomas and Son.

as a completely new approach to architecture which took full account of technical, economic and social conditions of life. He explained that architectural design should take care of the functional needs of the building and its users in the most efficient elegant way, using all the advantages of modern structure and technology. The movement rejected learned academic formulae or historic styles in design; it called for entirely new solutions. In a paper given at the Royal Institute of British Architects in 1967 Sir Leslie Martin summarized the three powerful lines of thought which characterized the early modern movement – first there must by a systematic re-examination of human needs; second, the full use of modern technology; finally each architectural problem should be reassessed and thought out afresh.

The influence of the modern movement in Wales before the Second World War was far greater than the relatively small number of buildings might suggest. Houses provided perhaps the most frequent evidence. The few known good examples are of the 1930s and significantly, perhaps, all are near the sea, at Llandudno, Borth near Aberystwyth and Penarth. Stylistically, many buildings of this period exhibit characteristics of the modern movement. Its influence is discernible in art deco and stripped classical and the streamlined styling of this period.

Two major buildings of this period in Wales, Swansea Guildhall and the Temple of Peace, Cardiff, both by Percy, later Sir Percy, Thomas, show the influence of the modern movement. They have the typical simple geometry of form and large areas of plain external wall. Criticized in the past as stark and almost neo-fascist, both buildings are now recognized as fine examples of their time. The Guildhall – built in 1934, is spatially generous with a richness of materials and decoration carried out to the highest standard of craftsmanship and this at the middle of the depression. The later Temple of Peace – 1938, is smaller and simpler, with a more re-strained use of decoration. Where this does appear internally it is very much in the style of the late thirties. The dramatic main hall is unmis-takably twentieth century. Flooded with light from elegant floor to ceiling windows the aisles are formed by square black fluted marble columns between which hang handsome pendant lights – collectors' pieces of art deco design.

The most significant major post-War development in Wales is seen in its new towns. Their importance is greater since their scale and complexity extend the architectural dimension to that of urban de-sign. Cwmbran new town, begun in the 1950s and Newtown, Mont-gomeryshire in the late 1960s showed that development corporations with their architects, planners and engineers, could produce new work of a high environmental quality.

Cwmbran new town, created to relieve extended journeys to work in the Torfaen area, incorporated the old industrial villages of Pontnewydd and Cwmbran and includes a series of newly built resi-dential neighbourhoods complete with shopping and social facilities, all in accordance with good planning practice. The town centre is

The central square and Congress Theatre, Cwmbran new town – a safe civic space for relaxed pedestrian circulation and enjoyment, designed by the Development Corporation.

St Mary's Close, Newtown, mid Wales. Flats and maisonettes in a sensitively landscaped pedestrian precinct by the chief architect, Development Board for Rural Wales.

entirely pedestrian with peripheral and underground car parks as an integral part of its design. New industrial parks, a rational road network and good social facilities, combined with generous landscape planting, produced a high overall standard of design.

Newtown, a charming mid-Wales town, was expanded with new housing neighbourhoods and substantial new industrial estates, aimed at stemming depopulation in rural Wales. With improved shopping in the town centre and better social and educational facilities it sets an enviable standard for its residents. Together, Cwmbran and Newtown represent successful architectural, planning, economic and social experiments which are valuable examples for the rest of Wales and the United Kingdom.

In addition to the new towns, a number of other planning proposals of the 1960s and 1970s were aimed at reducing rural depopulation in mid Wales. Selected country towns were studied including Aberystwyth, Rhayader, Brecon and Llandrindod Wells. Comprehensive planning reports were prepared by well-known consultants to assist the local authorities and the Welsh Office in future development. In practice, the reports, although advisory, proved useful guidelines and helped to focus attention on the particular character and quality of each town and how it might be enhanced and protected in the future. For example, the report in 1974 for Brecon confirmed the need for a major bypass to reduce the enormous volume of through traffic which choked the streets. The bypass was subsequently built. There were also recommendations regarding the way in which the historic central area of the town should be conserved. As a result, the worst effects of predatory commercial development, evident in other towns in Wales, have been avoided.

How, then, was the post-War need for housing generally met? Much of it is indistinguishable from pre-War work with relatively little evidence of innovation in lay-out, design or building quality. However, the award scheme – Good Design in Housing – organized by the Welsh Office jointly with the Society of Architects in Wales, has stimulated design and certainly raised standards substantially in recent years.

Special housing for the aged and disabled poses a particular challenge. There is a need to balance the provision of efficient services for people collectively with a sense of individual personal care and intimacy. In direct response to this challenge we have several award-winning projects – the Albert Edward Prince of Wales Home at Porthcawl, the Hafan Elan housing at Llanrug near Caernarfon, Trinity Court housing at Rhyl, Hanover Court at Rhos-on-Sea and most recently, the Coleshill Centre at Llanelli and the Cefndy Hostel for the Mentally Handicapped at Rhyl.

The Albert Edward Prince of Wales Court home for the elderly at Porthcawl, Mid Glamorgan. Designed by the Percy Thomas Partnership the illustration shows the main dining-room terrace and lily pool.

With the increased prosperity of recent years, people are taking a more active part in improving their own personal environment, their houses, gardens and flats. A national awareness has resulted in the provision of DIY stores where a lively demand has produced remarkable results. These private improvements demonstrate an encouraging potential for civic pride and its wider implementation beyond the garden fence.

A passion for learning and education is traditional in Wales. Important evidence of this is seen in the great range of new provision for higher education which forms the other most significant post-War architectural development. The colleges of the University of Wales offered a great architectural challenge. Following the recommendations of the Robbins Committee in the 1960s, a major university expansion programme got into its stride. The university colleges in Cardiff, Swansea, Aberystwyth and Bangor, all moved forward with new projects. The large teaching hospital at the Heath, Cardiff, had to train many more doctors and their pre-clinical studies of anatomy, biochemistry and physiology, had to be provided for at the University College. New buildings for this purpose, together with the Faculty of Economics tower, were built at the north of the Civic Centre at Cathays Park. The accommodation required did in fact exceed very substantially the level anticipated and this made the construction of multi-storey buildings inevitable. Fortunately, the architects' proposals to take in part of the adjoining College Road, and thereby extend the original site, helped to limit the overall height of the new buildings. A new music department was fitted neatly into nearby Corbett Road. To the east a new Students' Union building and the Sherman Theatre followed.

At Swansea, the university college had by 1958 realized that even with a number of new buildings already completed, their beautiful site at Singleton Park required urgent reappraisal to meet the pressure of expanded departments and halls of residence. A plan was commissioned and work began on the first new building proposed – the small department for social studies. This was immediately followed by multi-storey student halls and a new library, linked to the one built before the War. New departments for the arts and sciences followed and eventually sites for more student residence had to be found some distance away at Hendrefoelan. The college at Bangor similarly expanded on its urban campus, still dominated by the splendid Edwardian building of R. T. Hare. All three of these colleges were on relatively restricted sites, resulting in high-density building development to meet the needs for substantial new accommodation.

The University College of Wales at Aberystwyth, however, had to meet serious limits to its expansion many years before. The distinguished Victorian building of Old College on the sea front could not be extended. Development had begun before the War at the college's new site at Penglais on the slopes above the town. A series of earlier plans for the campus had resulted in a somewhat mixed pattern of building. Here, too, in 1965 a development plan was commissioned and Principal Thomas Parry and the President, Sir David Hughes-Parry took the courageous decision to implement its first stage – a Great Hall with Bell Tower and the Students' Union (see colour section). This was to form the new centre for the college on a site in the middle of what was then open fields. The plan proposed that these buildings together with a new library would rise on three sides of a broad paved concourse, the fourth side open with views westwards to the sea. The design of the assembly chamber of the Great Hall itself was based on the traditional form of the Welsh chapel to provide an appropriate sense of intimacy and participation. Subsequently, a theatre, halls of residence and arts teaching buildings have been erected. The architectural and landscape proposals in the plan have helped develop a unified college campus at Penglais.

A university should offer ideally a beautiful and civilized environment for its students and teachers. High above the town, with breathtaking views over Cardigan Bay, Penglais campus must surely be one of the finest and most dramatic university sites in Britain. The harmony of this development arises from the enlightened policy of the college and its successive presidents and principals who, with their colleagues, have shown confidence in the appointment of a co-ordinating architect, which has helped to ensure continuity of the initial design concept over the past twenty-five years.

A steady programme of expansion was also undertaken at the small University College of St David's in Lampeter which is unique in having a fine collegiate building by C. R. Cockerell, which was completed as long ago as 1827. During the last thirty years this has been supplemented by a wide range of new teaching accommodation and student facilities in idyllic rural surroundings.

Industrial development has been profoundly important in post-War Wales. In the 1950s the new Abbey steelworks at Margam and the tin-plating works at Trostre and Velindre were impressive in size and complexity. They formed articulate industrial compositions and their architecture clearly expressed their function. Later the steel-rolling mills at Llanwern, with a three-mile succession of plant and buildings used strong primary colours to give a dramatic and exciting

Inmos Microprocessor factory, Newport, Gwent, by Richard Rogers Architects Ltd is dramatized by advanced structural techniques and positioning major ducts and service plant outside the main building envelope.

new vision of industry. Travelling past the works on the London main line, inter-city passengers had a memorable reminder of the process within the mills themselves – the heavy steel ingots progressively reduced to thin strips of steel racing along the rollers in competition with the speed of passing trains. The progressive weathering of the buildings over recent years has been softened by the landscaping, the now mature trees screening the works from the traveller's gaze.

Reflecting the enormous changeover from coal and steel-making to manufacturing and science-based industry, new industrial building has been of critical economic importance. The work of the Welsh Development Agency in south and north-east Wales and the Developments Board for Rural Wales, has produced a number of excellent buildings and set proper standards of design to private developers and their architects.

If heavy industry has seemed dramatic in its visual impact some of the new science-based technologies have also made a significant impact architecturally. The earliest of these was the Brynmawr

Rubber Factory completed in 1951. Of exciting innovative design its main production area was spanned by nine shallow shell concrete domes. The Parke-Davis pharmaceutical plant near Pontypool was sensitively designed to exploit its rural setting to advantage. Amersham International laboratories at Whitchurch used high-technology building materials which emphasize the scientific and clinical nature of the product — radio-isotopes. It also helped to identify the different functions of the building elements on the site. (See p. 23.)

The Inmos microprocessor factory, another high-technology building at Newport, uses its external roof structure and its series of major service elements to dramatic effect. More restrained in its country setting on the edge of Newtown, the textile printing factory for Laura Ashley was designed to give this large building a more human scale. Traditionally hung wall tiling is used to do this and to express the intricate and delicate patterns of the fabrics produced.

In addition to those already mentioned, a variety of other building types have appeared in Wales during the past twenty-five years. A selection of those which have had major awards show how architects responded successfully to their clients' many different functional needs. The Llwydcoed crematorium near Aberdare in 1971 achieves a sense of quiet repose in its grouping of chapels and courts, its white rendered walls and slate roofs are characteristic of buildings in this wind-swept upland setting. The small Welsh Presbyterian chapel, Capel-y-Groes at Wrexham 1984, is unpretentious with restrained handsome detailing. With walls of honey coloured brick and a slate roof, it sits comfortably on its site among trees. (See p. 212.)

The main centre for the Welsh Folk Museum at St Fagans near Cardiff was designed to avoid any stylistic conflict with the many other different buildings of the adjoining folk park. It is planned for easy and relaxed movement of visitors through the galleries which provide a neutral architectural setting for the exhibits themselves as the focus of attention. Its light grey brick walls and horizontal emphasis help the building to fit in restfully within the woodland park background. Unlike most buildings, museums have to be designed for continuing growth and the master plan, prepared for St Fagans in the 1960s, is still the basis for its current, eighth, development stage. (See colour section.)

With the advantage of being far smaller than earlier major district general hospitals, two of the recent new generation of community hospitals have achieved a reassuring sense of human scale. These at Mold in Clwyd and at Ystradgynlais in Powys are both designed with low overhanging pitched roofs and walls of warm patterned

The community hospital at Mold, Clwyd by the chief architect, Welsh Health Common Services Authority is one of a new generation of small hospitals. Informal in character with low sweeping roofs it has a reassuring human scale.

brickwork of a domestic character. Their sensitive design avoids any institutional air and gives the patients a feeling of relaxed informality, complementary to their medical care.

The international concern which arose in the late 1960s and early 1970s as to the quality of many individual buildings and of the appearance of towns generally was shared in Wales. The sophisticated steel and glass grid of Mies Van der Rohe had become debased into the crudest curtain wall. Cheap wall cladding systems became a dull formula for enclosing any type of building. Poor technical performance and weathering often led to leaking walls and drab exteriors. Similarly, difficulties with the heavier factory-made structural systems, particularly as applied to multi-storey flats like Ronan Point, destroyed much public confidence in modern building technology. Inadequate knowledge and experience of performance in use of these systems, together with competitive cost-cutting in the building industry, were blamed for these failures. Although much of this was outside the architect's direct control the profession suffered a loss of public confidence.

Le Corbusier's vision of homes in crystal towers rising from broad green parks was lost in its application to existing urban settings. Dull versions of his proposed towers appeared in most larger towns and cities. These initially seemed something of a status symbol for larger housing authorities like Newport, Cardiff and Swansea. They helped, of course, to increase residential densities and economize on land and were regarded as interesting focal points in housing layout design. In some cases they were successful, but many were found wanting in two important respects. The Cardiff flats at Butetown illustrate this well.

The first problem arose from the post-War planning technique for 'comprehensive redevelopment' where the bulldozer was brought in to sweep away large areas of old residential neighbourhoods. The houses of Loudon Square, which would now be regarded as recoverable and renewable, were demolished to make way for two blocks of multi-storey flats of frightening scale and incongruity. This ruthless process destroyed the existing close-knit social patterns of the area. The rehoused residents found themselves remote from their original neighbours; old social relationships were greatly disrupted. Furthermore multi-storey flats were found in time to be particularly unsuitable for families with children. They felt isolated on upper floors, remote from play areas and other social facilities easily reached from traditional houses.

In parallel with work of this kind, the centres of larger towns were being developed with buildings, often of indifferent quality and appearance and with a scale and character of threatening anonymity. Promises of the modern movement seemed to be increasingly unfulfilled. There was a growing public awareness of the unsatisfactory quality of the built environment.

The process of urban clearance and rebuilding was seen by the late sixties to be losing the urban quality of towns in both Europe and North America. The informed public was becoming dissatisfied by this process and discouraged by the results of modern architecture. Much of post-War development was disliked because it appeared too plain and uninteresting and most of all, anonymous. The characteristic purism and lack of decoration of the modern movement was also a perfect basis for reducing building cost and using a minimal specification. Cheap buildings, especially evident in their external cladding, were ideal for speculative developers. Their inadequate long-term performance and poor weathering qualities were matters of little immediate consideration.

Gathering public concern became a major force in generating an international conservation movement. In Britain it helped to bring about the Civic Amenities Act of 1967 and subsequent planning legislation which focused attention on the loss of older buildings of all kinds and the inappropriate character of much of which replaced them. Old familiar buildings, which gave identity to a place and were often held in public affection, disappeared – the Old Market at Merthyr Tydfil, the Old Town Hall at Bridgend, the Westgate Street Fire Station in Cardiff and more recently the Cory Hall and Capitol Cinema among many others.

As with the modern movement the conservation movement had a social dimension. The process of public participation, already an accepted principle in town planning, emerged in the 1970s in projects like the Byker wall in Newcastle and in the community architecture movement. This recognition of the user's value in the design process, especially in housing, was important. Sadly its real effect has been limited in practice so far but its influence is growing.

Nevertheless, the conservation movement became a widely popular reaction against earlier post-War clearance. Once again older buildings seemed more likeable than the bland anonymity of the new and the devil the public knew looked preferable after all. Encouraged by that British sense of compromise to retain the best of the past alongside a better new seemed a good answer. Intellectual support for this change of view came from Robert Venturi and his adherents and led to a better understanding and re-evaluation of earlier architecture. Conservation with both popular and theoretical support had become manifest. The revival of traditional or regional local vernacular style in building — the neo-vernacular — had arrived.

Vernacular building had been of interest to architects at the turn of the century and, understandably, it was the late Victorian and Edwardian period which again attracted attention. In Wales, as in the rest of Britain, steeply pitched roofs replaced flat roofs, there were dormer windows, string courses in stone or brick with patterning of facades, rustic and cast-iron features and decoration, all assembled to produce a familiar, even 'cosy corner' effect. Houses, hotels, shopping centres and supermarkets could all be given this treatment, often with architectural wit and enthusiasm. Larger complexes were sometimes treated like groups of farm buildings or village halls decked out with appropriate details: weather vanes, clocks and lanterns. Indigenous buildings materials used included stone, slate, tile and timber and less concrete. Account has been taken of the local building styles so that neo-vernacular buildings fitted in more harmoniously in areas of older buildings in both town and country.

This architectural trend has been parallelled by greater public interest in ecology and the 'back to nature' wholefood trend in foodshops and supermarkets, and the revival of Victorian interior decoration for houses as well as Victorian-style clothing.

The rehabilitation of existing buildings, many of which might earlier have been demolished, was a major reversal of the comprehensive redevelopment approach and has had many advantages. Skilful architectural design enables old buildings to be adapted for completely different uses, keeping their most attractive features and integrating any new building work in a sympathetic way. Architects have shown great ingenuity in transforming a wide range of redundant buildings to entirely new purposes. Churches have become offices, farm build-ings clubs, coach-houses museums, warehouses hotels and so on. The advantages of these transformations have not only been economic, as the capital value in existing structures is often considerable, but have also helped to retain familiar and often well-loved buildings keeping the urban character of the place and complementing the existing context.

Another aspect of the conservation movement has been the con-scious revival of historic styles, particularly the classical. In its tradi-tional form this was entirely contrary to the original idea of the modern movement. But it has proved welcome to architects with clients who wish to express their conservatively traditional values architecturally. The classic idiom has also been used to very different effect, in what has become generally known as the post-modern style. The range and variety of post-modern work demonstrates its hybrid nature. Modern techniques are combined with traditional and his-toric elements with contrast and wit. The results are often stimu-lating, sometimes bizarre, but always the intention is to be 'different', a quality achieved with varying success architecturally.

In general the conservation movement has helped architects to relate their work more effectively to the public at large. This has often been done by using familiar architectural features to achieve better understanding of the architect's intention. There have been, of course, disadvantages in that some recent building has become poor pastiche or even caricature. Criticism of some speculative housing developments as 'Toytown' and some of the more extravagant examples of major buildings as 'carbuncles' are widely understood. But the most important result of the conservation movement has been the growing public awareness that a lively dialogue between the architect and society is essential to the well-being of our built en-vironment. Good buildings take account of the full range of the clients' needs and should be designed from the inside outwards. It is important that they are judged this way too rather than just from their external appearance.

Independent and increasingly effective pressures to improve mat-ters have come from a number of amenity societies. The Civic Trust for Wales has helped in the past twenty-two years, to establish civic societies through the Principality. With its help and that of its national counterpart in London, it has been able to influence both local authorities and their planners as well as architects and their clients. Many architects are often themselves members of local civic societies. The aim of the Civic Trust is to stimulate public awareness

The conversion of Spillers and Bakers old grain warehouse at Atlantic Wharf, Cardiff Bay, is a fine example of a conversion and renovation of a major Victorian building into modern flats. It was carried out by Lovell Urban Renewal with UMT Architects.

of the need to improve the quality of our surroundings and to use every reasonable means to this end. The recently awarded further financial support from the Welsh Office for this endeavour is particularly encouraging.

The Victorian Society and the Council for the Protection of Rural Wales are also helpful in this context. The first Building Preservation Trust for Wales was formed in Cardiff in 1985. Such Trusts aim to preserve and reuse buildings which can form part of our architectural heritage. The Prince of Wales Committee too has been particularly effective in generating a better understanding and appreciation of the built and natural environment. It has helped to initiate and implement a wide range of improvement projects throughout Wales, many of them involving school children and young people.

The process of urban growth and renewal is a continuing one and there have been many substantial changes in towns throughout Wales since the War. Some significant examples of architectural interest occur in Swansea, Caernarfon and Cardiff. Swansea was doubly unfortunate in not only losing the whole of its central area through enemy action in the War but in having it rebuilt so soon after on a conventional road framework. Many of the new buildings there were mediocre in quality and design. In great contrast to this has been the demanding but splendid renaissance of the lower Swansea Valley with the transformation of a vast area of industrial dereliction to new industrial estates, landscaped parks and major sporting facilities.

This development is to continue down the River Tawe, past the city's docks to the sea. On the west side of the river, the redevelopment of the south dock into Swansea Maritime Village is already one of the most successful examples of urban renewal in the whole of Europe. The old dock has been transformed into a handsome marina with boat and chandlery facilities, flats and restaurants surrounding the water in the most congenial way. Older buildings have been successfully rehabilitated for new uses, including a large warehouse which is now an industrial and maritime museum. The maritime village has provided Swansea with a new dimension and a welcome contact for the public with waterside recreation and the sea. (See colour section.)

A very different, but equally successful, scheme on a smaller scale is the new Gwynedd County Headquarters building at Caernarfon. This large new complex has been integrated into the old medieval urban framework, with great sensitivity. Adjacent listed buildings have been carefully retained or rebuilt as part of the project. Advantage has been taken to create new pedestrian squares and covered walkways. The scale, form and character of the new work is very much in harmony with the neighbouring buildings, not least the ancient castle. The result is a classic demonstration of urban conservation and good manners in architecture, paying full respect to the context of this distinguished historic town. (See colour section.)

St David's Centre and Concert Hall complete the east side of The Hayes in Cardiff. The architects, Seymour Harris Partnership, have designed the facade to retain a harmonious scale with adjoining buildings and ensure a successful containment of this very congenial urban space in the city.

Cardiff has been fortunate in being something of a late developer in post-War urban renewal. A number of grandiose, and architecturally inappropriate, development schemes for the centre of the city were, for various reasons, abandoned over the years. Instead, the outworn core has more recently been replaced by a relatively conservative development – St David's Shopping Centre. This has taken reasonable account of the existing context while taking advantage of direct links into surrounding shopping streets. The most attractive of these, the pedestrian precinct extending from St John's Church, past the old library to The Hayes, provides a western entrance to the centre. Adjoining the entrance, St David's concert hall has proved a tremendous new asset for music in south Wales. The concert hall is impressive internally with easy access from a series of public foyers and gallery spaces. The building has a limited frontage to the street with an irregular stepped facade which reduces its external impact architecturally but avoids conflict with the old surroundings. The shopping centre itself has smooth generous malls directly linked to existing major stores and convenient external entry points.

Enormous changes in the mining valleys of south Wales have radically improved the urban context. The depressing old image of abandoned mine workings and threatening black coal tips is giving way to green valleys and sparkling streams. The old mining towns support new cleaner light industry and are involved in a continuing programme of rebuilding and improvement. The Valleys Initiative of the Secretary of State for Wales seems likely to accelerate this steady process of urban renewal.

The Valleys Initiative is only one of several important developments in which architecture will play an integral part. A new barrage at the mouth of the River Tawe at Swansea is now under construction. This will create a new water area for marina and other uses and stimulate redevelopment of the adjoining areas to the east. Grosvenor Square Properties have recently proposed a well-designed new housing and commercial scheme – Port Tawe – which, like the Maritime Village will form an attractive new area for Swansea. The city council too has put forward new proposals to pedestrianize and landscape the city centre.

The proposed barrage to enclose the new Cardiff Bay is potentially one of the most comprehensive and exciting projects of the twentieth century. The intention is to re-unite the city centre of Cardiff with its waterfront and establish the area as a centre of excellence for innovation and urban renewal. As a major step in this direction South Glamorgan County Council, in partnership with Cardiff Bay De-

velopment Corporation, have demonstrated their own support by locating their new headquarters at the south end of the old Bute East Dock. This has generated much public confidence in the eventual achievement of the many advantages promised. Waterside development all around the long coastline of Wales has followed a study commissioned by Wales Tourist Board in 1982 for potential marina sites. Many of these are now to go forward. Other schemes like the Rhondda Heritage Park and the Ebbw Vale Garden Festival represent exciting new opportunities for the future. The major programme of refurbishment and extensions in the National Museum of Wales have already provided a dramatically improved context for our works of art. These together with current work at the Welsh Folk Museum at St Fagans will confirm the international significance of Wales for our collections and exhibitions.

Many major building projects have a substantial engineering content. Civil engineering work like bridges, barrages and major roads are of considerable visual and architectural significance. They will form an increasingly important aspect of new building work in Wales.

Economic growth in recent years has meant increasing investment in the urban infrastructure and buildings in Wales and a dramatic

The new South Glamorgan County Hall forms the vanguard of a major programme of urban renewal in Cardiff docklands. With a base of buff brick and a dramatic composition of ascending dark slate roofs it takes full advantage of its splendid waterside position on the old Bute East Dock.

improvement in the scope and the quality of architecture. The public level of expectation from the architect's work has risen substantially, and the general standard of design has improved accordingly. This is due not just to clients and their architects, but to the many other professionals involved within the design and construction process. The state of architecture in Wales now is probably more promising than ever before. There is, however, room for further improvement in that only about 37 per cent of annual building work carried out involves the services of an architect. An increase in the contribution of the architect to the total would certainly be helpful to the quality of our urban surroundings.

Many of the architects now practising in Wales, studied at the Welsh School of Architecture in Cardiff. The excellent progress of the school under the guidance of that gifted teacher, Professor Dewi-Prys Thomas, has been continued by his successors and a dedicated teaching staff. Also at the university college, the Department of Town Planning has achieved a fine reputation throughout Britain.

Notwithstanding the great improvement in architecture in recent years, architects have faced increasing criticism. Better public awareness of architecture and a more articulate climate of opinion is developing. The current wave of objection from HRH The Prince of Wales in his television film and his recent book *A Vision of Britain* is significant in that it expresses much of what many people feel. A great deal of what Prince Charles recommends, however, is familiar ground to most architects. Much of the content of his book is based on material provided by architects themselves and few would disagree with his 'Ten Principles'.

One of the Prince's expressed objectives is to challenge the 'professional establishment' and support the opinions of the layperson. In so doing the Prince appears to saddle architects with the whole responsibility for what is wrong with our towns and cities. This does not seem fair. The wishes and decisions of private developers, public authorities and agencies, and the government itself, are the major determinants of what architects are able to do and where they do it. The architect does not fix the budget for building cost and it is this which is often the most important factor in determining the final quality of a building. As in most other matters, society will only get the quality that it is prepared to pay for.

More information and publicity about architecture will ensure its future well-being. This field has been largely untapped in Wales by writers and journalists. When shall we see a regular weekly article on architecture or urban design in a Welsh magazine comparable with

Lewis Mumford's famous 'Skyline' series in *The New Yorker* or Jonathan Glancey's more recent articles in the *Independent*? When will television in Wales produce a series as enjoyable and informative as Alec Clifton-Taylor's 'Six English Towns' (he eventually covered eighteen!)

We have a rich vein of excellent architectural material which could be presented in an informative and exciting way. It would have considerable general interest as well as commercial value for tourism and incoming industry. It would help within the school curriculum to give children a fuller understanding of their surroundings, and it would reinforce public consciousness of our own rich architectural heritage, leading in turn to the development and maintenance of high standards.

The refurbished circular gallery at the National Museum of Wales, Cardiff, is part of the first stage of a major expansion programme by Alex Gordon Partnership. Precise control of light and ventilation is provided to ensure ideal conditions for viewing and for the works of art.

Surely the Prince of Wales is right in his object to stimulate discussion 'about the design of the built environment' and 'to re-kindle an alert awareness of our surroundings'. It is unrealistic and probably undesirable to look for universal agreement on architectural style and taste. Controversy itself is evidence of increased interest and vitality and, as a public art, architecture is likely to benefit from this process. Prince Charles's own active interest should therefore be welcome.

A public well informed about architecture is more likely to be sensitive and discriminating about its urban surroundings. It is also likely to produce more demanding clients and, one hopes, many more patrons of the art of architecture. Architects invariably do their best work in such circumstances. Surely this is what we would all like to see in Britain and certainly in Wales. Good architecture is a pleasure to see and a delight to experience. There is already much of it in Wales to enjoy. There can be much more. To those as yet unaware of this encouraging prospect the motto of the City of Cardiff may be apposite – 'Deffro, Mae'n Ddydd!' – Awake it is Day!

A TOUCH
OF MAGIC
ON THE ROAD

JOHN PETTS

IN Wales, praise be, it is our privilege to live in a land of rocks and mountains, velvet hills, streams and tumbling falls of silver waters, rivers with leaping salmon and trout, placid lakes reflecting sun and sky, shores of wide sand and mighty cliffs, surf and breaking waves, fields, trees and forests, all alive and enriched with birds and beasts. The impact of man is seen in roads and bridges, the rearing of flocks and herds and the burgeoning of green acres, and in industry with the manufacturing of steel, the mining of fuels and the magical making of things.

Considering a small country so crammed with a myriad fascinating subjects to capture the eye of the artist, the interested observer has often posed the understandable question: surely the response to all this wonderful subject matter, all this exciting form and line, all this colour and texture confronting artists of similar aim and vision, must have resulted in the creation of a national school of painting? The true and disappointing answer is, 'No way'. This is a situation which, in my view, takes some understanding. Naturally, such a picturesque country has attracted professional landscapists and amateur sketchers for some centuries but, sad to say, following the post-War development of an awareness of modern art in Wales and the growth of art education through our schools and art colleges, too many of our rising young painters have turned sophisticated eyes outside Wales to the dazzling achievements of fashionable painters in London, Paris and New York. Understandable yet sad, this desire to be modish has led to the turning of blind eyes to rich and natural sources of inspiration. Unhappily this attitude has resulted in some paintings in Wales which can only be called pseudo art, as apish in style as a teenager's hair-do. These immature painters, by now, I hope, have learned the painful truth of the couplet that 'those who strive to keep abreast, are bound to end up second best'.

I have heard reasons galore trying to excuse or explain away the lack of a living tradition in Welsh art ... 'The people were too poor.' 'They had to work too hard.' 'There was no patronage.' 'They were forbidden by the chapels: like the wanton theatre, art, being bound up with the enjoyment of the senses, must be taboo, to the extreme Puritan, the work of the Devil.'

Peasants in Poland, though horny-handed from their work in the fields, covered the walls and ceilings of their cottages with delicate appliqué designs cut from richly-coloured paper. The elderly Matisse used the same language when not fit enough to stand and paint. What we are considering here is 'the impulse to decorate', that most valuable gift which is by no means common to all cultures: the given instinct to use colour, texture, mass and line as a special poetry to delight the eye, as music pleasures the ear.

Jingoism and truth are awkward bedfellows. East of the Urals, we are told, there are some folk who are sure that Shakespeare was a Russian, that the apple dropped not on Newton's head but on a Slav's. Such perversion of the truth in the promotion of 'nationalistic' identify is not uncommon. It should not surprise us therefore that any attempt at a comprehensive history of art in Wales should be eyed with caution. In its anxious search for corn in Egypt, it could be tempted to go too far and dig too deep, and so be unable to resist pouncing upon any evidence of the visual arts in the Principality in any period and lay claim to it as Welsh. Wishful thinking, laced with scarcity value, is very strong drink to the historian who is not too sure of his ground. At the same level we can find sophisticated Celtic metalwork, superbly crafted in the Early Iron Age and dug up in Anglesey by bulldozers excavating a new airfield, proving that the incendiary match struck by Saunders Lewis and friends in Llŷn was not the only notable event brought about by the advent of an English airfield. And what of the fine calligraphy and illumination of those Cistercian scribes brought over when the Normans set up the monastery at Margam?

This land of Wales, bound to other lands and cultures by the sea-routes from Spain, Brittany and the Hebrides, has had living art connections with the Middle East, with the early Coptic church. There are beasts carved on capitals in Egypt that might have crawled from Norse ship decorations to the fantastic church of Kilpeck in Gwent. Students sailed far to land at the small port of Hodnant near St Illtud's church of Llantwit Major in south Wales, to join the saint's college where they studied both ploughing and philosophy. Confronted by such quirks of geographic art history, Wales can lay no claim to parentage or inheritance. Yet we can be quietly aglow with a little pride on discovering that our Dark Ages had their own special light.

As we move forward in time, we have to face the fact that any search for a truly indigenous art of quality in Wales is fruitless before the eighteenth century. Even then, with art education non-existent, the squirearchy went to London for paintings to decorate the walls of its mansions. This demand brought into Wales travelling limners, hack-workers able to supply landscapes and portraits. Some settled, and local artists developed to fill a need. Early portraits show not only 'the squire and his relations' but other stations such as harpists, prosperous tradesmen and gamekeepers. Further, the developing interest

in topography and nature and the production of books on these subjects created a need for illustrators and engravers. A notable example
was Moses Griffith, manservant to Thomas Pennant, trained by his
master to illustrate his *Tours in Wales* in 1784. Prolific as well as
gifted, Griffith is reckoned to have made over 2,000 topographical
drawings for Pennant. The lesson here seems to be 'create the need
and the artists will appear'. Is not the truth of this being demonstrated some two hundred years later?

The so-called Romantic movement in art and literature of the late
eighteenth and early nineteenth centuries can be said to have been
anticipated by the Welsh poet John Dyer in his much anthologized
poem *Grongar Hill* with its language of extravagant eulogy in praise
of the Tywi Valley much praised by Wordsworth and influencing, it is
said, Gray's *Elegy written in a Country Churchyard*. This movement
gained astonishing popularity and became a 'fashionable way of
thinking and creating' in both artistic and literary works. The extrav-
agance of its attitude was echoed in the words of Archbishop Herring
who, after a visit to 'Wild Wales' wrote 'I have been greatly terrified
with something like the rubbish of creation'.

In Wales the three classifications of laudable landscape were to
become accepted as 'the sublime, the beautiful and the picturesque'.
Contemporary writing is crammed with descriptions of rugged scenes
as 'awesome, fearful, tempestuous, full of grandeur and awe, majestic
and sublime'. This attitude also found visual expression as English
painters wrapped themselves up and moved into Wales for the drama
of its landscape and weather. If asked which landscape painters of
distinction were drawn to Wales during this period, the straight
answer seems to be ' *all* of them' – all the acknowledged masters of the
time, including David Cox, Thomas Rowlandson, J. C. Ibbetson, J.
M. W. Turner, Paul Sandby, John Sell Cotman and Thomas Girtin.
These artists could be called foreigners on tour, marvelling at the
varied visual wonders of a new landscape. The 18-year-old Turner,
for instance, made a series of spirited drawings during a walking tour
across south Wales.

The best-known native Welsh landscape painter of this period is, of
course, Richard Wilson. Born near Machynlleth in 1713, he started
with that favourable background for future fame, the son of a Welsh
clergyman who gave him a classical education. This must have influenced his approach to painting landscape, for he acknowledged the
influence of Claude and Gasper Possin. In the 1740s he set up a studio
as a portrait painter in London, later making the fashionable and
profitable move to Italy where he painted devotedly from nature in

the Campagna and soaked himself in the style which never left his work. After some seven years he returned to London, continuing to paint modish landscapes aimed at buyers who had made the Grand Tour. He painted views of England and Wales, too, all with the required look of Italy. His was a large commercial output but, in spite of this realistic productivity, he fell on hard times, and in 1776 he was appointed Librarian of the Royal Academy, a post regarded as a sinecure for the needy artist.

Earlier we gave some thought to why Wales has produced no recognizable and fruitful Welsh School of Painting, in the sense of a lively and original group of creative artists of similar aim in a productive and stimulating get-together – 'knocking spots off each other' would be the colloquial term. Sometimes we cannot help but wonder: 'What, no Impressionists? No Fauves? (We have *some* 'wild beasts' surely?) No Barbizon School? No Norwich School? What about an *Ysgol Eryri* or *Grŵp Morganwg* ?' Since no vivacious and fertile group has yet appeared, we have to concern ourselves with individual artists of achievement.

As we move into the middle of the nineteenth century – amazing! Behold, we have a sculptor! George Gibson is the name. Born at Gyffin, upriver from Conway in Gwynedd, apprenticed at an early age to a sculptor in Liverpool. He came to the notice of a perceptive patron, William Roscoe, who recommended him to the imaginative sculptor, Henry Fuseli RA, Keeper of the Royal Academy Schools in London (where, God bless, entry has always been on merit alone, with no fees charged). Eventually, Fuseli steered Gibson to Flaxman, who steered him to Rome. There Gibson set up his studio as a professional, with many important commissions coming his way, including a coloured statue of Queen Victoria for the grand staircase of Buckingham Palace. Gibson made a popular hit with his life-sized marble nude *The Tinted Venus*, which is said to have caused a sensation when exhibited in a Greek temple specially designed for it at the London International Exhibition in 1862. Clearly, Gibson liked his marble flesh-pink, for he coloured a total of five life-sized replicas of *The Tinted Venus* during his lifetime. He worked in Rome for forty-eight years, amassing a large fortune. Labelled a neo-classicist – a sculptor influenced by early Greek art – Gibson was an excellent traditional draughtsman and, as a carver, a superb craftsman. Unfortunately, by today the passage of time has caused much of his work to remind us of the angels on tombs in Victorian cemeteries.

From now on the story of art in Wales continues to be one of comings and goings: the entry of artists from England and abroad, attracted by the dramatic beauty of the country, and the exit of talented local artists trying to make good in more prosperous environments. By the mid-1890s the work of the Pre-Raphaelites was in evidence, the one Welsh painter to be noted both for his contacts and for his achievements is Henry Mark Anthony. Through his friendship with Ford Madox-Brown, Anthony was connected to the Pre-Raphaelite Brotherhood (PRB). He had spent some time with the Barbizon School in France and was a friend of Corot. In technique he acquired a breadth of handling which brought high praise from friends in the PRB who regarded him as 'like Constable but better by far', and further that he was 'the outstanding painter in England'. (There is a painting of Tintern Abbey by Anthony in the National Museum of Wales.)

Edward Burne-Jones, a native of Birmingham, versatile painter, and designer of tapestry and stained glass for the William Morris firm of craftsmen, counted Rossetti and other Pre-Raphaelites among his friends. He has a number of works in Wales, including a large west window in stained glass in St Deiniol's church, Hawarden, (given in memory of their father by Gladstone's children), and a window in Llanwenarth Citra church, near Abergavenny. Another important Pre-Raphaelite work in Wales is the triptych painted by Dante Gabriel Rossetti, commissioned in 1856 by Llandaff Cathedral, which shows a Nativity group in which are included portraits of the artist's friends. Unfortunately, the three panels have suffered from a lowering of tone due to a misuse of oil and varnish.

Despite having breathed sad sighs over the lack of groups of artists in Wales, tribute must be paid to the setting up of the Royal Cambrian Academy (RCA) in 1881. Its aim was high: to establish a national academy of art in Cardiff (not a capital city at that time). This seemed a pipe dream in the face of a lack of funds and a worthy headquarters. The latter problem seemed to be solved, pro tem, by the offer by Lord Mostyn of the fine Tudor building of Plas Mawr in Conway at a peppercorn rent. The Academy moved there in 1884 and has remained there ever since, quietly playing its part as a centre for artists hailing mainly from north Wales and the west Midlands, yet sadly taking little part in the cultural life of the whole of Wales. Many believe that the Academy, boasting such a noble title, could come into its own if it would only gather up its fading skirts and fly down from its north-east hideaway to our capital city. Certainly the consideration of such a move would take a selfless resolution, but it is clear to many with experience of the art scene in Wales that, having taken the plunge, the Academy would never look back once fully involved in

Snow above Beddgelert *by Kyffin Williams.*

the lively and varied, comprehensive world of contemporary art in Wales. In many ways the RCA has done its best to move with the times and to widen its aims and standards by inviting artists of stature, such as Kyffin Williams and Will Roberts, to join its ranks as Honorary Academicians. This is a realistic opening move, and we watch the next with interest. I remember Lily, daughter of Clarence Whaite, the President of the RCA at the time, recalling in her seventies the excitement of a young girl at the visit of Queen Victoria to the opening of the Academy at Plas Mawr in 1884. A contemporary photograph shows the frock-coated academicians and councillors meeting the royal train at Conway station. Queen Victoria's reign was a heyday for art and artists in Britain. One popular painter, Frederick Leighton, was even raised to the peerage, the only one in art ever, it seems, before or since. Members of the new and increasingly prosperous middle class were becoming patrons. There was money for the doggy pictures of Edwin Landseer (how evocative of the period is the title *Dignity and Impudence*).

In a more respectable category there appeared the sculptor Goscombe John: born in 1860, the son of a Cardiff wood-carver, he moved to London at the age of twenty-one to work for the sculptor Thomas Nicholls. Gaining a studentship at the RA Schools, he worked hard there in the evenings and won the Gold Medal, which enabled him to tour Europe. In Paris he studied the work of leading European sculptors, especially Auguste Rodin, to whose studio he was a frequent visitor. On his return he set up a studio in London where he established a growing practice, increasing in reputation as a frequent exhibitor at the RA to which he was elected in 1909. A knighthood followed two years later. Such success in the metropolis brought commissions from even the officials of his native city and beyond, and so Welsh collections acquired many of his works. He became a staunch supporter of the idea of encouraging Welsh art in Wales.

Born not in Wales but in Bruges, yet hailed as another noted Welsh artist of this period was Frank Brangwyn. Made an RA in 1919 at the age of fifty-two, he was knighted for his achievements over twenty years later. He was a lively and talented painter of large rumbustious murals (some would say of vulgar exuberance) in rich colours. There are typical examples of these in public buildings in London and America. His designs for murals in the House of Lords, however, brought him much trouble. Rejected after heated arguments, on the grounds of unsuitability, eventually they found a permanent home in the Guildhall, Swansea, which many people consider a happier place for them, their colourful gaiety and full designs seeming in better accord with concerts of music than with the solemn deliberations of peers in the Victorian Gothic of the Upper House in Westminster. However, in any setting, they would remain a decorative *tour de force*. The panels were once described as 'a fairground harvest festival in Covent Garden market'. Could it perhaps be said that the House of Lords has need of such colourful relief? Brangwyn's works always carry a powerful sense of scale and the architectural strength in his design is enriched by the vitality of his draughtmanship. These qualities enliven his large etchings which have found a respected place in national collections worldwide.

We now come to a period of exciting change in the story of art in western Europe. The loose term 'modernism' might be used to cover what was happening as the new century advanced, and the new labels were Cubism, Fauvism and the bold movement into Abstract Art, lit by the explosive name of Picasso. In Wales, increasing awareness of

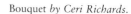
Bouquet *by Ceri Richards.*

these influences was spread in several ways — by the growth of illustrated art books, by enlightened art education, and especially by
artists fired by the new flames. In some instances the last two
categories were occupied by the same important figure: Ceri Richards
comes at once to mind.

Ceri Richards was born at Dunvant near Swansea in 1903 and,
from a generation of brilliant students at Swansea School of Art, he
became the finest artist. Abstract in the construction of his paintings,
in London exhibitions of the 1930s he was linked with Henry Moore,
Ben Nicholson and John Piper. Much influenced by the modern continental masters, Picasso, Matisse and Max Ernst, it could be said
that both as a painter and a teacher he did much to spread the gospel
of modernism, sowing on the fertile ground of the time, learning new
visual languages, gathering expressive material to enrich his own
powerful and individual vision. In Wales he certainly opened our
eyes, shook us out of sluggish visual habits and gave us so much
through his art. (I am thinking especially of the lovely *Cathédrale
Engloutie* series which reminds us that Ceri was a man of music as
well as painting.)

Augustus John was another west Wales native whom we are proud
to own. Never directly influenced by any of the 'isms', yet, with his
superb draughtsmanship, intense colour and bravura brushwork, he
brought much that was new to art in Wales. Born in Tenby in 1878,
son of a Haverfordwest lawyer, he was trained at the Slade School,
where he added to the tradition of fine drawing of the human figure.

Little girl with a large hat and straw-coloured hair *by Gwen John.*

In the years before the First World War, he made a brilliant series of small landscape paintings, a direct response to nature, vivid in colour and contrast. These made their mark on his contemporaries especially on a fellow-Welshman, James Dickson Innes from Llanelli. A close friendship developed between the two young painters. In 1911 they shared a painting expedition to the mountains of north Wales which resulted in series of landscape studies of identical approach, brilliant in colour and strength of statement. In some of these only the signatures clarify their identify. For reasons of income, John developed his gift for portraiture, while Innes returned to the mountains he loved to paint in the southern Pyrenees, at Callioure, where he stayed for reasons of health, since he suffered from tuberculosis. Three years after his expedition with John, he died aged twenty-seven, while John developed into the most brilliant portrait painter of the age.

Augustus John's sister, Gwen, also trained at the Slade. Hers was a great and special talent, with a personality so very different from that of her extravagantly Bohemian brother. Gwen was shy and withdrawn, introvert. Her painting was full of subtle grey tones, her subjects were of absolute simplicity: a small empty table in an attic window became a visual poem. She never married, never fought for what the world calls success. She did not return to Wales after her studies in London and never painted in her native land. In 1903 she moved to France and felt at home in the austere life of convents where she had friends who sat for her.

To support herself Gwen John worked as a model in Paris studios. An artist of sensitive perception, Gwen John must have been well aware of the value of her service, and it must have been a matter of pride when she was engaged to serve in the studios of the sculptor acknowledged to be the greatest of his age, Auguste Rodin. At the height of his fame at the age of sixty-three, his projects called for many life models. From her experience, Gwen John proved a valuable assistant who became a close friend. The value of the contact was two way, for the sculptor encouraged the painter and passed on to her his belief in the reward of hard and devoted work. She has left behind her a host of delicate paintings and drawings, many of which are now in the collection of the National Museum of Wales. Her work was held in high esteem by her brother. At an exhibition in the Leicester Galleries in London, Augustus John, holding one of his sister's small paintings, was heard to say: 'One day someone will say "Didn't Gwen John have a brother?"'

In the early part of the century a widening interest in the visual arts in Wales became evident. One aspect of this was increasing patronage and sponsorship. In 1920, Gregynog Hall, a mansion near Newtown was bought by two sisters, Gwendoline and Margaret Davies, granddaughters of David Davies of Llandinam, who had built a fortune from developing coal transport and docks enterprises in south Wales in the middle of the nineteenth century. These ladies had plans for developing the arts in Wales. Gregynog was to become a centre for exhibitions, with studios for pottery, concerts of music and a printing press for producing fine books. The most successful of these ventures was the press, which, by the employment of skilled typographers,

Aphrodite in Aulis *by David Jones.*

wood-engravers and bookbinders, produced a series of very fine volumes which brought world-wide praise. (Now under the aegis of the University of Wales, Gwasg Gregynog has continued to produce fine books since its revival in 1974.) Years later, these same generous and perceptive ladies were to put Wales and Cardiff on the world's art map by presenting their superb art collection, including fourteen impressionist paintings, to the National Museum.

Another important art enterprise in a rural setting in Wales was the arrival of Eric Gill with his family and colleagues in 1924 at Capel-y-ffin at the head of the lovely Honddu Valley in the Black Mountains, north of Abergavenny. Gill was anxious to make a fresh start in a new place after the failure of the Guild of St Joseph and St Dominic at Ditchling in Sussex. One clear distinction set this enterprise apart from others: it was based on a unifying belief in the importance of creative art and craftsmanship under the aegis of the Roman Catholic faith.

This was a heyday period for Gill, with many commissions demanding his attention. In the four years at Capel-y-ffin, he carried out projects in sculpture, wood-engraving for illustration, and the design of typefaces for printing. John Rothenstein has spoken of a visit to Capel-y-ffin that while being shown round by Gill they passed through a room where a studious young man was sitting drawing. Outside, Gill said quietly: 'Take note of that young man. He's going to do great things. Never mind Eric Gill and the rest of us, *he* is the gifted one who will be known. His name is David Jones.' In the sixty years since, this has proved a truly discerning prophesy.

The time at Capel-y-ffin was the first adult visit of David Jones to Wales. He has proved such a rare and special person that he can be hailed unhesitatingly as one of the truly important figures in the art of Wales in this century. Jones was born in Brockley in Kent, his father being a Welshman from Holywell in Clwyd. His nature, interests and inspiration cannot be summarized in a paragraph. His religious instinct was intense. He was fascinated by the ancient myths and legends of Wales and had a great love for the sea and landscape. He had been profoundly moved by his experiences as an infantryman in France in the First World War, which found expression in his first book *In Parenthesis* in 1937. He was also that rare figure, scarcely to be found since William Blake, a creative artist gifted in both word and image.

The first comprehensive retrospective exhibition of the works of David Jones, organized by the Welsh Committee of the Arts Council in 1954, toured Wales before being shown at the Royal Scottish Academy and finally at the Tate Gallery in London. It opened the eyes of so many to the rich heritage created by this gifted man, and taught us much about the value, the wonder and, especially, the mystery of true art.

The list of important influences in the development of art in Wales in the past three decades and the number of artists who have made a name is now so long that we can but touch upon them. The name of

Man planting *by Will Roberts.*

John Kyffin Williams, the doyen of Welsh painters in oils, would be the first to spring to many minds. Considered to be the ideal figure of the native artist in Wales, living and working in his own country, and taking as his subjects its dramatic mountain landscapes and his characterful fellow-countrymen, he is held in high esteem and affection. He is also a writer and lively raconteur. A Royal Academician and a prolific worker, he handles paint with zest and bravura, laying on a thick impasto with a direct assurance of design.

Another acknowledged painter of importance is Will Roberts of Neath. A powerful draughtsman, his work always carries its own dignity: landscapes of mood, strong in design, and portraits of discerning characterization. His figures, like Millet's, are informed by the nobility of labour, and his pictures are always rich in expressive colour.

Based in west Wales, Arthur Giardelli is respected both for his influence as an art educationist and as an adventurous designer. His creative and original constructions in relief, using multiple fragments of materials such as slivers of wood and metal, are carried out with infinite patience and craftsmanship. Robert Hunter, of Carmarthen, is a gifted painter with a strong sense of design and colour, with the courage to experiment with both. It is more than high time that our public buildings made fuller use of such a decorative artist among us. John Elwyn, though based in Hampshire, where he was art lecturer for many years, has never really left his native Dyfed, since he returns there constantly for study and inspiration. With a fine sense of colour, his paintings carry a strong feeling for atmosphere and place. (See colour section.)

It is very clear now, in retrospect, that the past thirty years or so have been a specially burgeoning and fruitful period for the visual arts in Wales. The 1960s were a time of lively change, when artists questioned themselves and each other, looked around and abroad, and, in south Wales in particular, many ran the gamut of a host of fashionable styles and coteries under such banners as Funk-Art, Op-Art, Pop-Art, Happenings, names as fantastic as some of the pop groups of the time. Though much was ephemeral, it all served a purpose, a visual sparring and flexing of muscles, a seeking for new art forms and language and a shedding of old prejudices.

This whole movement was enhanced by the foresight of Leslie Moore, the devoted and pioneering art organizer for Glamorgan, a

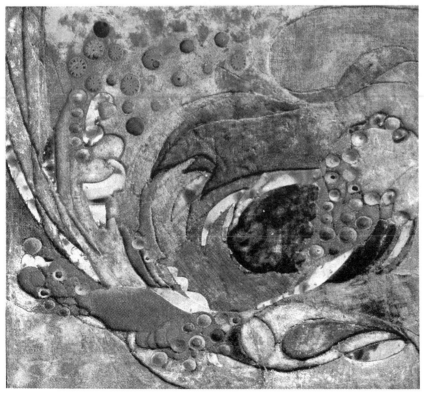

The sea has many voices *by Arthur Giardelli.*

Courtship by Michael Flynn.

painter of verve himself, who added to the flames of controversy at his annual summer school at Barry, by bringing to the staff an enterprising group of known avant-garde artists and sculptors in new materials. Led by the forthright Tom Hudson, they liked the climate and stayed, eventually joining Hudson in a powerful team when he became the new Director of Studies at Cardiff College of Art. Now they are well-known figures, including Michael Tyzack, Terry Setch, Alan Wood and Laurie Burt. A colleague of similar stature, Head of Fine Art in what is now called the South Glamorgan Institute of Higher Education, is Welsh painter Glyn Jones.

Newport College has also held distinguished artists and sculptors on its staff: sculptors Hubert Dalwood and Anthony Stevens, and painters Ernest Zobole and John Selway. Jeffrey Steele became one of the best-known Op artists in Britain, while Thomas Rathmell, the former Head of Fine Art, occupies a special place as a traditional figurative painter of refinement. Jack Crabtree was given leave of absence to benefit from special honours: first a Gregynog Fellowship, to develop his work in the quietness of Powys, then, most enterprisingly, the National Coal Board awarded him a fellowship to study the life and work of the pits, both on the surface and underground, an opportunity of which he took great advantage, enriching his work and vision.

Other colleges in Wales have benefited from distinguished tutors: in Swansea, the Stained Glass Department, under Tim Lewis, has become a leader in its very special field, training designer-craftsmen who are making a name world-wide. In Aberystwyth, David Tinker, both by his teaching and as a versatile exponent in painting and sculpture, made the Art Department in the University College of Wales a lively centre for study and exposition.

Other important figures stand out for their individuality and single-minded development of their special gifts. In north Wales, Jonah Jones is versatile in many materials, notably figurative sculpture and beautiful letter-cut inscriptions in slate and stone. In the south both Peter Nicholas and David Petersen are strongly individual and versatile in the use of materials while, in the slate-quarry town of Bethesda, at the gate to Snowdonia, Peter Prendergast, born in Abertridwr in south Wales, has settled in an area that he loves, painting what he finds in a direct and spontaneous way. His work is strong and assured in statement. He could be described as 'a painterly painter'.

An artist of rare quality who stands alone in contemporary Welsh painting is William Powell Wilkins. He lives and works quietly near Carreg Cennen Castle in Dyfed. His canvases are of modest size; his subjects some landscapes but mainly interiors with figures, nudes and

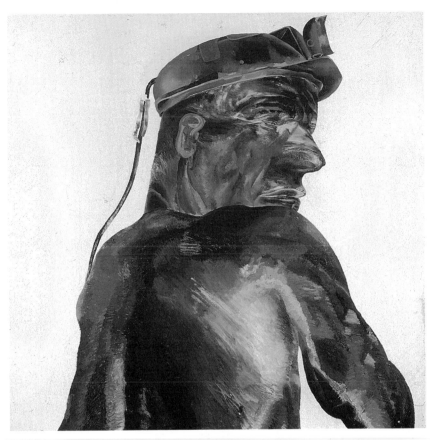

Miner of G6 face *by Jack Crabtree.*

still life. All is carried out with exquisite care, slowly realized with contemplation, his paint quality and texture *dwelt* on. It is clear from his admirers and patrons on both sides of the Atlantic that they *love* his work. (See colour section.)

By now, we are too used to expecting a wince of pain whenever Ireland hits our awareness; however, we can rejoice at the presence in Wales of Irish sculptor and ceramist Michael Flynn, known as a stimulating lecturer visiting many of our art colleges, and ceramics consultant in Cardiff. An Oriel 31 Touring Exhibition, sponsored by the Welsh Arts Council, was shown in Wales and the rest of Britain in 1989 and aroused wide interest. Here, at last, we have a fine and compelling draughtsman, devoted to expressing the human condition. In bronze and raku, his work explodes with dynamic energy, at once exultant and ominous. He *thinks*, too, and myth means much to him. He uses words as well: his titles evoke and explore. His art is wholly concerned with the throbbing and whirling spirit of life which torments and delights us.

Bethesda quarry *by Peter Prendergast.*

The 56 Group is an exhibiting co-operative of leading artists and sculptors in Wales who have felt the need to raise particular banners which imply that modern Welsh artists should be more widely shown. Since its inception, the Group has shown many exhibitions of high standing in Wales, and has also pioneered in sending exhibitions of Welsh art to Europe and the USA. There is also now a Welsh Sculpture Trust to help to place three-dimensional works firmly on the map of Wales. One of the trustees is our distinguished portrait sculptor Ivor Roberts-Jones. Under the guidance of the Trust our first open-air sculpture park has been created on the wide acres of Margam Park in West Glamorgan. This would have been unthinkable not so long ago.

The Contemporary Art Society for Wales is another older-established organization which has done valuable work in making artists and their works more widely known in Wales. Founded in 1937, its main aim has been to encourage the purchase of contemporary paintings, so giving a stimulus to artists, while at the same time widening the public interest by presenting its purchases to galleries, colleges and public institutions. The responsible task of selecting works for purchase is given to a different member each year. Over the years an important and most varied collection of works has been bought, exhibited and distributed, so the whole nation has been enriched.

Of the national institutions in Wales honouring the visual arts in painting and sculpture, pride of place must be given to the National Museum in Cardiff, whose art department, as well as building an increasingly representative permanent collection, has grown in international status following the gifts and bequests of the Davies sisters of Gregynog. Cardiff is now an essential port of call for anyone devoted to French nineteenth-century painting. In Aberystwyth, the National Library of Wales also mounts a regular series of exhibitions, and is steadily building a collection of contemporary Welsh painting.

In west Wales, at Picton Castle in Dyfed, is the Sutherland Gallery, under the aegis of the National Museum, devoted to an important selection of his paintings and drawings given by Graham Sutherland himself. In a special sense, this generous gift is a tribute to Wales (and especially to Dyfed) for the acknowledged impact of the landscape on the artist's work. The city of Swansea is fortunate in having the Glynn Vivian Art Gallery, which, sponsored by the local authority, is forward-looking and alert, bringing lively exhibitions before the public. It also provides a valuable service through visual interpreters acting as a link between the art and the gallery visitors, especially the children. In Llandudno, the Mostyn Art Gallery is the main art centre for north Wales, forming its own exhibitions as well as displaying others. The gallery has a valuable sense of public relations, providing lectures, teachers and working studio facilities.

It must be acknowledged, however that the greatest impact on the increase of art awareness, the encouraging of a wider appreciation of the visual arts and the growth of indigenous art in Wales, has been the devoted work of the Welsh Arts Council, which, by 1967, had been freed from the control of its parent body in London. Though financed by central government funds, this meant complete autonomy in the way in which it administered its affairs, and how and where it spent its money. Over the years the Council has dispensed grants to artists and craftsmen, art societies and other organizations, formed and sent exhibitions on wide tours, assisted special projects and lectures, aided special commissions, subsidized schemes for artists in schools, aided travel for study abroad, and so on. Altogether, with so many artists and organizations benefiting from these imaginative and varied ideas and schemes, the Council can be said to have carried out its difficult tasks with such foresight that it is impossible to contemplate progress in contemporary art in Wales without it.

So, over the past forty years, the story of art in Wales is the recital

Portrait of Colonel Sir William Crawshay *by Ivor Roberts-Jones.*

of steady, astonishingly varied and lively growth. Never before have there been so many practising artists, designers, sculptors and craftsmen scattered throughout Wales, so many galleries with full displays, so much public interest, so much buying of works of art. Before this period, who could have imagined a large open art exhibition at the Royal National Eisteddfod, thronged with visitors in eager discussion and argument? Today this is taken for granted.

This road of progress is remarkable, and the question is bound to arise: where do we go from here? And other questions follow: Why have we still no Welsh Museum of Modern Art? Why no City Art Gallery in Cardiff? Why are so few artists of achievement honoured by the Gorsedd at the Royal National Eisteddfod or in the Honours Lists, for that matter?

If I could wave a magic wand and blow a rousing trumpet from the shining peak of Snowdon, what would be the cry? Bless us with an increasing awareness of the importance of the vision of artists in opening our eyes. Bless us with sensitive and perceptive art sponsors with deep pockets. Bless us that original works of art in our houses might become as important as our three-piece suites; that we might become as proud of our contemporary paintings as we are of our cars; that we flourish a print of a new Welsh wood-engraving with the exultant glee usually reserved for the acquiring of a ticket for the next international game at the Cardiff Arms Park; that we bring in from overseas more artists of achievement to discuss and hob-nob with our own; that local authorities appoint committed and gifted art interpreters to act as links between exhibitions and the visiting public, especially our children; that roving and hungry art patrons might multiply, and O finally that we could all be blessed with an increasing vision of knowing the mystery, the magic – and yes, the *love* that is deeply implicit in that special word: ART. ('Nonsense', cry those who drop bricks on the polished floor of the Tate Gallery ...)

DRAMA

TRANSPORTING A SENSE OF PLACE

MIKE BAKER

THERE is ample evidence that the dramatic arts are in the vanguard of defining a new Wales. Welsh performers, writers and directors want both to entertain and provoke thought. If Yeats is right that out of the quarrel with others we make rhetoric, out of the quarrel with ourselves we create poetry, then the new dramatic traditions should not fear the quarrel.

New traditions must challenge the old and the borrowed. If the theatre of Wales is to be truly unique and invigorating then it must be wary of the seduction of the developed literary theatre of England. It is only some twenty years since professional theatre took root in Wales and already an amazing diversity of styles is emerging.

Firstly, there is what might be called a 'home service', a belief that audiences have the right of access to live theatre in their own locality, indeed designed for the locality. Then, there is a vibrant wave of young writers challenging the traditional motifs of Wales and examining the conflicts of contemporary life. Also, there is true internationalism; with artists seeing themselves not only as citizens of Wales but as part of an international artistic community. Satisfyingly, an international audience is approving. There is also a precious, (in the best sense), attitude toward theatre for young people. Moreover, there is access to a good technically equipped theatre building within forty miles of every part of Wales.

Within the fractured mosaic of indigenous styles — for our traditions are young and incomplete — the emerging theatre of Wales is radical and fascinating.

An excellent illustration is offered by the spectrum of events which burst from and in Wales over the summer of 1989. Among the beneficiaries of one event were the citizens of a European province not unlike Wales, that of Friesland in northern Holland. Even after the 1,500-strong audience had left the converted ice rink in Leeuwarden, the empty arena still reverberated with the epic rhythms and images of *Gododdin*. As drunk on the power of the performance as were the depicted men of Catraeth on mead, the Frieslanders were still hearing echoes of another tongue. *Gwŷr a aeth Gatraeth gynt*: (Men went once to Catraeth). The Welsh tongue in Britain has a similar position to that of Friesland in the Netherlands: both are minority languages in regions with some yearning for full nationhood. *Gododdin*, by the way, was chosen by the British Council as a flagship promotion under a new Britain in Europe initiative. And so, that summer in 1989 the spectacle of the *Gododdin* unfolded around and between audiences in their thousands in Italy, Germany, Holland and Scotland, the property of the Welsh theatre company, Brith Gof. It is stunning that

Brith Gof's highly acclaimed production of Gododdin, *performed in Wales, Scotland and Europe.*

Wales stands forward in international theatre in this way, to hear the language of Wales in performance in Friesland as in South America in 1988.

That summer also, professional theatre companies from Wales conquered Scotland under the collective banner 'Raiders of the Western Shore'. Strong new plays were the export commodity in English *and* in Welsh as seen at the Edinburgh Fringe Festival. Reviewing one of the Welsh plays in Edinburgh, the *Guardian* proclaimed that 'there

Anthony Hopkins

seems no doubt that contemporary Welsh culture is experiencing a resurgence and breaking out of national boundaries'. That is review-speak for a wave of exciting new work which is attracting a great deal of public attention. The author and director of one play was, according to one critic 'trying to create Welsh characters whose identity is not tied to tall hats, leeks or the past legacy of bards'.

A legendary raider of an eastern shore, America in this case, was Madog. This twelfth-century Welsh prince, son of Owain Gwynedd, with his crew reputedly interbred with the native Mandani Indians so that in the eighteenth century a certain John Evans could journey from Wales in search of a mythical Welsh-speaking tribe. In the summer of 1989 not only the Welsh and English languages but also Gujerati and a full vocabulary of performance ideas used the myth of Madog and the journey of John Evans at the Samaj community centre in Grangetown, Cardiff. The style and belief of the company, aptly named Theatr Taliesin Wales, is to build productions with participation by Cardiff's ethnic minorities, along with visiting professionals from far afield. And so the multi-ethnic Cardiff audience danced and then sat in fear as if they were the congregation, with John Evans preaching Baptist hellfire to them.

Of Welsh actors and artists working in more conventional theatre styles, in theatre, film and television, we must avoid the temptation to corral and type. Each is unique. While all of us of lesser talent ape the follies and styles of the gifted and lucky, the truth is that both the good and the committed stand apart. As Melvyn Bragg writes in his biography of Richard Burton: 'He was like no one else and the power of that singularity was what he drew on ... for his talent to act, to still an audience and to fill the screen, this was drawn not from technique, nor from imitation, but from himself.'

By the October of 1989, both Siân Phillips and Anthony Hopkins (whose natural technique and presence give him the distinction and the burden of the description 'Wales's greatest living actor') were leading West End casts while Peter Gill, distinguished theatre director and writer of plays on his Cardiff upbringing, was director of the National Theatre Studio. Peter Gill, described by director William Gaskill as arriving on the London Royal Court Theatre scene as 'suddenly there like a changeling. Black haired, skinny, a dock worker's son from Cardiff ... with his great strength in his ability to take a piece of human activity and focus on it with such care that it acquires a luminous life beyond its function'.

Memories are long as far as the famous Welsh faces who achieved international fame. Not all feel forced to carry the equipment of dark

Siân Phillips

intensity and self destruction. Emlyn Williams gave his name to the studio theatre auditorium in Theatr Clwyd, Mold which stands in his old county of Flint. On the occasion of the theatre's tenth anniversary, the Theatr Clwyd Company gave a vintage production of *The Corn is Green*.

The establishment of HTV, then TWW, as the regional independent television station for Wales owed much to the dedication of Stanley Baker. Although such contributions are soon forgotten, taken for granted or perhaps, more healthily, replaced by later generations, the spirit of individual performance is available on film. Of character actors the late Huw Griffith and the much-alive Meredydd Edwards are held in deep affection. Huw Griffith's dour undertaker is particularly well remembered as BBC Wales regularly broadcasts *Grand Slam*, Gwenlyn Parry's fictional account of an excursion to Paris from a Gwendraeth Valley village to see Wales play France in Paris. For many, *Grand Slam* is the definitive modern portrait in conviction and humour, performed by a happy mixture of three generations of Welsh actors, with Huw Griffith and Windsor Davies alongside the youthful Siôn Probert, Dewi Pws and Sharon Morgan. From the same generation, Dafydd Hywel among many, is crossing easily from Welsh to English, notably in such films as *The Happy Alcoholic* and *Coming Up Roses*.

There are many examples of Wales providing performers and artists of skill and originality to drama entertainment within Wales while also fuelling the repertory of international television and film – Angharad Rees and Hywel Bennett, Philip Madoc, Emrys James, Rachel Thomas, Glyn Houston, Mike and Robert Gwilym. Two young actors who should be watched for the future are Richard Lynch and Paul Rees, respectively playing leading roles in the Karl Francis film *Boy Soldier* and a major drama series directed by Richard Altman on the life of Van Gogh.

The memory of those who both made and were their own drama is preserved and enhanced by some extremely clever character performances. The wit and unique standpoint of writer Gwyn Thomas, who died in 1981, is captured beautifully in Glyn Houston's one-man virtuoso celebration. Not only Gwyn's verbal facility and his humanity but also his sheer likeness, the whole essence of the man, appears before us. Most recent in solo performances as Dylan Thomas is Robert Kingdom (a sell-out in the Edinburgh Festival in summer 1989) whose appearance is uncanny, his delivery inspired.

For some more militant Welsh people such names exemplify the self-mutilating tendency of Wales, that which is supposed to have

Theatr Taliesin's performance of Madog.

ultimately destroyed Dylan Thomas – namely, generosity to strangers. Though none of those mentioned, nor many other excellent artists working in the wider British or international drama media, is likely to consider himself a charitable donation to help out the ailing English.

But there must be no doubt that the peril of a small nation is its economic inability to retain those whose gifts attract them to richer palettes, bigger stages. No one should deny that Wales has something to offer the traditional British stage.

The charge that there is no theatre of Wales is plainly wrong; but it would be equally wrong to imagine that a grand literary theatre tradition will spring into being overnight and, indeed, in itself be an appropriate model. Think of how long it took for the Royal Shakespeare Company and the Abbey Theatre in Dublin to become established. Professional theatre created in Wales, as distinct from that toured into Wales, is still young.

In the autumn of 1989 Wales's national daily newspaper noted 'the truth is that Welsh people are notoriously difficult to attract to the theatre. Indeed, Wales has a reputation of being, in terms of drama, something of wasteland'. As an alternative to politely inviting the journalist in question to search for the Mandani Indians, we can further consider the events of that year.

In July, those with a particular advantage could view a world turned upside down. More accurately *A World Turned Upside Down*, an hour of magical beauty in an imaginary land created in a schoolroom by Hijinx Theatre. Among the elements contributing to its charm were old Moravian folk-songs. The story highlighted loyalty between friends and coping with change. It was of immediate attraction to its young audience, children with a qualification which gave them this particular advantage that afternoon. For this was a unit for children with special needs, some with a mental handicap. It is for this audience that the uniquely gifted Hijinx Theatre create their work.

This was a very different audience from those who filled theatres in three corners of the Principality to see Welsh actors of the conventional stage in their prime, particularly Philip Madoc (no relation to the Mandani) as the oily media Welshman Alun Weaver CBE in *The Old Devils*, a production which toured from the largest English language company Theatr Clwyd. They enjoyed another style of Welsh theatre which had them laughing at Kingsley Amis's unutterably sour view of Wales and its language. Perhaps the key fits again: provocative and entertaining.

The Old Devils proclaimed a view of Wales very distant from that of a small school in Gwynedd, in the village of Waunfawr. This is a community of the kind possibly referred to by the poet T. H. Parry-Williams 'There's Snowdon and its crew; here's the bare, naked land; Here's the lake and the river and crag; to be sure, Here's where I was born.' On a day in that warm June, the children were restless as the term was coming to an end, and because the local theatre in education company Cwmni'r Fran Wen had arrived to present its show *Plethu Gwreiddiau* (Plaiting Roots). Characters in the story, interestingly again looking at friendship and loyalty, frequently questioned the

Cwmni'r Frân Wen's performance of Plethu Gwreiddiau.

children from within their roles. At one point a character asked the question 'How does somebody feel when they go to a new school for the first time?' A black child immediately stood up and replied in perfect Welsh: 'Nervous and a bit scared but excited at making new friends'. The action continued. The programme ended to the delight of the teachers and children. The company toured on along Kate Roberts's Lôn Wen to Rhosgadfan, and the following day to Llwyngwril and Llanegryn. Participation by children excited by their experience was always lively, though never as surprising as that day in Waunfawr when a small child of Nigerian parents spoke up in the language of Gwynedd. Healthy drama explores conflict, and what greater conflict affects us all than in the perspective of young children, where our personal and social worlds just refuse to fit!

One of the many roles undertaken by Wales's network of county-based theatre in education companies is that of giving confidence in Welsh by means of theatre stimulation to young children whose first language is another, usually English. These are partnership funded: an arrangement unique in Britain, perhaps even world-wide, where costs are shared between the Welsh Arts Council, the local education authorities and the regional arts associations. This arrangement of tri-partite funding allows performances – or programmes since the work is both of theatrical and educational value – to be offered free at the point of contact to the classroom. This enables broad freedom of expression and opportunity. How otherwise would a permanent professional team of five be able to offer a fully researched and rehearsed half-day production to an audience of thirty in a small village school in the shadow of Snowdonia? Such a national framework of theatre provision for our young people is justifiably a source of pride.

Perhaps the foremost drive in the home service is *brogarwch*, a care and love for the locality and its people. This is most typically found as community theatre, written or devised specially for a locality and taken to its audience in village halls and centres where local people are used to meeting for other reasons. Among the most successful is Theatr Bara Caws (it means bread and cheese) who tour in and from the predominantly Welsh-speaking county of Gwynedd. When planning a recent six-week tour of different village halls each night, their administrator had to turn away a further three weeks' worth of engagements.

Always fully booked also are Theatre West Glamorgan, who work in English and Welsh, touring to similar home villages from Swansea in the south. The first observation to be made by a visitor to Wales, would be that both Bara Caws and Theatre West Glamorgan offer a strong sense of place. It is, perhaps, this 'belonging', a desire to create a theatre which grows from a love and a care for local people and the heritage and future of the locality, which is a dominant strain in the theatre of Wales. There is a strong body of opinion that these companies – and there are another six or seven who work to a similar credo – are the real incarnation of a national theatre of Wales, or at least the foundation for its future being.

In the Welsh-language calendar, the first week of August is notable for the Royal National Eisteddfod. In 1989, the village of Llanrwst and the people of the Conwy Valley in Gwynedd hosted Europe's largest competitive and participatory itinerant arts festival. Remembering Yeats, perhaps, there was controversy over the medal awarded for the best new play: argument over what is best in a small nation's creation of a new heritage.

Meanwhile there was a choice of four professional productions each night, six companies in all attracting more than 6,000 *eisteddfodwyr* as audience. And the variety – two devised shows strong on satire, an adaptation from a literary classic, a new social drama, an experimental piece with a cast of two men and two video screens, a packed-out show for children. An extraordinary mosaic of styles which, along with other companies, represents Welsh-language theatre greeting the 1990s.

Wales not only has a developing indigenous theatre tradition, but also the buildings in which to welcome audiences. For while we have been concentrating on the developing traditions of theatre created in

Cheryl Campbell and James Faulkener in Theatr Clwyd's production of The Constant Wife *by Somerset Maugham.*

Wales, it is the arguable right of our citizens to have access to the best which can be toured from Britain and abroad.

Most recently, the refurbishment of the 1904 Cardiff New Theatre has been completed with open foyers, traditional winding stair and improved auditorium. Inquisitive journalists have revealed exciting proposals for a new opera house in the regenerated Cardiff docklands, and another prestige venue is planned for Llandudno. As each reaches the drawing board, it follows the wave of the last fifteen years to upgrade or erect anew custom-built, technically equipped theatres: the Swansea Grand, the Torch Theatre at Milford Haven, Theatr Y Werin at Aberystwyth, Theatr Ardudwy Harlech, Theatr Gwynedd Bangor, Theatr Clwyd Mold, Theatr Hafren in Newtown and the Sherman in Cardiff. These are the best of those professionally-managed playing spaces of which Wales can be proud.

In summer 1989 something important closed. This could lead, however, to another sign of contemporary, even radical theatre having achieved popular appeal as in spring 1990 the Moving Being Company reopened its redesigned and filleted St Stephen's Church in the Mount Stuart area of Cardiff Butetown. This company mounted spectacular productions of the Mabinogion and intends to stage Shakespeare, Webster and challenging contemporary writing in the vaulted surroundings of the renovated Cardiff church.

If the theatre of Wales shows such new vitality, the question may well be asked: what of the classics of Wales? Can they be relevant today? One place which proved that they could be was Gilfach Goch, in an economically depressed community near the Rhondda Valley. A professional writing about amateurs runs the risk of appearing patronizing, at very least condescending, but the genuine emotion left after *How Green Was My Valley*, must be declared unapologetically as heartfelt and as admiring. The director and adaptor is a professional in social work, an amateur in theatre, which is to say that he is not paid for it and does not do it full time. He adapted the novel and directed local amateur actors and musicians in a production that for clarity, entertainment, yes *and* social relevance was memorable to the professional eye.

This was an example of another piece in the mosaic – community drama, perhaps it could be catalogued as part of the 'home service', defined as performed drama built on local participation. How local can you get? The faces of the cast performing their ancestors in a play written about that same valley, to a painted backdrop of mountain which, had it and its retaining wall collapsed, would have revealed the real McCoy, the rolling hills and valleys of Rhondda, hiding the horizon as if the mountains of the moon.

Merlin the Magician *performed by the Moving Being Theatre Company at St David's Hall, Cardiff.*

So what do we have? Theatre and drama of Wales definitely *of* but not restricted *by* its parish boundary. A belief in the crucial importance of belonging to Wales yet with a fully paid-up membership of the international community. Here are theatre traditions in which a respect for the masterful characterization of an Anthony Hopkins is as important as the clarity of a special production for disadvantaged children; where a packed community centre in a Valleys' town is as satisfying an achievement as the ovation in one of our cities' plush auditoria; where argument still rages as to whether a true national theatre of Wales exists or can only be if it is The National Theatre of Wales; where reassurance is gained from our friends in Friesland and where the search for Madog continues.

In such a new Wales, we should not fear the diversity, the energy, the audience or the quarrel.

On the road to Aberystwyth *by John Elwyn.*

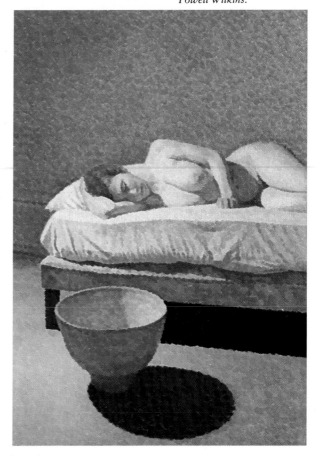

Nude with a bowl *by William Powell Wilkins.*

St Francis preaching to the birds *(All Saints' Church, Penarth) by John Petts.*

Campus centre of the University College of Wales, Aberystwyth. From left to right the library, great hall, bell tower and students' union grouped around the main pedestrian concourse facing Cardigan Bay.

The Marina Village at Swansea is one of the most successful urban renewal projects in Britain. Its nautical character is reinforced by the use of docks' building vernacular as well as the moored yachts and ships.

The new galleries of the Welsh Folk Museum at St Fagans are grouped around a courtyard. The masterplan is designed for continuing expansion to meet increasing acquisitions and visitors.

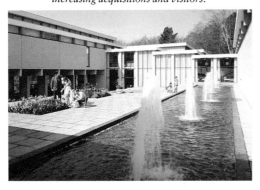

Right. Gwynedd County Headquarters shows how well a modern building can be fitted into an existing ancient town. The architects have created a sensitive urban composition and provided much-needed new accommodation near Caernarfon Castle.

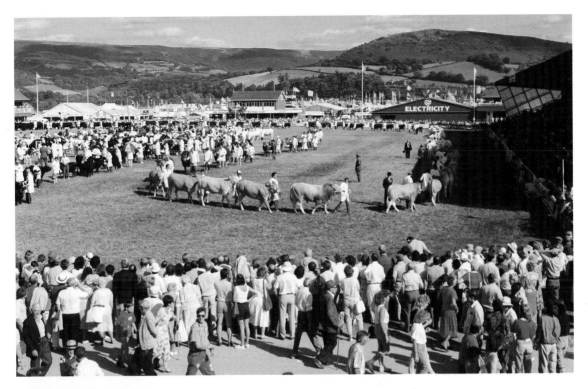

The Royal Welsh Agricultural Show, held annually at Llanelwedd near Builth Wells in Powys, attracts more than 200,000 visitors to its four-day programme of events.

Pencarreg reservoir is one of a chain of four large reservoirs in the Elan Valley, set against a background of wooded hills and vast open moorland. The ecology of the valley with its numerous plants and wildlife draws many visitors to this remote and fascinating area.

Dinas Brân Castle is perched 1,000 feet above the town of Llangollen, home of the world-famous international eisteddfod held annually in the town.

The five-kilometre sweep of Rhosili Bay lies at the western extremity of the Gower Peninsula, officially designated an area of outstanding natural beauty.

PRAISE THE LORD! WE ARE A MUSICAL NATION

GERAINT LEWIS

IN the nineteenth century, Brahms described England (and probably by implication Britain) as 'the country without music' – 'das Land ohne Musik'. Deliberately exaggerated and, doubtless, unfair though the comment may have been, it is certainly true that England at that time possessed no composers on Brahms's exalted level, whatever the general quality of her musical life. By 1902, however, Richard Strauss could propose a toast at a dinner in Düsseldorf after the second German performance of *The Dream of Gerontius* 'to the welfare and success of the first English progressivist, Meister Edward Elgar, and of the young progressive school of English composers'. The twentieth century has seen the flowering of an English musical renaissance, and a handful of her greatest composers counted among the most important of any on an international plane.

The Welsh on the other hand, from the travels of Gerallt Gymro to the affectionate parody of Dylan Thomas in *Under Milk Wood*, have enjoyed a musical reputation, and Wales is stereotypically regarded as 'the land of song'. This notion, however, has little, if anything, to do with the actual composition of music by Welsh composers, and this paradox has naturally exercised the minds of those who have fought to change such a situation. In 1971 in his contribution to the volume *Artists of Wales* William Mathias wrote, 'Perhaps the real problem lies in the fact that the Welsh have somehow been persuaded into thinking that they are a musical people. As a result they have the greatest difficulty in taking music at all seriously, preferring rather to place a high value on its social usefulness'. In the same volume another major Welsh composer – Daniel Jones – put his finger on glaring practical deficiencies: 'At the time when I am writing this, there are in Wales far too few halls suitable for orchestral concerts, and there is not a single theatre ideally fit for the production of opera. I end on a plaintive note. Where, oh where, is our National Orchestra of Wales?' Mathias was careful to sketch a background to his challenging statement, while sensing a wind of change blowing gently: 'If it took the environment of Vienna to develop the skill of a Schubert or Beethoven, Wales had no comparable artistic milieu and hence, no creative musicians of this stature. At long last we are beginning to develop the institutions vitally necessary to a truly musical culture; but a change of attitude is what is most needed.'

Twenty years on there has certainly been a change or consolidation of attitude in many quarters. A significant number of the potentially vital institutions have developed dramatically and changed the face of practical music-making in Wales, so that the perception of music within Wales, and of Welsh musical activity in the eyes of the wider

world, has flourished in a remarkable way. In recording this transformation of the Welsh musical landscape, it is to be hoped that the
impression of a genuine sea-change will emerge, even though we will
need to question whether the change of attitude for which William
Mathias called is genuinely deep-rooted or merely a reflection of an
institutional sense of responsibility.

The paradox of a 'musical nation' for a long time 'without music' is
perhaps not as surprising as it may seem. A curious frisson was
triggered in my mind on coming unexpectedly across a review in the
New Musical Express in September 1989 of a production by Brith
Gof, with music by Test Department, called *Gododdin*. Reading the
article just outside Edinburgh, where Aneirin in all probability wrote
the poem in the sixth century, heightened the synchronicity – but I
was most struck by two sentences which I took partly, and for this
purpose out of context: '"Gododdin" is a step back into the distant
past to capture the future.' Secondly:- '"Glasfedd eu hancwyn"
towers above everything else . . .' The oldest poem in the oldest living
European language has the power and immediacy to resonate in
movement and music today. The frisson came to some extent from
stumbling across the long-familiar words in such a surprising context. From the perspective peculiar to this chapter, it seemed to eluci-
date a special aspect of the interrelationship of words and music from
a Welsh standpoint. There is a remarkable meshing of the two in this
poetry: from the verbal composition flows a sound which verges on
song. As Professor A. O. H. Jarman has written of the performing
tradition which created and sustained *Y Gododdin*: 'The sounds of
the poem, its rhythms, cadences, stresses, consonantal and vowel
correspondences, the reciter's voice-inflexions and indeed the entire
musicality of his mode of declamation were therefore of its very
essence.'

> Gwyr a aeth Gatraeth, oedd ffraeth eu llu,
> Glasfedd eu hancwyn a gwenwyn fu
> Trychant trwy beiriant yn catau,
> A gwedi elwch tawelwch fu.

That cumulative impact of contrasted internal rhymes was surely
shaped in sound and, though it may seem obvious, it is worth stress-
ing that for at least three centuries it is likely that the epic survived
purely *as* sound, preserved by means of an oral tradition until it was
recorded by a scribe in what is known as Llyfr Aneirin in the thir-
teenth century (though other manuscripts may have existed as early as

the ninth century). After all, there is a specific blurring in Welsh – one of the medieval scribes, in an interpolated addition, wrote 'Hwn yw y Gododdin; Aneirin ae cant' (This is Gododdin; Aneirin sang it). The use of *canu* (to sing) to convey the act of poetic creation has survived in Welsh to this day. The oral declamatory tradition (necessitating the reciting of complex patterns alongside the retentive power of memory) in time must have encompassed a directly musical projection although its nature inevitably remains largely conjectural. The quality of implicit musicality in itself, though, does help to explain the marked preference which the Welsh have always had for *vocal* musical expression, either in terms of music stemming directly from the poetry as heightened declamation (as in *cerdd dant*) or simply as 'song' in all its guises, from spontaneous folk-song to sophisticated 'art' song.

Nevertheless, evidence of the deliberate marriage of words and music in a secular sphere does not seem to have survived in manuscript form from the pre-Renaissance period, even though such a troubadour tradition would have been a natural development and part of a general European culture to which a figure like Dafydd ap Gwilym so obviously belongs. We do know, however, from the observations of Gerallt Gymro in *The Description of Wales* (1194) that the Welsh were naturally drawn to singing in harmony, and that they seemed to be prodigiously gifted in performing 'instrumental' music. He refers to 'skilled and rapid execution of the fingers' and 'tremulant notes and intricate organa of many voices'. He may be describing the instrumental transcription of religious music – a common hybrid derived from a genre which in its pure form was certainly to be found in medieval Wales, since it was recorded in the poetry; but it is sadly tantalizing that none of this music has survived in transcribed form (assuming that it might have existed as such) where there is, on the other hand, such an abundance of literary manuscripts.

Similarly, although there is abundant documentation of the activities of the highly organized schools of Welsh harpists well into the sixteenth century, only one major source of their music and its notation survived, the famous *Musica* neu *Beroriaeth* which Robert ap Huw copied in 1613 and which Osian Ellis has suggested was already virtually incomprehensible to the generation of harpists following its circulation. But in recording the dying art of a nation already cultivating a foreign idiom it mirrors the decisive schism which shaped the future of Wales after 1500. The enlightened aristocratic patronage of poets and musicians in medieval Wales was emasculated by the political and cultural upheaval triggered when the

Tudors assumed the English throne, thereby shifting the focus of Welsh courtly life eastwards. The 'royal' Welsh harpist now became a common phenomenon at the Court of St James. Whatever character had belonged to native Welsh music (and it may have been both strongly individual and healthily mainstream) now became a largely dependent imitation of English and continental models – flowing freely even into the 'rediscovery' of the *Antient British Music* by John Parry and his contemporaries, which was palpably fraudulent. The poetic tradition survived, even if temporarily diluted, but the notion of a musical 'high' art withered before it could flourish. Thus, Wales was consequently deprived of an indigenous classical musical tradition.

Those tricks of historical fate which left Wales a materially deprived country following the Industrial Revolution and consequent exploitation were one reason why there was no infrastructure of professional music-making in Wales in the early twentieth century. Daniel Jones's plea in 1971 is a powerful reminder that the situation was a long time changing. Only by the second half of the 1980s did Wales finally have a full symphony orchestra of the size needed to perform a work like Stravinsky's *Le Sacre de Printemps*, which was first performed in 1913. But the 'institutions vitally necessary to a truly musical culture' are at last in place and furthering the sophisticated development of music in Wales.

The attempts to build a professional orchestra in Wales were chequered and interrupted. Sir Henry Wood conducted the inaugural concert of the optimistically assembled National Orchestra of Wales in Cardiff's City Hall in 1928. The orchestra folded due to lack of financial support from the Welsh councils. Significantly, though, the concert was broadcast. Before the Second World War the BBC formed a tiny studio orchestra which, though disbanded when war broke out, was subsequently re-established and eventually developed into a viable symphony orchestra over a thirty-year period. This gradual growth to full symphonic strength has been possible because of a durable partnership between the BBC and the Welsh Arts Council. This blossomed at a time in the mid 1970s when national BBC restructuring threatened the survival of the orchestra. Welsh foresight won through not only to ensure survival, but to enable the orchestra to expand numerically and to tour the length and breadth of Wales so that it could at last assume its role as the national orchestra of Wales in all but name.

Since the opening of Cardiff's St David's Hall in 1983 the BBC Welsh Symphony Orchestra has had an official 'home', acclaimed as one of the finest in Europe. A deliberate cultivation and successful achievement of international standards has followed inevitably, and

The BBC Welsh Symphony Orchestra on tour in Siberia.

Dame Gwyneth Jones from Gwent won international fame as a dramatic soprano in Verdi and Puccini roles before gaining further renown as a Wagnerian heroine.

with the additional financial input of Sianel Pedwar Cymru (Channel Four Wales) the orchestra enjoys a reputation as the most televised in Britain, thanks to the enlightened attitude of broadcasting hierarchies in Wales. In addition to its role as a national orchestra and in broadcasting, the BBC Welsh Symphony is increasingly recognized as an international orchestra. It has played to popular and critical acclaim in the great concert halls of the world – the Golden Hall of the Musikverein in Vienna, the Concertgebouw in Amsterdam, Leipzig's Gewandhaus, Berlin's Philharmonie, the Philharmonic Hall in Leningrad, and many others. The list grows yearly and the orchestra has already been invited to return to many of these prestigious venues. The future for the orchestra looks rosy, and plans for a series of independent commercial recordings can only help to raise its profile.

The story of the Welsh National Opera (WNO) is a similar one. The traditional Welsh love of singing and the profusion of great Welsh singers provided a natural background for the forming and nurturing of a national opera company. From its largely amateur origins in 1946 the venture seems to have been blessed with a remarkable spirit of adventure and success. It has also had to battle against considerable odds in terms of financial outlay and conditions of performance. But its strength shines through despite the fact that Wales still lacks a purpose-built opera house. Consequently, an inevitable but sad paradox is that Wales has been largely deprived of grand operatic opportunities to hear its great native singers. Gwyneth Jones, Margaret Price, Helen Watts, Elizabeth Vaughan, Sir Geraint Evans, Stuart Burrows, Delme Bryn Jones, Gwynne Howell, Robert Tear and many others have naturally been attracted to the greatest operatic stages of the world. Although many of these international figures have subsequently accepted invitations to perform with WNO, the cramped conditions of Cardiff's Edwardian New Theatre present an ultimately unsatisfactory compromise.

One of the leading lyric tenors of the last thirty years, Stuart Burrows has sung in nearly all the major opera houses of the world and has appeared at the Metropolitan, New York, more frequently than any other British singer.

The solid foundation of the WNO – as with the BBC Welsh Orchestra – was established gradually. By the early 1970s it had its own fully professional chorus and orchestra which have proved themselves to be the backbone of the company. It has tackled the staple operatic repertoire from Mozart, Rossini, Beethoven, Verdi, Wagner, Puccini to Strauss with consistent success and stimulation. Moreover, it has proved that it can succeed where others failed. Epoch-making productions of Britten's *Billy Budd* and Tippett's *The Midsummer Marriage* in the mid 1970s rehabilitated these masterpieces and drew national and international attention to the company, which then proceeded to champion the neglected operatic canon of Janacek. Welsh National Opera's standards of performance, production and design are widely recognized to have challenged those of all the other leading British companies and have led to increasing recognition abroad. When the Welsh National Opera is invited to perform two complete *Ring* cycles in Covent Garden and to take its production of *Falstaff* to Milan and New York it is superfluous to underline that something quite remarkable has been achieved. Plans currently under discussion to build a special opera house in Cardiff's dockland development must be a major priority for the future development of an institution of which Wales can be proud.

Robert Tear, the versatile Barry tenor has made a special reputation as a performer in the operas of Benjamin Britten. His flair for characterization has been applauded from Covent Garden to Vienna and Moscow.

If the Welsh National Opera and the BBC Welsh Symphony Orchestra are the jewels in the Welsh crown among performing institutions a number of others also deserve mention. The National Youth Orchestra of Wales was founded in 1946 and has served as an invaluable training ground for young Welsh instrumentalists. Administered by the Welsh Joint Education Committee it has travelled widely as a consistent ambassador for music-making in Wales and for

Welsh National Opera's performance of Falstaff *produced by Peter Stein, with Donald Maxwell in the title role and Cynthia Buchan as Mrs Quickly.*

Bryn Terfel, the 24-year-old baritone who was runner-up in the 1989 Cardiff Singer of the World Competition and won the international lieder *category.*

Welsh music. The development of this orchestra into the next decade is likely to be particularly exciting. In recent years its role has been supported by two enterprising sister-organizations – the National Youth Brass Band and the National Youth Choir of Wales. Both offer specialist intensive training and demonstrate effectively the versatility of young Welsh musicians.

In the second half of the 1980s two institutions were established which reflect, on a smaller scale, the work of the BBC Welsh Symphony Orchestra and WNO. The Welsh Chamber Orchestra concentrates on the repertoire for small orchestra which was once the daily diet of the BBC Welsh Orchestra, as it was known for a long time, but which it has had to neglect as its profile has changed. Another vital role which the Welsh Chamber Orchestra performs is the encouragement of Welsh composers. As yet, this has not been a priority of Music Theatre Wales, a company based at St Donats in the Vale of Glamorgan. Its challenging style of performance in the works of Maxwell Davies and Philip Glass has established a platform for modern music-theatre in Wales which should thrive into the 1990s.

There appears indeed to be a thirst for musical activity in many parts of Wales, as demonstrated by the creation of two organizations in north Wales – Opera Gogledd Cymru (North Wales Opera) and the

North Wales Philharmonia. In an area which suffers, perhaps in-evitably, in terms of shortage of live performance when compared with the south, these two bodies will perform a useful function.

A traditional feature of the musical life of Wales which has taken on a new dimension is the Festival. Ever since the Lord Rhys held his courtly contests at Cardigan in 1176 the Welsh have had a reputation for musical performance and competition, a reputation which con-temporary eisteddfodau maintain. The role of the small local eistedd-fodau in Wales should be noted alongside the significance of the Royal National Eisteddfod. They stress the importance of a healthy amateur tradition which cultivates high standards of performance. The Llangollen International Eisteddfod has warmly extended this tradition to the whole world.

Alongside these festivals the post-War years in Wales have seen the flourishing of a remarkable network of professional festivals – from Swansea, established in 1947, to Beaumaris in 1986. Llandaff, Cardiff, Fishguard, North Wales (St Asaph), Vale of Glamorgan, Gower, Aberystwyth, Lower Machen and Llantilio Crossenny – the range is considerable and each has its own character and in-dividuality. They provide a valuable focus for the musical life of an area, by attracting renowned artists and, in particular, encouraging new works. Such a role has been evangelically espoused by the Guild for the Promotion of Welsh Music, founded in 1950 by John Ed-wards. It is eloquently represented by the journal *Welsh Music* which appears three times a year, and embodied in the Welsh Music In-formation Centre within the University of Wales, College of Cardiff and funded by the Welsh Arts Council.

The Welsh Arts Council is central to much of the musical activity within the Principality. In one way or another it supports practically all the organizations I have mentioned. If its role is essentially that of provider, it does also possess the power to shape a policy through the patronage it provides. Another significant source of patronage has developed through the increasing role of broadcasting. The dividing line between artistic endeavour and the provision of entertainment is one that has been fairly well protected in Wales in what are generally Philistine times.

Education has suffered from a different brand of problem – one that has seen to it that since 1980 a climate of continual financial str-ingency has been imposed upon the British universities. Wales has to rejoice in the fact that the closure of the oldest-established Depart-ment of Music within the University of Wales at Aberystwyth, less than a century and a quarter after its foundation, is a 'rationalization' which will make it easier for the departments at Cardiff and Bangor to survive. These two departments were enlarged and modernized during the 1970s by Professors Alun Hoddinott and William Mathias respectively. When both retired prematurely in 1987/8 their Chairs were left empty. Cutbacks and rationalization procedures have, perhaps inadvertently, affected the prestige attached to the public perception of music within the University. Internally of course there are considerable moves and developments which reflect a determination to expand and consolidate and it is crucial to the future of higher education in Wales that no further cutting is endured. Another major institution – the Welsh College of Music and Drama in Cardiff – has had a turbulent history during much of the 1980s. With a magnificent site and, like its University counterpart over the road, a purpose-built and lavishly-supplied building it has strong assets which the recent change in musical administration will doubtless put to good effect in the interest of continued effective training of young musicians.

A crucial question however, remains. What of *music* in the new Wales? Have we at last our Bach and Handel? All the orchestras, opera companies, festivals, Arts Councils, universities, colleges and broadcasting organizations can, with money and administration, be set up and run. But composers are born, not made – as Alun Hoddinott has said, 'Music chooses you, and you have to go along with it because there is nothing much you can do.'

The institutions outlined above are ultimately essential to composers, and necessary for them to thrive. The institutions themselves will never, however, guarantee the emergence of great composers. Universities and colleges can instil competence, and individual teachers can inspire. An orchestra or opera company can provide a budding composer with the thrill of hearing a great work 'live' as opposed to through the clinical perfection of a compact disc – but in today's cost-effective climate such a composer is hardly likely to hear his own efforts. Roles have changed, and the struggle is different.

A composer, as William Mathias said, needs an 'artistic milieu' in order to flourish and for the so-called 'classical' composer it is difficult to perceive what that might be in today's Wales. The composer still has to fight for a place in society. Contemporary music does not play a socially useful role in Wales and composers do not feel that there is an audience which actively wants them to compose. The nearest thing to a genuine supply and demand only exists in the ephemeral world of Welsh pop music. What then does a composer do?

The potential roll-call of Welsh composers is long and distinguished. It becomes even longer and less distinguished if extended.

The catalogues of the Guild for the Promotion of Welsh Music are impressively comprehensive and provide eloquent testimony to the enormous outburst of creativity amongst Welsh composers since the Second World War. It has to be recognized that many important Welsh composers of the late nineteenth century and early twentieth century were hampered by the lack of those practical institutions which have since been established. Their talents were considerable – had Joseph Parry been born in Milan or Munich he could possibly have gone straight to work in an opera house and developed as a Verdi or Wagner. But however heroic his efforts he did not, and could not become a Welsh equivalent of either. Although both Morfydd Llwyn Owen and David Vaughan Thomas composed vocal works of lasting beauty and quality, they aspired towards orchestral and instrumental expression which could not in reality find fulfilment. Subsequent generations have grafted themselves to a slowly established indigenous tradition while observing the need to keep abreast of musical developments in England and abroad.

David Wynne, Grace Williams and Daniel Jones belong, historically speaking, to the generation of Walton, Tippett and Britten, and arguably represent the first mature flowering of modern Welsh composition. Wynne and Williams, in fact, had very close links with Tippett and Britten respectively. Grace Williams (1906–77) will probably be remembered as the first major Welsh composer to make a significant and potentially lasting impact outside her native country, on equal terms with others of her generation such as Elizabeth Maconchy and Edmund Rubbra perhaps. She succeeded in what was largely (*pace* Morfydd Llwyn Owen) a man's world, and succeeded, too, in discovering a winning way of conveying her Welsh musical heritage quite unselfconsciously – her *Fantasia on Welsh Nursery Tunes*, and on a different level, *Penillion*, are definitive orchestral projections of Welsh folk material and idioms which remain unsurpassed. Her distinctive and naturally lyrical voice was most characteristically deployed in vocal music, but she had the courage to risk ambitious large-scale works – Symphony, Violin Concerto, opera (*The Parlour*) and mass (*Missa Cambrensis*) which called for a full range of compositional resources and imaginative power, with great success. But, and this will become a common complaint, they have not been given their proper due in performances in Wales.

David Wynne deliberately cultivated an advanced European musical idiom which distanced him from his audience at home without, paradoxically, ensuring him a wide acceptance outside Wales. He was acutely aware of the linguistic problem which faced him and of a degree of pressure from within Wales, partly inspired by Vaughan Williams, for the conscious cultivation of a national language based on folk-music. He characteristically looked further afield writing: 'Admiration of Bartok should have led me to follow his example and likewise to have attempted to seek out an idiom based upon Welsh folk-music. However a comparison of our native folk-music with the folk-music which was available to Bartok showed that, from a compositional point of view, Welsh folk-music was decidedly inferior in its rhythms and melodic systems. Moreover, by the end of World War II, the time for conscious Nationalism was over. Music was undergoing one of its periodic changes of emphasis, where composers were now thinking in terms of new idioms and forms based on an extension of modalism into free atonality, or in terms of the strict serialization of all the elements which constitute the material of music.'

Wynne remains a maverick figure – held in high esteem and affection by generations of pupils, and a prolific composer of works which have largely fallen into neglect following his death. A late developer who seemed at times to plough consciously a lonely furrow (though he could write socially 'useful' music when so called), his exploration of serial language and a highly individual notion of music-theatre placed him outside the emergent mainstream in Wales, and it is difficult to assess his contribution as a whole in any sense of justice when his output is so shamefully neglected.

Daniel Jones's innovations have been applied most directly to matters of rhythm – he invented a system of 'complex metres' which he has used with consistent ingenuity. Although he has composed operas and a notable cantata *The Country Beyond the Stars*, Jones is at heart an instrumental composer with a major canon of twelve symphonies and a vast quantity of distinguished chamber music to his credit. Yet again, however, his output enjoys the tributes of lip-service paid lavishly, but far more rarely does it receive regular performances. His strongly romantic expression may have rendered him unfashionable outside Wales and it is true, perhaps, that his reputation in his later years has depended on a series of now deleted commercial recordings sponsored by the Welsh Arts Council which have taken his music around the world without generating a quantity of significant live performances beyond the Welsh festivals. The irony is that Daniel Jones's early reputation was established in London in the late 1940s and early 1950s – but the significance of his contribution is sure to be recognized as time passes and his output is reassessed.

In the shadow of these three pioneering composers, other distinguished Welsh figures wrote distinctively on more intimate levels. Mansel Thomas and Arwel Hughes played a vital role as musical administrators within the BBC at a time when they were able to build its orchestra gradually and establish the foundation of musical patronage as a commissioning body, a role which has since developed steadily. Although they will be remembered most significantly as vocal miniaturists, this should not obscure their considerable natural gifts as composers on a larger scale. Two composers of vocal music who will be sung as long as the Welsh language survives are Meirion Williams and Dilys Elwyn-Edwards – genuine miniaturists who recognized the fact and developed their special gifts accordingly.

Most of the Welsh composers born before 1940 were either wholly educated or completed their education outside Wales, usually in London. Not only that, they had to find their feet outside Wales. They needed to fight for recognition from London and other major English regional orchestras – in direct competition with the finest composers of their generation at home and abroad. The two Welsh 'second-generation' composers whose talents were immediately recognized on such a level were Alun Hoddinott and William Mathias. Hoddinott's first five symphonies were given their initial performances by the Royal Liverpool, BBC Symphony, Halle (nos. 3 & 4) and Royal Philharmonic Orchestras respectively, and Mathias's two by the City of Birmingham Symphony and Royal Liverpool Philharmonic Orchestras. The fact that their most recent have been played (Hoddinott's sixth in 1984) and commissioned (Mathias's third for 1991/2) by the BBC Welsh Symphony Orchestra is appropriate recognition of established eminence and an indication of the new stature enjoyed by the orchestra.

It is acknowledged universally that Hoddinott and Mathias have given Welsh music an international profile. Their names are now virtually inseparable after a manner with a long and distinguished musical pedigree – Bach and Handel, Haydn and Mozart, Beethoven and Schubert, Brahms and Liszt, Bruckner and Mahler, Britten and Tippett – Hoddinott and Mathias repeat the pattern, for the first time in the history of Welsh music. Such a pairing does not invariably reflect shared characteristics. It is instructive, therefore to observe what Hoddinott and Mathias have in common and what the comparison underlines as illuminating differences.

Both are from south Wales, and after education to university level in Wales studied in London, returning then to the country of their birth to follow dual careers as composers within the University establishment (Hoddinott for a while at the Welsh College of Music and Drama and then at Cardiff University, Mathias at Bangor). Both

Pembrokeshire-born William Mathias has composed well over one hundred works including symphonies, concertos, oratorios and a special anthem for the wedding of Prince Charles and Princess Diana in 1981.

achieved national and international recognition very quickly – Hoddinott with his first Clarinet Concerto at the 1954 Cheltenham Festival, Mathias with his Clarinet Sonatina (at the 1957 Festival) and Divertimento for Strings – all works which were swiftly taken abroad. One of Britain's most prestigious music publishers, Oxford University Press signed both as house composers when they were still in their twenties. Commissions from leading British festivals followed in profusion and both responded with challenging works which consolidated their early reputations.

In 1967 and 1970 respectively they became Professor and Head of the Music Departments at Cardiff and Bangor, remaining until 1987/8. In 1967 and 1972 they founded respectively the Cardiff Festival of Twentieth-Century Music and the North Wales Music Festival and remain involved, Hoddinott from 1990 as president and Mathias still as artistic director. They are both enormously energetic, prolific composers and their works are performed and broadcast world-wide. Both have contributed significantly to the major musical genres, and since 1988 have been able in large measure to concentrate exclusively on composition.

Such similarities are essentially superficial and coincidental. In purely musical terms it is too easy to pinpoint crude differences, and to suggest that Hoddinott's work is essentially dark and tense while Mathias's is light and free. Hoddinott's popular *Welsh Dances* (of which there are now four sets) are entirely felicitous, joyous and exuberant and these characteristics continually imbue his most serious work as a natural part of the discourse. Mathias's *Requiescat* is a brooding, elegaic canvas of deeply sustained, unresolved tension and this vein can be traced throughout his mature work. It is, nevertheless, more common to think of Hoddinott in terms of the powerfully dramatic, atmospheric tone of *The Sun, the great luminary of the universe* and *Lanterne des Morts*, and Mathias as the infectious, affirmative celebrant of works like *Dance Overture* and *Celtic Dances*. This simply proves that both composers command a very wide range of expression and that it is misleading to define their musical personalities in a limited and ultimately redundant manner.

In linguistic terms both set out from a tonal, neo-classical base. Hoddinott's natural chromatic expansion of his idiom to encompass a free yet disciplined brand of serialism has remained with him. It defines his complementary sense of a tonal pull to the language, allowing him a rich flexibility and redefinition of tonal concepts from a different perspective. Mathias, on the other hand, after a brief early flirtation with serialism found his natural, instinctive musical personality in terms of strongly rooted tonality with an evocative modal freedom, which later veered towards a degree of serial organization *within* the framework in which his ideas developed.

More profound polarities emerge in structural terms. Hoddinott's cast of mind is quite distinctly Romantic and decorative and is at odds with the Germanic sonata archetype. His preference is for the Italianate forms of toccata and aria, where he can exhibit opposing tendencies towards strict, virtuosic tautly-palindromic (running music in reverse as it were) organization, alongside a lyrical, improvisatory freedom. Mathias, on the other hand, is a classicist who has adapted the sonata concept to his own purposes for dramatic ends in which the firm feeling of framework and structural expectation can be blurred and transformed by the flexibility of discourse within the structure.

Alun Hoddinott, a prolific composer of symphonies, concertos and operas won a European reputation at an early age.

Hoddinott's orchestral and instrumental catalogue is daunting – ten piano sonatas, four violin sonatas, six symphonies, over fifteen concertante works to list abstract genres alone. The composer's sixtieth birthday year (1989) saw a prodigious stream of major works for orchestra – a symphony for organ and orchestra, *Star Children* (enthusiastically acclaimed by audience and critics alike at the Proms) and the singular honour of a commission – *Noctis Equi* – for the great Russian cellist Mstislav Rostropovich and the London Symphony Orchestra.

While both Hoddinott and Mathias have three string quartets to their credit, Mathias's instrumental output is markedly less prolific – two piano sonatas, two violin sonatas, two symphonies and eight concertos. But Mathias increasingly has won regard as a writer of choral music – not only on a large scale with major works like *St Teilo*, *This Worldes Joie*, *Lux Aeterna* and *World's Fire* – but also, specifically, for performance in church. This is a role rare in our time and one in which he rejoices. The commission to write an anthem for the wedding of the Prince and Princess of Wales set the seal on this aspect of Mathias's creativity but much of this activity is now restricted of necessity to selective commissions. Many of these are from the United States and as the most celebrated composer of church music in America, Mathias visits the country at least twice a year for major festivals of his music.

Hoddinott's energies have been more regularly directed towards opera. Welsh National Opera has produced one opera by each composer – *The Beach of Falesa* (1974) and *The Servants* (1980). Whereas Mathias has yet to follow the latter – a gripping and melodramatically claustrophobic scenario adapted specially by Iris Murdoch from her stage play, which was realized in vivid musical life – Hoddinott has followed his lyrically atmospheric adaptation of Robert Louis Stevenson with a Stevenson sequel for television – *The Rajah's Diamond*. This was the composer's second television opera, following *The Magician*. The two works were separated by a delightful children's opera drawn from Hans Christian Andersen, *What the Old Man Does is Always Right*. The grandly drawn juxtapositions of pageantry and intimacy of Hardy's *The Trumpet-Major* (1981) was the third opera Hoddinott wrote in partnership with Myfanwy Piper (Britten's librettist for *The Turn of the Screw*, *Owen Wingrave* and *Death in Venice*) whose husband, the distinguished painter John Piper also designed *What the Old Man Does* in 1977. After turning to Flaubert for a choral and orchestral presentation of *The Legend of St Julian*, Hoddinott and Piper are currently collaborating on a chamber-opera drawn from Balzac.

Both Hoddinott and Mathias have written works for many of the greatest Welsh singers of our time who have acted so effectively as Welsh musical ambassadors – Geraint Evans, Stuart Burrows, Kenneth Bowen, Robert Tear, Stephen Roberts, Helen Watts and others, and the Welsh identity of their music in itself is a fascinating focus for projecting Wales to the world. Yet they are not composers who use Welsh folk elements as a basis for their language – as David Wynne analysed, that era is essentially past.

Professor Basil Deane has put his finger on what he feels to be Hoddinott's Welshness: 'The national flavour of his music derives from his own personality; it is a matter of mood rather than material, of atmosphere rather than structure. There are dominant characteristics in Hoddinott's music which betray a Celtic rather than an Anglo-Saxon temperament; obsessive drive, sombre brooding, rhetorical lyricism, fiery outbursts, and, embracing all of these, a love of language itself, a delight in virtuosic manipulation of the means of communication.'

Mathias, for his part, has himself defined what he senses as the qualities of Welsh art in an archetypal manner, and which are reflected in the character of the new Welsh music: 'It is an art of paradoxical contrasts – brightly jewelled colours contrasting with dark introspection, declamation with tenderness, and intellectual tautness with an almost improvisatory lyricism.'

Wales is indeed fortunate that her two greatest composers are currently at the height of their powers with many more years of music to contribute. Although there is a proliferation of Welsh composers actively writing from all generations, no younger composer of com-

Sir Geraint Evans in the HTV Wales production of Alun Hoddinott's What the Old Man Does is Always Right.

parable reputation has yet emerged. The following composers (a selective and disparate list) have all contributed and will continue to contribute significantly to the Welsh music of our time – Ian Parrott, Robert Smith, Mervyn Burtch, David Harries, Jeffrey Lewis, Brian Hughes, Richard Elfyn Jones, Richard Roderick Jones, David Nevens, John Metcalf, Gareth Glyn, Robert Swain, Lyn Davies, Dalwyn Henshall and Martin Davies – but it would not be realistic to claim that any of them enjoys a position either outside or within Wales remotely comparable to that of Hoddinott or Mathias. It is ironic that the enormous growth in musical provision in Wales has not been matched by a comparable emergence of a younger generation of composers on a par, for argument's sake, with John Tavener, Oliver Knussen or George Benjamin, to restrict the comparison to England alone.

But as the pre-eminent Welsh composers, Hoddinott and Mathias are among the most celebrated British musicians of our time and are also, of course, regarded as figures of international significance. While they have long been regarded as essentially 'conservative' figures (though such distinctions have barely applied in Wales) intent on working within an eclectic, yet in each case, highly individual formulation of a comprehensible *lingua franca*, there is now a perceptible shift away from a pejorative dismissal of such a stance. Neither Hoddinott or Mathias has ever bowed to the often illusory fashions of the decades during which they established their distinctive voices.

They have succeeded in large measure because of this independence. The increasing 'pluralism' of today's musical climate has served to break down certain barriers of a narrowly linguistic nature – *what* a composer says is now often considered to be more important than *how* he says it. Above all else these two great composers have the gift and power to communicate, and this is perhaps where the strength of their very Welshness lies.

In the years ahead we can look to both Hoddinott and Mathias for further works of enrichment, eloquence and excitement. The musical regeneration in Wales cannot be strictly thought of as a renaissance when there was not, in reality, a golden age of music to be rediscovered. But in reaching back to the intangible past for artistic characteristics embedded in the Welsh psyche both composers represent a burgeoning spirit which is in the profoundest sense a reflowering. Their greatest music enshrines the image expressed in Dylan Thomas's 'Author's Prologue' to his *Collected Poems*, the last three lines of which preface the finale of Mathias's Second Symphony (*Summer Music*):

> My ark sings in the sun
> At God speeded summer's end
> And the flood flowers now.

WE ROCK TOO – BILINGUALLY!

DEBORAH COLE

Cardiff-born Shirley Bassey has been an international star for thirty years.

Iᴛ is not only in the more highbrow areas of opera and choral singing that the sons and daughters of the land of song have made an international impact. Tom Jones and Shirley Bassey are household names that almost every age group in countries all over the world would recognize – but many people are unaware of the talented Welsh musicians who have shot to fame in the world of rock and pop music.

Swansea-born John Cale, for example, was a founder member of one of the most influential rock groups of the 1960s – the Velvet Underground. The son of a coal-miner and a schoolteacher, Cale went to America on a Leonard Bernstein Fellowship but abandoned his classical studies after meeting composer John Cage and other avant-garde figures. The Velvet Underground rebelled against the prevailing hippy mood of peace and love and left a lasting impression.

In post-Velvet Underground years, Cale turned his talents to composing and producing for a host of stars but still found time for more than fourteen solo albums. Despite his long career, his work has always defied categorization, ranging from classical collaborations with symphony orchestras to raucous rock and folk influences. He long ago adopted America as his home and rarely performs elsewhere, but he made a welcome appearance at St David's Hall in Cardiff in July 1986.

Among the Welsh success stories of the 1960s were Amen Corner. The seven-strong band of youngsters from Cardiff and Newport who began playing with local bands at the tender ages of fifteen or sixteen, had a hit with their first record, 'Gin House' which was released on Decca's Deram label in 1967. Six more hit records, including 'Bend Me, Shape Me' and 'Half As Nice', followed, but in 1969 the band, who shared a palatial London mansion and lived the high life, split up. Their last album, titled The National Welsh Coast Live Explosion Company, was released in the week the break was announced.

This was by no means the last that was heard of the lazy, laid-back individual style of vocalist Andy Fairweather Low. On the contrary, his solo single 'Wide Eyed and Legless' was a world-wide hit and his albums have achieved respectable sales. From his Cardiff home he has travelled all over the world playing with a variety of other successful musicians and was seen on Top of the Pops in 1986 playing guitar on Samantha Fox's single 'Hold Tight'.

Others who achieved fame and fortune in the same era as Amen Corner included Dave Edmunds, whose Cardiff band Love Sculpture shot into the charts late in 1968. This sudden success, with Edmunds's lightning-fingered version of Khachaturian's Sabre Dance, took even the band by surprise. In fact they did not hold together long and in 1970 the singer and guitarist, who was born in Cardiff in 1943, scored himself a number one hit with 'I Hear You Knocking' which sold three million copies and topped the charts all over the world.

The record was the first release on Gordon Mills's new MAM label but it was recorded in a stable converted to a studio at Amberley Court, Rockfield, Monmouth by Charles and Kingsley Ward – a facility that was used by many big-name musicians including rock band Black Sabbath and Andy Fairweather Low.

Tom Jones who still stars in shows in the United States has returned to Wales to establish his family home in the Vale of Glamorgan.

That stable became Rockwell Studios and Edmunds eventually formed his own Rockfield record label. His Top-30 hit 'Baby I Love You' was issued on that same label and he used the studio's electronic gadgetry to play all the instruments himself as well as providing lead and backing vocals.

Edmunds also turned his talents to producing records by The Flamin' Groovies, Brinsley Schwartz, the legendary Welsh rock band Man, Del Shannon and many others. In 1973 he became musical director and a featured performer in the film *Stardust* and the following year went on tour. The end of 1975 saw the birth of the next successful Edmunds band – Rockpile, featuring bassist Nick Lowe, guitarist Billy Bremner and drummer Terry Williams – an association which lasted until 1981.

Swansea-born Terry Williams is another success story. He has put Wales on the map as drummer of Dire Straits, one of the world's supergroups whose Brothers in Arms album was a major hit in more than twenty countries. On return trips to Swansea Terry is often to be found teaming up with friends and local musicians for concerts and charity events.

Even before Dire Straits he was no stranger to the limelight. He was a member of the Welsh rock band Man who somehow managed to become a legend in their own lifetime and still occasionally stage one-off comeback concerts. Gruelling tours, sometimes playing thirty dates in thirty-six days, ensured that they became known the length and breadth of Britain. They also toured Europe, America and even Iceland.

Cast in the same mould were heavy rock band Budgie. This threesome originated in the Cardiff music scene around 1967 and their first major breakthrough came when they were discovered by Black Sabbath producer Roger Bain. The original line-up featured bassist Burke Shelley, guitarist Tony Bourge and drummer Ray Phillips. In 1973 Phillips was replaced by Pete Boot who stayed with the band for only a short time and was successfully replaced by Steve

Shakin' Stevens – the Cardiff singer who played Elvis Presley and went on to top the charts himself.

Williams, who was still there many years on. Budgie recorded five albums for the MCA label before signing to A & M.

To all intents and purposes Racing Cars was another Welsh band that appeared to enjoy a meteoric rise to stardom in 1977 with 'They Shoot Horses Don't They?' The virtues of this single were extolled by disc jockey John Peel, the arbiter of modern music taste at the time, who placed it above classics from the Beatles, Rolling Stones and Bob Dylan. The five band members were in fact far from starry-eyed new-comers to the music scene – they were old hands who had worked long and hard in many a local band to achieve success. Sadly, their well-deserved acclaim was short lived. A change in musical tastes and, perhaps, a lack of exposure consigned them to the list of one-hit wonders relatively quickly.

Swansea-born Bonnie Tyler, the husky-voiced star dubbed the female Rod Stewart, has never suffered that fate. Since topping the charts in 1976 with her first hit 'Lost in France' she has managed to stay in the limelight. Her first American hit was 'It's a Heartache' and her LP Faster Than the Speed of Night was a roaring success shooting straight to the top of the British charts and going platinum in six other countries. She has actually achieved something that no other Welsh vocalist can boast – she reached Number One in the American Billboard top 100.

One of twelve children brought up in a council house in Cardiff, Shakin' Stevens is one of the hottest properties in the music business with an impressive string of hits behind him and adoring fans who write him thousands of letters a week. But for Shakey, alias Michael Barrett, it was a long hard road to the top. When he left school a teacher told him, 'I hate your voice, but keep up the singing – someone else might be fool enough to like it.' The 15-year-old was an up-holsterer by day and a singer by night and after a few false starts with bands that obviously did not have what it takes Shakin' Stevens and the Sunsets were conceived.

For years the band toured up and down the country playing at colleges and clubs in time-honoured tradition, one of many 'local' bands trying to make the big time. Like many other local Welsh groups of that era – Kimla Taz, Eyes Of Blue, Night Time Pipeline, Electric Circus, Memphis Bend, Stone Idol, Good Habit, Farmhouse and others too numerous to mention – they developed a following all over the United Kingdom and were popular in Germany. But success and discovery evaded them. Probably it was a dearth of competent managers and promoters that was largely to blame, since there was no lack of talent in the Principality. Another factor has always been the

The Alarm from north Wales have established a huge following.

reluctance of London-based and biased record companies to look beyond their immediate environs.

It was the West End musical Elvis, which featured Shakey as the star in the middle part of his lifetime, that set Stevens on the path to stardom. He joined the musical in December 1977 and when the show closed nineteen months later he was a polished stage performer ripe for the journey to the top. His first hit was 'Hot Dog' and his second 'Marie Marie', but neither bore comparison with the impact and success of 'This Ole House', followed by smash hits 'Green Door' and 'You Drive Me Crazy'.

A Cardiff pop duo Waterfront achieved megastar status in America after their single, 'Cry', entered the Top Ten. They were the first Welsh band to appear on the television show American Bandstand for nineteen years. Both former pupils of Howardian High School, Cardiff, the pair signed a major record contract some two years ago and have been travelling almost non-stop across Europe and America since. Their second single, 'Nature of Love', entered the British Top 40 and landed them in hot water when the steamy video made to accompany the song was banned by censors both at home and abroad.

In the 1980s, other chartmakers have included north Wales band The Alarm who formed in 1981 and built up a fanatical live following before scoring a hit with '68 Guns'. This was the first in a series of triumphant top twenty hits – and albums Declaration, Strength, and Eye of The Hurricane all achieved gold disc status. In 1987 they were among the bands who supported supergroup U2 at the National Stadium concert in Cardiff where they completely upstaged more famous names. In subsequent concerts at Cardiff and London, The Alarm were supported by the Welsh language bands Anhrefn and Llwybr Llaethog, proving to large audiences that Welsh could be more than a medium for singing hymns in choirs.

Alarm's fourth album, Change, was released in September 1989

Ar Log, Wales's foremost folk group.

and on one track, 'A New South Wales', the band teamed up with the Morriston Orpheus Choir and members of the Welsh Symphony Orchestra. Lead singer Mike Peters learned Welsh after marrying a Welsh-speaking Prestatyn girl and the band released a bilingual single to coincide with the album.

The Welsh-language music scene has gone from strength to strength since Welsh nationalist singer Dafydd Iwan and Huw Jones founded Sain record company in 1969. They and folk-singer and composer Meic Stevens did much to lay the foundations on which groups like Ar Log, Ceffyl Pren, Edward H. Davis, Cyrff and Geraint Lovegreen, and soloists Geraint Jarman and Heather Jones were able to build. There are more than a hundred Welsh-language bands playing in Wales today. Some such as Cyrff and Jess are professional and travel extensively outside Wales while blues singer Steve Eaves and the lively satirical music of Geraint Lovegreen have become permanent fixtures of the Welsh-language scene. Geraint Jarman, a poet, actor and writer as well as a singer, has done much to popularize modern Welsh-language music, ably backed by musicians of the calibre of guitarist Tich Gwilym who has been a feature of the south Wales music scene in many and various bands currently the Superclarkes, since the 1960s.

Tich Gwilym is one of the many dedicated and talented individuals, such as Tommy Riley, Mickey Gee, Gary Pickford-Hopkins, Martin Ace and Wales's answer to Otis Redding, Laverne Brown, who have helped to make the Principality's pubs and clubs lively and interesting places of entertainment. It would be a sad day if the land of song's live music venues ever faded away but, thankfully, that looks extremely unlikely.

LITERATURE

OF POETRY, PARADOXES AND PROGRESS

R. GERALLT JONES

As it moves towards the magic metamorphosis of 1992, Wales offers to the new Europe two quite distinct and separate literatures; two literatures, rather, which are too often thought of as quite distinct and separate. Simplistically, one represents the literary output of some 80 per cent of the population, the other some 20 per cent. Such a tabloid analysis of the situation, however, would ignore the fact that much of the English-language literature of Wales owes a great deal to the past and present life of Welsh-speaking Wales. The greatest contemporary English-language Welsh poet, R.S. Thomas, is a Welsh-speaker and a fervent cultural nationalist; one of the most distinguished English-language novelists, Emyr Humphreys is a Welsh-speaker who has recently taken to writing and publishing verse in Welsh, while the decidedly non-Welsh-speaking Alexander Cordell has successfully captured a mass-market audience with historical novels about a proletariat whose lives were lived in Welsh. Many English-language poets draw heavily on the myth and legend of the nation's past, a body of imaginative experience expressed and conserved through the medium of the Welsh language. And, distinct though the two literatures are, they both face similar problems of identity and similar problems of survival. Both are threatened and overshadowed by the existence, within two hundred miles of the Welsh border, of the most affluent, the most hyped, the most marketable and the most metropolitan of all world literatures, that which is written in English and published out of New York, London and elsewhere by the vast publishing conglomerates of the western world. That being the case, both the literatures of Wales show clearer signs of life than one might perhaps expect. Both might well also see, in the approach to Europe, new horizons and new opportunities.

The survival of any literature at all in the Welsh language, catering at the end of the twentieth century for a readership of little more than 60,000, is a miracle in itself. (One cites a figure of 60,000 because, although the number of those speaking Welsh in Wales is perhaps some eight times as many, the figure represents reasonably accurately the number of people who buy any kind of printed material in the Welsh language.) It is a miracle because of the smallness of the market. It is also a miracle because the existence of a rival literature written in an ancient language within a brief train journey of London has always been steadfastly ignored by the London literary establishment. Writing in the Welsh language is never referred to in English literary periodicals, even in a marginal way; it is as though it never were.

And yet there is a paradox at the root of all things; and the abiding paradox here is that the British state, through the medium of the Welsh Office and through subsidies devolved from the Arts Council of Great Britain to the Welsh Arts Council and in turn to the Welsh Books Council, does a great deal to breathe life into a literature that it does not really believe exists. In terms of intellectual energy and motivation, Welsh-language literature has either had to be self-sufficient or to seek associations with languages and literatures outside the United Kingdom. Traditionally, in spite of the promptings of Saunders Lewis and others, it has followed the first course, feeding largely on its own past and drawing heavily on Celtic myth and legend and on the indigenous forms of Protestant Christianity that both generated and marketed writing in the Welsh language during the eighteenth and nineteenth centuries. There are signs that it may now be looking more readily towards sources outside itself, and this is a point to which we must return.

T. James Jones, the Crown bard at the Newport Royal National Eisteddfod in 1988.

Traditionally also, there has been a dichotomy within Welsh-language literature itself. In the distant past, it was a division between the qualified professional poet resident in the great houses of the nobility and the wandering bard, not so strictly trained nor so highly regarded, and condemned to entertain the populace. In more recent times, this division manifested itself in the regular use, during the early decades of this century, of the terms *bardd coleg* (college poet) and *bardd gwlad* (country poet), to indicate the distinction not only between the tutored and the untutored but also, more significantly, between the abstruse and the accessible. It is perhaps significant that the term *bardd coleg* later gave way to the term *bardd tywyll* (obscure poet) while the term *bardd gwlad* gained a progressively higher status as the committed voice of the people.

One dwells upon poetry rather than on any other form of literature because the poet is still pre-eminent in the field of Welsh-language writing. Names like Bobi Jones, Alan Llwyd, Bryan Martin Davies, Nesta Wyn Jones, Gareth Alban Davies, Menna Elfyn, Dic Jones and a score of others indicate that a strong body of contemporary verse is continuing the outstanding achievements of major poets like Waldo Williams, Euros Bowen and T. Glynne Davies during the sixties and seventies. The ancient disciplines and the standards of excellence achieved by the Poets of the Princes and the Court Poets have etched themselves deeply into the Welsh psyche, so that poetry is still regarded by many as a superior form of literature to prose. This is certainly how things are seen from the outside. Despite the National Eisteddfod's continuing and repeated attempts to upgrade prose writing and dramatic writing by declaring their Prose and Drama medals to be of equal value to the Chair and the Crown, the major poetry awards, the mass media still insist on choosing the bardic ceremonials for saturation coverage and for live transmission to the English.

To return to the dichotomy. It is born in modern times of a natural and inevitable dilemma afflicting a literature fighting for its life within a small and diminishing market. Those who care for Welsh literature, those who write it and read it, would be happy to feel that there was work of genuine quality, work born of original and contemporary talent, still being written in this ancient language. They are not always convinced, however, that such work will find a ready audience. So, side by side with the search for new and exciting writing, there is a constant demand for work which will be 'popular'. Even in a heavily subsidized situation, there exists the feeling that the writer should aim to become a genuinely populist author, for the sake of the language. The author who writes in a minority language is always saddled with the task of keeping the language alive by appealing to as many potential readers as possible. It is not necessarily a role that is consistent with the creation of serious literature. And so the *bardd coleg* and the *bardd gwlad* soldier on, the one represented by the books and periodicals selected for subsidy by the Welsh Arts Council on a basis of excellence, the other by the popular autobiographies, often ghost-written, and the pulp fiction demanded by libraries and supported and even commissioned by the Welsh Books Council, which tackles well the difficult task of encouraging and supporting literature at all levels.

This, however, is in itself a tabloid presentation of a complex situation and it will be useful to analyse in more detail present patterns of subsidy within a situation which is so heavily dependent upon it. Apart from the specifically scholastic publishing activity generated and supported by the Welsh Joint Education Committee, public subsidy for Welsh writing is administered on behalf of the government either by the Welsh Arts Council or by the Welsh Books Council. Very few Welsh books are published without any subsidy at all. Nor would it be possible for most of the numerous Welsh-language periodicals to appear regularly without support from one or other of these organizations. This should occasion neither criticism nor surprise. The concept of state subsidy for minority literatures within multicultural states is well established world-wide, and literatures like those of Catalonia, the Basque peoples and the national republics of the USSR receive an incomparably higher subsidy than that which supports Welsh-language writing within the United Kingdom.

Bearing all this in mind, Welsh-language literature, as it moves into the 1990s, represents a brave and lively effort to sustain a broad spectrum of genuinely contemporary writing, in spite of all the difficulties. There are no obvious giants; the last survivors of the golden generation born around the turn of the century died in the 1980s, Saunders Lewis, Kate Roberts and John Gwilym Jones. But there is much activity, a good deal of it of a high standard. It is also, on the whole, activity which is both more outward-looking than Welsh literature in general has been since the days of Dafydd ap Gwilym, and more positive and less obviously afflicted by the gloom of a failing culture than it was in the 1980s. Writers seem determined to write, and to write in Welsh, come what may. Younger novelists and writers for television like Siôn Eirian, Alun Jones and William Owen Roberts may still struggle, as does a slightly older, highly successful novelist-turned-script writer, Eigra Lewis Roberts, to escape from the huge shadow of Kate Roberts, but their voices are modern, positive and unmistakably of their time; young poets, often aggressively accessible, almost succeed in taking their medium for granted.

Eigra Lewis Roberts, one of the foremost contemporary Welsh-language novelists.

In support of all this, the Welsh Books Council administers a grant of some £400,000 annually from the Welsh Office and £180,000 from the Welsh Arts Council. This provides grants to books and periodicals, and support services for book design and the editing and processing of manuscripts and typescripts. The Council is also increasingly involved in the marketing of books and periodicals through the Books Centre, which serves as a central clearing house for publishers wishing to use it. The Council even goes so far as to commission books, and uniform series, in areas where it is felt that there is an inadequate supply of reading materials. This is particularly the case where books for children and young people are concerned. The Welsh Arts Council itself operates in a more selective way, giving grants to specific works of quality, offering bursaries to enable writers to release themselves from full-time employment to complete a literary project, awarding literary prizes, and giving block grants in certain exceptional cases, like the Welsh-language poetry publishing house, Barddas, which is also now branching out into literary criticism and even into the field of creative prose, and the fine-art press, Gwasg Gregynog. It is intended that the activities of the two major donors should complement each other, and by and large they do.

William Owen Roberts, an exciting young novelist who has brought a new dimension to Welsh-language fiction.

During 1988–9, under this umbrella of variegated subsidy, 488 titles were published in the Welsh language, including over two hundred children's titles. At the same time, the Books Council offered subsidies to some dozen periodicals, varying from *Sothach*, a pop and

A variety of Welsh-language periodicals subsidized by the Welsh Books Council.

rock publication aimed at teenagers, to *Prentis*, a magazine specifically targeted at Welsh-learners, to *Pais*, a women's magazine. The Arts Council tends to support more upmarket periodicals, like Yr Academi Gymreig's Welsh language quarterly, *Taliesin*, and the long-standing critical-philosophical publication, *Y Traethodydd*. The roles of the two bodies are less clear-cut in this area than they used to be, however, in that the Books Council also supports a religious periodical, *Cristion*, while the Arts Council gives substantial support to a recently established general-interest contemporary review, *Golwg*, edited by Dylan Iorwerth, a journalist with wide experience in the mass media. What is clear is that the regular appearance of a wide variety of periodicals offers plenty of opportunity for general reading in Welsh, and at the same time provides a platform for aspiring writers. The editors of a literary journal like *Taliesin*, for example, have been able to publish the work of upwards of a hundred authors over a period of two years.

If one then is to return to the actual scope and substance of work of genuine creative calibre emerging from all this activity, one has to reiterate that poetry is still the flagship, as far as traditional literary genres are concerned. If poetic activity is widespread and often substantial, with some honourable exceptions, the lack of substance in the field of the contemporary novel is disappointing. This is no doubt partly the result of factors already referred to: the strength of the poetic tradition, and the demand, in the field of prose fiction, for 'popular work' which is easily accessible. What most people require from the Welsh novelist is the traditional well-told tale; Catherine Cookson, after all, is more in demand on library shelves than Gabriel Garcia Marquez. But there is another factor, one that is particularly relevant in an age of increased commercial awareness. Quite simply, the Welsh writer cannot earn a living by writing novels in Welsh; novels do appear, and there are some talented contemporary novelists. But they cannot build a developing career as novelists, in the way an English or French or Spanish novelist can. The poet is accustomed to living within a social context where his writing is regarded as a part-time aberration. He or she can flourish notwithstanding. The prose writer, however substantial, may well require a different kind of motivation. And the truth is that such motivation has to some extent been provided over recent years by the undoubted success of the Welsh-language television channel, S4C; Eigra Lewis Roberts, William Owen Roberts, Siôn Eirian and others are enabled to live their lives as professional writers because of S4C.

It is now possible for a Welsh-language writer to earn realistic television fees for writing formula-scripts for Welsh-language soap-operas like *Pobol y Cwm* and *Dinas*. If that writer is willing to spend some portion of time researching and writing documentary programmes in addition, then it is just possible to become a full-time professional writer in the Welsh language without ever publishing a book. While it can be most beneficial to an established writer to augment a normally paltry income from book royalties by writing also for television, it is also true that a great many aspiring and potential young writers are drawn, like moths to a candle-flame, by the lure of television before they have ever learnt the rudiments of the writer's craft, and are probably, as a result, lost to literature for ever. Those who might have written social novels satirizing Peter Walker's Wales, or embarked on imaginative experimentation in fiction, feeding on the very internationalism which television itself has brought to the Welsh language, are probably researching other people's programmes and contributing to the lowest common denominator of saleable soap. It would be pleasant to think that S4C, moving into the decade of the new Europe under its new Director, could become as aware of its possible role as a partner in the creation of serious literature as sound radio was in the 1950s and 1960s, and at the same time of its already imminent power to frustrate literary development.

Before leaving literature in the Welsh language, one should mention one other ambivalent development which has taken place in recent years, and which offers both an opportunity and a threat to serious literature. This is the growth of the professional theatre company, locally-based, specializing in community theatre and often handling themes of direct contemporary relevance. At their best, in the early productions, for example, of the north Wales company, Bara Caws, the work of such companies fills the void created by the lack of substantial social comment in the contemporary novel: it is sharp, moving and intelligent. At its worst, however, it is barely literate, and the practice that has recently developed, whereby the actors themselves write their own scripts as they go along, often without any noticeable command of language, can lead to the performance of material whose linguistic and literary standards are low indeed. Such companies should be persuaded that the writing of plays is a wordsmith's art and that actors are not necessarily playwrights.

It is clear that there is an audience for live theatre in the rural setting; it is admirable that professional companies, once again mercifully still subsidized by the Arts Council, exist to fulfil the needs of such an audience. The exciting Theatrig company, Bara Caws at its best, Cwmni Cyfri Tri and others have shown that these needs can be met with original work of a high quality. As in the case of S4C, one hopes that such companies, and those responsible for funding them, can see the value of patiently fostering high standards in the literary aspects of their work as well as in their techniques of performance. The opportunity for partnership clearly exists, but the current demand for 'bums on seats', in this as in so many other fields, militates against excellence.

It might perhaps seem, at a casual glance, that none of these complications is likely to apply to Welsh writing in the English language. Such writing is, after all, a part of English literature, a contribution to the vast flood of creative expression written and published in a world language. This is, of course, to some extent true. It is possible for a Welsh author writing in English simply to become one more English writer. These authors are often highly successful in their appeal to the mass-market and become celebrities in the world of hyped-up fiction. They might be said to include Craig Thomas, Ken Follett and Leslie

Thomas. In their case, however, as in the case of some politicians, one assumes that their Welshness is coincidental and that they do not therefore come within the scope of this chapter. Let us rather consider the writer whose Welshness is part and parcel of his image of himself as a writer, who writes out of Wales if not of Wales, whose experience is a Welsh experience.

Such writers face a more subtle market problem than Welsh-language writers do, but a genuine one nevertheless. Just as it has been true that Welsh-language writing has simply been regarded as non-existent by the London literary world, it has also been true, and it remains so, that what is regarded as 'regional' writing in English finds it equally difficult to attract notice, particularly if that 'region' is part of the United Kingdom. It therefore follows that the existence of support organizations like the Arts Council and the English-language section of Yr Academi Gymreig are almost as vital to English-language writing in Wales as their counterparts are to Welsh-language writing. (The Welsh Books Council, although its editorial, design and marketing expertise is available to all Welsh publishing, irrespective of language, does have a particular responsibility for Welsh-language writing, as far as grant-aid is concerned.)

The Welsh Arts Council would regard itself as having a responsibility to provide even-handed support to work of literary merit in either language. It therefore gives grant-aid to periodicals like *Planet*, *Poetry Wales* and the *New Welsh Review*; it awards bursaries, prizes and residencies in exactly the same way as it does in the Welsh-language context and it supports Wales-based publishers producing books by Welsh authors and books of particular Welsh interest; Seren Books, a recent and successful development of Poetry Wales Press, is an excellent example of this, and they now publish a wide range of creative work.

In spite of the fact that Welsh Arts Council literary prizes have been awarded during recent years to writers of Welsh birth who have long since distinguished themselves in the wider literary world like Bernice Rubens and Dannie Abse, it is probably fair to assume that most grant-aid is used to help writers who are not yet known outside Wales or whose work is so specialized or so 'regional' in nature that it is never likely to attract the attention of those who are not conversant with the Welsh experience.

As far as the nature of the work is concerned, one has to note once more the scope and quality of poetic activity. It is, of course, true beyond Wales that recent years have seen a resurgence in poetry. We have seen a proliferation of poetry competitions, some of them lucra-

Dannie Abse, poet, dramatist and novelist, is best known for his poetry and public readings of his work.

tive, and a growing interest in readings and in poetry workshops. This has been reflected within Wales, where the recent move to establish a residential writers' centre in Gwynedd was initially motivated by the remarkable popularity of the Arvon Foundation centres in England.

Inside the world of poetry, it might be thought that the gaunt figure of R. S. Thomas would dominate the scene. In a sense he does; he is certainly the best known and most highly regarded outside Wales of any Welsh writer since Dylan Thomas. But he is in no sense typical of his fellows. Rather than becoming, like the other Thomas, a kind of talisman for Anglo-Welsh writing, R. S. Thomas in his seventies straddles uneasily the two cultures of Wales and typifies more readily the traditional angst of the Welsh-speaking writers of previous generations than the more cosmopolitan social concerns of most of his contemporaries, whichever language they use as their medium. He does, of course, speak Welsh. He is a member of the Welsh section of Yr Academi Gymreig. He takes it upon himself to make apocalyptic comments regarding the state of the language and the decline of social structures. He is in some ways far more attuned to the social climate of his adopted Dwyfor than to that of Anglicized Wales. In many ways he stands apart.

It might be thought that another distinguished poet already mentioned, Dannie Abse, typifies more readily the stance of many Welshmen who write in English. He is certainly Welsh; he is conscious of his Welshness and he writes and speaks of it. But his Wales is not Welshspeaking Wales; it is Cardiff. And his roots do not lie on a Ceredigion hillside; they lie in the Welsh-Jewish community of the capital. His Welshness is a subtle and complex thing, interwoven with many other strands in his upbringing and in his adult environment. In any case, though I began by emphasizing the interdependence of Welsh-language and English-language writing in Wales, the very nature of that interdependence is much more subtle than it used to be. The days when the 'Indeed-to-goodness' school of Anglo-Welsh writers presented a bizarre Welsh-speaking cartoon to an amused English-speaking world are by and large over. The modern Welsh writer writing in English is either not particularly concerned with Welsh Wales at all, he regards it with a distant casual interest or he or she acknowledges a dependence upon it and treats of the two cultures as essentially one.

There are certainly many younger writers by now who come into the first category. Among them one could name poets such as Tony Curtis, Robert Minhinnick and Duncan Bush and novelists such as David Hughes. Their personal Wales like that of Dannie Abse, is in fact an Anglicized urban environment, neither rural nor Welsh. It is out of this that they have come and it is of this that they write. The Valleys of south Wales, however, were Anglicized so recently and so rapidly that the very linguistic rhythms even of these writers are permeated by the cadences of Welsh. And even they cannot avoid coming into contact with S4C.

As far as those who are more conscious of the relevance artistically of their Welsh identity within a wider historical context are concerned, many more bridges have been built between the two cultures during recent years. Two distinguished poets, Gillian Clarke and Anthony Conran, exemplify this. Gillian Clarke, active with The Welsh Academy and poetry workshops within Wales, but also widely known outside Wales and much in demand for poetry readings, has learnt Welsh and lives in rural Ceredigion. Anthony Conran, who

Gillian Clarke is among the most-read contemporary Welsh poets writing in English.

edited the *Penguin Book of Welsh Verse*, and has translated a great deal of Welsh verse into English, was recently the author of a play, *Branwen*, which was a re-creation of one of the Mabinogion tales, and drew upon the mythology of earlier times to make comments of contemporary relevance. Anthony Conran, in fact, is by no means the only Welsh poet writing in English to draw widely on Welsh myth and legend as a basis for his imagery.

Another important contributor in the process of bridge-building during recent years has been the magazine, *Planet*, edited by Ned Thomas, another Welsh-speaker. Since its re-emergence, it has made strenuous efforts to survey the whole of Wales, and often to represent in English the views and attitudes of Welsh-speakers. It is one of very few publications which review Welsh-language books in English, and the whole publication, although living up to its subtitle of 'The Welsh Internationalist' in the breadth of its horizons, presents a positive and well-informed sense of Welsh identity. It and the improving Welsh-language periodical *Golwg* complement each other, and to read both is to get an increasingly rounded view of Wales and the world through the eyes of the Welsh.

For a literature that has produced outstanding writing in the field of the novel and the short story in the past, it is perhaps disappointing that present-day Welsh writing in English has not produced a body of fiction to compare with its verse output. There may well be many reasons for this, and the lack of specific motivation may be one of them. The advent of television, with its emphasis on the simplistic story-line, may be another. It is perhaps significant that a prose-writer of considerable talent, Alun Richards, has written his best-known work for network television. (It is interesting that the Academi has very recently recognized the need to encourage fiction by offering substantial prizes for short stories through its John Tripp Award.) Yet another reason may be the climate of the time. It seems to be in the nature of the Welshman that his literary talent is for work on a small scale, for lyric poetry and for short stories. The poem is in favour at present, the short story is not, and there is a very restricted market indeed for good short stories.

The answer, where the novel is concerned, may be simpler still. If the literary scene in Wales appears at present to be most lively in its poetic activity, that may largely be as I suggested earlier because the successful writers of fiction are in any case likely to become part of the general spectrum of fiction in the English-speaking world, unless, like Emyr Humphreys, they have a conscious commitment to Wales and a need to work within a Welsh context. Emyr Humphreys is perhaps the most consistently stimulating of such novelists now writing, and he, like R. S. Thomas, is much associated with Welsh-language matters, and he writes for television in Welsh, but he, like Thomas, is in many ways a solitary figure.

Nor should it be forgotten, however, that writers who have adopted Wales and have written of it as it were with an outsider's eye, have made substantial contributions to our understanding of ourselves during recent years, from Bruce Chatwin in *On The Black Hill* to Kingsley Amis in *The Old Devils*, not to mention Jan Morris and her vivid evocations of the ethos of place.

Finally, it may also be worth noting again that the huge international publishing houses which now dominate the London scene do not react favourably to fiction which is too 'regional' in character, as that, in their view, restricts the market potential. There may well now be a case for funding bodies to consider specifically supporting the publication of high-quality fiction within Wales itself, in the same way as they have successfully encouraged the publication of poets through the Poetry Wales Press and others, and a start has in fact been made, in the way Seren Books has successfully embarked on the publication of novels.

Emyr Humphreys has been awarded the Hawthornden Prize and the Somerset Maugham Award. His highly acclaimed novels include Flesh and Blood, Salt of the Earth *and* A Toy Epic. *He has also published books of poetry and non-fiction in Welsh and English.*

In any case, whichever language is our medium, we cannot avoid the truism that we live in a visual age. In some senses, our best 'novelists' in the future may well be committed and independent-minded film-makers like Karl Francis, with his sharp portrayal of modern problems in the industrial wasteland. All writers have to take cognisance of the visual media, and should consider how to achieve creative compromises with what may seem at first sight to be the enemy. Similarly, those who work creatively in film and television might well look more positively at the possibility of co-operating more fully with writers working in traditional genres. On the whole, if one accepts the negative aspects I noted earlier in the article, the advent of S4C has brought some positive benefits to Welsh-language writers: it has, to a limited extent, worked in tandem with established writers, it has brought an air of contemporaneity to the ethos of the language and it has created a wider audience for the language itself. It cannot be said that the broadcasting media have done similar favours for the English-language writer in Wales. Long before the establishment of S4C, the opportunity had been there for both the BBC and successive independent television companies to represent Wales to the world through the medium of Anglo-Welsh writing. That opportunity is still there and is still little used. One hopes it may be possible to develop more fruitful partnerships in the future.

Looking to the future, different kinds of opportunities present themselves. It may well be opportune for both the literatures of Wales to look very positively indeed at the new horizons which will be opened up by the opportunities of 1992. As I write, wider and more apocalyptic developments in Europe make it impossible to judge what other opportunities may recur. In any case, the nation-states of mainland Europe are, by and large, better disposed than England is to the concept of cultural and linguistic minorities, and more interested in the human experience encapsulated within such minorities. We ourselves, in turn, insular as we are, whether we write in Welsh or in English, need to get used to becoming more multilingual, to laying ourselves open to translation, to becoming more literate in the literatures of Europe. Both in the richness of its past, in legend and myth, and in the melting-pot of its present search for indentity, Wales clearly has a distinct contribution to make to the literatures of Europe. It may at last become possible for it to make that contribution without first going through the fine strainer of London taste and the London market. To return to our central paradox, however, it will no doubt continue to be necessary for it to do so while depending for its survival on a substantial subsidy from the British state.

SPORT FOR ALL AND THE NEW RICHES

DAVID PARRY-JONES

As a young cricketer I played neither the hook nor pull shots at the crease. My runs for Cardiff High School on plumb wickets at the old Harlequins ground in east Cardiff (now alas no more than an unkempt public park), for the Welsh Secondary Schools in Tests at Cardiff and Old Trafford, and for Oxford University Authentics, were chiefly grafted on the off-side, through mid-on or with leg-side glides and tickles. Not until my early twenties did I take the bull by the horns and begin striking short-pitched balls decisively to the square-leg boundary or over mid-wicket.

Modestly, I can state that this early deficiency had less to do with lack of ability or 'bottle' than with the circumstances that had shaped me as a batsman. The after-school cricket of my generation was mainly played in the network of suburban back lanes along which refuse lorries and car-owners drove to collect household rubbish or garage their vehicles. These narrow thoroughfares afforded strips of tarmac on which balls bounced truly, and were enclosed on each side by eight-feet-high walls which made a complement of fielders unnecessary. Where two or three were gathered together, there could be hours of pleasure, albeit hemmed in (dust-bins made sonorous wickets).

The drawback was that if you hooked or pulled vigorously the ball inevitably rebounded from the leg-side wall and sailed over the one opposite. This meant a time-consuming, and usually tension-fraught, call upon hostile neighbours to retrieve the vital piece of equipment. Confrontation was frequently followed by confiscation – and close of play. It was thus prudence and hard experience which confined the leg-side shots of back-lane batsmen to jabs or carefully guided pushes.

In the 1940s small sportsmen had to be opportunists. Soccer was staged (using an old tennis ball) in culs-de-sac with garage doors for goals. Towns and cities like Cardiff and Swansea boasted tennis-courts in their parks; but these were usually booked days in advance by 'big kids' with access to telephones and plenty of pocket-money. There were a few snooker halls where, again, booking in advance might guarantee an hour's play; but for a decent swim in uncrowded waters youngsters from Roath, Penylan, Llandaff, Cathays and the other Cardiff suburbs had to travel to Penarth, a journey involving a ten-mile return cycle ride and pocket-money for the ha'penny toll at the long-defunct single-carriageway toll bridge that once spanned the River Ely. Golf, skiing, squash, fencing, even boxing and athletics – these were sports that 'other people' played, usually the sons and daughters of better-off families who attended boarding schools.

In other words, outside the schools – whose playing fields and gymnasia, if they had them, closed at 4.15 p.m. sharp – facilities for sport and exercise were minimal. Looking back, it is remarkable how the instinctive desire to flex muscles, test stamina and compete with others still found outlets: in those back lanes, on partially-cleared bomb sites and in the fairly spartan municipal or private enterprise venues that existed.

A prime motive, of course, was the mimicking of heroes whose names we knew from radio commentaries and whose faces were familiar from smudgy photographs in the press. Hardstaff, Hutton, Hammond; Bleddyn Williams, Ken Jones, Macdonald Bailey, Bryn Jones, Ken Hollyman and Stan Richards – we lived and breathed their exploits by courtesy of the *Football Echo* and the Welsh Home Service, and impersonated them in our back-lane battles. Such men, and I daresay the girls worshipped Fanny Blankers-Koen and Louise Brough, were a constant challenge to the rising generation to emulate their achievements. Sometimes we could actually watch them in the flesh, at Cardiff Arms Park or Ninian Park; but for the most part distance lent enchantment: our heroes and heroines did not loom large in mid-close-up or action replay on living-room screens.

Star quality and the pursuit of excellence – and perhaps supremacy – are undoubtedly tremendous influences upon budding sportsmen and sportswomen. Welsh sport today has its world-class performers, and there is nothing new about that. There have been winners and champions at all stages in the history of games in Wales. They appear during four identifiable eras.

Primacy among the superstars of Wales must be accorded to Guto Nyth Bran, that legendary long-distance runner whose exploits can make even those of Steve Jones seem pedestrian. Guto could catch foxes in full flight; he could leap from bed to extinguish a candle and be back beneath the blankets before his bedroom went dark; and he beat the all-England champion in an epic race through Gwent before dropping dead at the finishing line. Like Pheidippides, you could say, he went out at the top.

But the personality cult that was Guto had few parallels in eighteenth-century Wales, whose sports pastimes were manifestly knock-about and made few demands upon individual skill and stamina. Saints' days and holidays were often marked by games and contests for which farmers and their labourers crowded into villages and market towns to compete at running, long-jumping, wrestling, bare-fist fighting, tug-of-war, and quoits. Parishes met in opposition, the losing side having to buy the *cwrw* (beer). Side-shows included cock-fighting and bull-baiting (Swansea boasted a corporation bull-ring). Horse-racing and hunting had many adherents who flocked to venues like Holywell, Chirk and Llangefni.

Cnapan was also played, a village-versus-village game that might involve 2,000 participants on foot or horseback. There were no side-lines or goal posts, victory going to the side that could remove the ball beyond recall. Towns as far apart as Dolgellau and Neath were taken over periodically by this all-in wrestling on-the-move, whose origins may lie back with the Roman legionaries based in western Britain.

Those Welshmen who took to the water, whether at sea or on rivers, usually had the very specific motive of catching fish for the table. But coracle races were common, with prizes at the end of the eighteenth century amounting to five guineas or more. Similarly, practical military considerations prompted the archery and shooting contests which were frequently staged at the great houses. Members of the Royal British Bowmen's Society, based at Wrexham, wore a green cutaway coat, buff waistcoat, lace jabot, yellow breeches and white silk stockings to take part in an annual shoot held between 1787 and 1869 and interrupted only by the necessity to fire at real targets during the Napoleonic Wars.

The retrospective view of Wales in the eighteenth century, there-fore, is of a vigorous, vital society with energy to spare and an unrefi-ned competitive instinct just waiting for laws, goals and targets to be formalized. This process was taking place, as luck would have it, at very close quarters: those most excellent formulators of rules and codes, the English, were busy bringing order to the violent leisure-time exchanges of public schoolboys by laying down strict conditions for contests, laws that settled disputes and, on the 'playing fields' themselves, goals, touch-lines and boundaries.

Oxbridge men like Rowland Williams (St David's College, Lamp-eter), W. P. Whittington (Landovery College) and J. C. F. Morgan (Cowbridge Grammar School) thus found ready acceptance when they set out to transplant enthusiasm for 'Rugby football' into Wales. Both in towns and out in the country there was an eagerness to accept the discipline of rules in the interests of bringing about a better, properly organized contest.

And, in response to this demand, came initiatives from landowners and the aristocracy who emerged as providers of the facilities that were needed. The Third Marquess of Bute gave Cardiff's cricketers permission to play on reclaimed land known as the 'great park' close to the Taff, extending the courtesy to Rugby footballers in 1876. Lord Tredegar's generosity assisted the establishing of a venue for cricket,

Rugby and other sports besides the Usk at Newport, similar developments taking place at Neath and elsewhere.

The energy and hunger for exercise and competition, therefore, were present in Wales; exiles and immigrants from England, and to some extent Scotland, had successfully demonstrated the extra fun that could be had through submitting to discipline; facilities were beginning to become available. How would the Welsh people exploit the potential of these circumstances?

First of all through clubs, whose formation and rapid strides ushered in the second discernible era in the progress of sport in the Principality. Young men who had learned to play the new 'team games' at their public schools carried their enthusiasm on into adult life and set out to perpetuate the practising of skills and the pleasure to be gained through playing games in congenial company and against mettlesome opponents. In modern parlance, they got their acts together, combining to agree laws and codes of conduct (or importing them from across Offa's Dyke) that made for meaningful competition. Experience of the hurly-burly of Rugby football prompted them to introduce common uniforms, as the best way of distinguishing team-mates from opponents. Their gatherings, often on patches of waste land or meadows lent by friendly farmers were dictated by geography and proximity; and the desire for local identity in order to test themselves against rivals from nearby towns and villages endured from an earlier age.

The first major Rugby clubs – and they remain the best known – were Neath, Llanelli, Swansea, Newport and Cardiff, all communities that had become swollen through economic forces in the latter part of the nineteenth century, and ones into which had poured immigrants from Scotland, Ireland and, most significantly, the west country of England. Firm 'fixtures' began to be struck – Cardiff and Newport initiated their venerable series of meetings on marshland near the estuary of the Usk in 1876. Results assumed importance for local pride, which was no longer confined to participants. There arose a need for independent arbiters – 'referees' – to rule on contentious issues of the play.

To regularize such developments and reach agreement on broader issues it was necessary to achieve a consensus; and this was secured by the setting-up of the Welsh Rugby Union in a meeting at Neath in 1881. From this stage it was a short step to the issuing of challenges to neighbouring national bodies. Thus Welsh representative teams took the field for the first time against sides from England, Ireland and

Scotland in 1881, 1882 and 1883, a first-ever victory being registered in Dublin in the 1881–2 season.

Meanwhile at Ruabon in 1876 a parallel development had taken place with the formation of the Football Association of Wales by the lobby which preferred to play the 'dribbling' game. Because of the early grip on southern Wales seized by the handling code, with its unique blend of skill, finesse and brute force, 'soccer' was a long time spreading over the whole of the Principality; but by 1907 a Welsh Championship had been formulated which was capable of attracting sixty or seventy entries, the number of clubs affiliated to the FAW rising by 1910 to 262. Cardiff City was founded in 1899, Newport County and Swansea (Town) following in 1912. Welsh international soccer teams played only sporadically until the early years of the twentieth century (and the laws had to be carefully explained to spectators in the south) but were soon drawing crowds of 15,000 and more. This 'explosion' of soccer has been ascribed to the disenchantment experienced by many spectators at the defensive tactics employed by leading rugby clubs, and the future of the 'dribbling' code as a gate-taking sport was assured.

After foundation, consolidation became the watchword with Rugby clubs adopting policies by which their future good fortune might be safeguarded. The truism was recognized that players' careers are finite, governed by fallibility of physique or the need to allot more time to earning a living. But club members whose playing days were over now proved willing to serve in an administrative capacity, as committeemen. Thus another valuable tradition became established whereby past players nurtured the ability of their successors and catered for their needs.

Decisions were taken to build or lease 'club houses' where players and spectators could foregather. Often, as at Neath, Aberavon and Llanelli, it is still possible to discern the early delineation of these arenas with their dual concept: a 'grand stand' offering a new overview of the play combined with an infrastructure where changing rooms, administrative offices and rooms in which to eat and drink could be incorporated.

The club, as an ensemble of active or recently retired players, was certainly the launch-pad which bore most sports in Wales into and through the first half of the twentieth century. Just as in Rugby and Association football, so in hockey, athletics, boxing, cricket, baseball, tennis and the rest, clubs depended upon individual initiative and energy; and from them sprang national teams and governing bodies, of which there were eighty-seven in Wales by 1989.

To a considerable extent the clubs delivered the goods, providing a viable and complex framework within which sportsmen could exercise themselves, compete with rivals, undertake a form of community service – and pursue excellence by, in the case of the few, being chosen for national teams. Thus sporting heroes began to emerge whose example shone brightly upon the grass roots and encouraged them to reach upward in turn. Let us pause awhile to mark achievements that have reflected on the name of Wales.

Billy Meredith, a wily winger, was a turn-of-the-century superstar in soccer's firmament; but it was almost certainly the 1905 Rugby victory over the first All Blacks which took the name of Wales from obscurity on to the world sporting map. Suddenly the little Principality bordering Britain's Atlantic coast had forced itself to the notice of the outside world, and the names of Gabe, Nicholls, Bush, Owen and others excited interest all over the United Kingdom. Welsh boxers made their mark: champions like Wilde, Driscoll and Petersen presaged the achievement of Tommy Farr, who went fifteen rounds with the then world champion Joe Louis in their world heavyweight title fight in the USA. Such men were the forerunners of post-War champions like Erskine, Richardson, Eddie Thomas, Dai Dower, the Curvis cousins and perhaps the most charismatic of Welsh fighters, Howard Winstone. This last-named stylist won a gold medal in the 1958 Empire Games at Cardiff and briefly held the world featherweight title despite the partial loss of fingers on his right hand in an industrial accident.

There was success in plenty for most followers of Welsh sport, and its up-and-coming aspirants, to cheer as the twentieth century moved along. Glamorgan County Cricket Club, founded in 1888, climbed from Minor County status in 1921 when a reluctant MCC accepted Norman Riches's team into the County Championship. In 1948 and after early heartaches and hiccups Wilfred Wooller led the Welsh country to a Championship victory (repeated in 1969) which brought the title out of England for the first time – and matched the feat of Cardiff City AFC who had won the FA Cup in 1927.

Ken Jones was a magnificent Rugby-playing athlete who captured post-War imagination with his track performance and medal during the 1948 Olympic Games in London and captained the Welsh team at the Vancouver Empire Games. But perhaps the most memorable moment in Welsh athletics came in 1964 at the Tokyo Olympics when the spindly long-jumper from Nant-y-moel, Lynn Davies, jumped 26 feet, 5½ inches to take the gold medal ahead of his great rivals Ralph Boston and Igor Ter Ovanesyan. (It is a curious aber-

Former Olympic gold medal winner Lynn Davies presents Colin Jackson with the award for 1989 Western Mail Sports Personality of the Year. Jackson went on to win a gold medal in the 110-metre hurdles at the 1990 Commonwealth Games.

ration that this personable man's great status and standing in world athletics do not seem to have been harnessed to effect in his native country.)

Predictably Rugby football played its part. Under John Gwilliam's highly-disciplined regime Triple Crowns and Grand Slams were won in 1950 and 1952, Lewis Jones and Cliff Morgan emerging as superlative entertainers and match-winners. Two decades later Barry John, Gareth Edwards, Gerald Davies and Phil Bennett were the stars who pulled in the crowds and continued to inspire the young.

Such sports relied mainly on muscle, stamina and the adrenalin released by the thunderous roar of big crowds. But suddenly, as colour television coincidentally disclosed snooker's singular appeal, the Welsh showed that besides giants of the open field they could throw up ice-cool champions of the baize, men who relied on finesse and a delicate touch. In the 1970s the immaculate Ray Reardon smoothed back his dark hair and won six world snooker titles. His achievements must have inspired the feats of amateur champions Doug Mountjoy (1976) and Cliff Wilson (1978), not to mention Llanelli-born Terry Griffiths, who took the world professional title in

1979 at his first attempt. These were the men who brought the inaugural World Cup to Wales in 1979 and retained it in 1980.

Other heroic feats have punctuated the century. Harry Llewellyn, on the horse Foxhunter, brought the Welsh an Olympic gold medal at Helsinki in 1952. Swimmer Martyn Woodroffe, a butterfly expert, achieved an extraordinary silver medal at the Mexico Olympics in 1968, while breast-stroker Pat Bevan won her gold in the Commonwealth Games two years later. Mike Davies, Gerald Battrick and, as a junior, J. P. R. Williams saw that their country was well represented on the tennis-court. Golfers like Dai Rees (one of Britain's most successful two or three David Cup captains) and David Thomas kept the Welsh profile truly international in their sport, and in 1987 Ian Woosnam was to spearhead the successful Welsh bid for the World Cup. There were even the throwers of darts, a sport in which Wales won the first-ever World Cup in 1977 and in which Leighton Rees became something of a cult-figure.

Ian Woosnam who with David Llewellyn won the World Cup for Wales in 1987 and took the individual title. He has been a member of the victorious British Ryder Cup team on three occasions.

Today's Colin Jackson and Steve Jones and their contemporaries are the latest part of a long, honourable tradition, the former following up his Olympic silver medal at Seoul with gold in the 110-metre hurdles at the Auckland Commonwealth Games of 1990.

There can be no doubt that the clubs have played an important part in nurturing ambitious, excellent sportsmen who carried the name of Wales to the top of the leader-board. As the post-War years went by, however, and political change brought in radical reforms on a broad front, it was only natural that games and sports should come under the microscope. Although theoretically open to all to improve and refine their skills, there was a growing feeling that clubs were for large sectors of the populace, particularly the young, distant and inaccessible places. This was particularly true of less spectacular, or fashionable, sports (the majority) which could not charge gate-money for the funding of broad-based development.

Steve Jones, the former world record holder for the marathon, at the 1989 Welsh Athletics Championships.

Nor did there appear to be opportunities for the ordinary Welsh person, who simply fancied a brush with games and exercise. The more delicate grass roots stood in need of cultivation; in addition to the warmth of a bracing sporting climate they required fertilization and nutrition. This required a political initiative, as opposed to the private energies which had given momentum to organized sporting activity in Wales between the middle of the eighteenth and nineteenth centuries. A third major era of development was at hand.

The 'think-tank' work for Britain as a whole, much of whose philosophy inevitably affected progress in Wales, was undertaken by the

Wolfenden Committee. Its report 'Sport and the Community' prompted the Labour Government of the mid 1960s to set up a Sports Council chaired by Denis Howell MP, a former football referee who was at the time a Parliamentary Under Secretary at the Department of Education and Science. This was the body which in 1965 established the Sports Council for Wales (SCW) with a brief 'to promote a properly balanced and co-ordinated improvement and expansion of facilities for sport and physical recreation to meet local and national needs; and to foster co-operation among the local authorities and voluntary organisations concerned'.

Alderman Philip Squire of Mid Glamorgan was its first chairman and, despite immediately encountering a period of stringent public economy which caused the government to defer expenditure on numerous capital projects, it set in motion the process which resulted in the opening of a National Sports Centre for Wales at Sophia Gardens, Cardiff, in 1971. This impressive complex on the west bank of the Taff has proved an admirable 'shop window' for sport in the Principality. It stages world championships and international events in a variety of sports; it acts as a home venue for some Welsh national teams; and by hosting courses it has become an admirable cramming school for sporting high-fliers in their quest for excellence. The Centre is, however, no more than the tip of what has grown into a very substantial iceberg. For threaded into the Sports Council for Wales's policies and attitudes there has always existed the maxim 'sport for all'; that is, the idea that opportunities for games and exercise should be brought within range of as much of the population as may from time to time seek them.

The collection and analysis of data, hitherto lacking, has been a prime weapon in this ongoing campaign. In order to prescribe, there needed to be diagnosis; and, in order to diagnose, information was required about the quantity and conditions of facilities for sport in Wales – whether natural or man-made – and about potential participants. Thus in its first decade the SCW initiated or backed a series of authoritative studies out of which aims and purposes could rationally be determined.

Following the old Central Council of Physical Recreation's summary of the needs of major sports entitled 'Sports Facilities in Wales' (1965) came 'An Initial Appraisal' (1967), a survey of swimming-pools, sports halls, golf courses and athletics stadia. Upon this were based 'A Standardised Assessment of Requirements of Provision' and 'Facilities for Sport' (both 1970) which detailed the requirements of governing bodies for international, national, area

Tracy Edwards, the first woman to win the Yachtsman of the Year Trophy. She was skipper of the Maiden Great Britain, *the first all-women crew to complete the 33,000-mile Whitbread Round the World Yacht Race.*

and county competition. 'A Strategy for Water Recreation' (1973) looked at the potential for recreation held out by Wales's lakes, rivers, reservoirs, canals and coastline; while the 1975 study 'Sport in Wales: Participation' detailed those who took part in games, and their numbers. These important documents highlighted the statistics and circumstances upon which an appeal to local authorities to redouble their efforts to support sport and leisure activities could be based. What had emerged between 1965 and 1975 was a broad consensus between governing bodies and the Sports Council for Wales (the quango) about the lack of space for games and sport, shortage of vital equipment, and poor or non-existent changing and spectator accommodation. 'This must affect the quality of Welsh performances and limit the experience of players,' stated the Sports Council for Wales in 1975, adding that: 'The responsibility for the provision or improvement of major sports facilities lies mainly with the local authorities.'

The response at the outset of the 1990s appeared to have been much more than satisfactory, since the Sports Council for Wales was able to report: 'There has been an increase in both popularity and frequency of participation in sport in Wales since 1977.' Not only had the public been coaxed, cajoled and sometimes coerced into changed attitudes and expectations by campaigns and clever publicity; but thanks to local funding, allied to centrally allocated grants and loans, there had sprung up a sleek new generation of 'sports halls' and 'leisure centres' where the populace at large could flex muscles, break sweat, kick balls, smash shuttlecocks or swim a few lengths. At last there was provision for the low-fliers as well as the champions and better-than-average performers.

Everywhere evidence can be seen of the vast sums of public money which have poured into satisfying people's new aspirations towards fitness and health. In the major cities and conurbations like Cardiff, Swansea and Newport, in smaller towns dotted throughout the Valleys and rural areas, and in up-country villages, all-purpose brick-built barns have sprung up in which anything from badminton to bowling and keep-fit to whist drives can take place. There has been a massive, and largely successful, drive to open up under-used school and college sports facilities during evenings and vacations. The Sport for All scheme means, too, that the elderly, the disabled and the unemployed can enjoy a weekly work-out at such premises.

Money has also been spent on the expert designing and improving of golf courses, on the installation of artificial cricket pitches, on the laying-down of running tracks, on the provision of swimming-pools and on the erection of squash courts. The Sports Council for Wales was able to state with some satisfaction and justification by 1988 that 'the existing supply of facilities for swimming, squash, tennis and golf is capable of meeting demand in the majority of districts in Wales'.

Occasionally special capital funding has led to the creation of a major International venue, the best example of which is the National Watersports Centre at Plas Menai between Caernarfon and Bangor, the only one of its kind in Wales and England. Although this kind of activity is in its infancy some 3,000 participants attended sixty courses of varying length in the year ending spring 1988, non-residential usage attracting a further 35,000 attendances. By any standards this is remarkable; but not to be outdone the National Sports Centre coincidentally quadrupled its attendances between 1972 and 1988 to 800,000.

Sports new to Wales have also been thrusting their way into the limelight. The Principality has acquired its own ice-rink in Cardiff (to supplement the one on Deeside) where large crowds pour in to cheer league contests. The Cardiff Devils, augmented with a quorum of highly-expert Canadians, swept triumphantly into the 1990s at the top of Britain's Heineken Premier Division. Wales's heartland has afforded testing routes for major British rally-driving events, with David Llewellin emerging as the United Kingdom's top driver. Not far behind him in the ratings lies north Welshman Gwyndaf Evans, a bus driver who has proved himself at home on any terrain in any vehicle.

At the same time as Joe – or Dai – public was discovering the joys of physical exertion and Sport for All was moving from a philosophy to a reality, the national shop-window managed to remain flush with glittering prizes. Between 1987 and 1989, for example, Clive Branson, an angler, Darren Morgan (snooker), golfers Ian Woosnam and David Llewellyn, bowler Janet Ackland and cyclist Sally Hodge were all world champions. Stephen Dodd became the fourth Welshman to win the British amateur golf championship during the 1980s, subsequently joining forces with fellow-Welshman Neil Roderick to help Britain win the Walker Cup for the first time on American soil.

And there were the sailors: surely the new presence of Plas Menai contributed to a four-pronged world title triumph that echoes the land-lubbers' feats. Tracy Edwards, inspirational skipper of an all-woman crew in the Whitbread Round the World yacht race, became the first female to be named 'Yachtsman of the Year' in 1989. Welsh

The Cardiff Devils, winners of the Heineken Premier Division and the Champions Cup 1990.

water-borne success was sustained by the pre-eminence of power-boater Jonathan Jones, a Fishguard bank clerk who became world champion for the second time in 1989 after surviving a serious crash. Lower down on the formula ladder Adrian Morse of St Clears won the British 750 title.

But although the balance between egalitarianism and the elitist quest for individual excellence has seemed to be about right, not everything in the garden is lovely. For example, the pattern of non-participation remains the same, with women, semi-skilled and unskilled workers and the unemployed lagging behind. Actual levels of participation are lower here than in England. School pupils exert themselves less frequently, and show less interest in sport as they grow older. At senior international level, despite the conveyor belt of stars, research shows that Welsh sporting performances relative to those of other countries declined overall in the decade from 1974 and 1985: 'In spite of national squad training systems and increased representative competition overseas, marked progress has not been made,' said the Sports Council. And there are still sports whose development is hampered by the lack of facilities capable of accommodating events of major importance.

Though there are – inevitably – ongoing arguments, sometimes heated, about priorities and the cutting of the financial cake, the Sports Council for Wales has none the less done well to identify many of these problems and shortcomings, and to eliminate a number of them. Undoubtedly there has been a transformation of which it can be proud. It has shown itself capable of enlightened thinking about what goals can or should be targeted and achieved; and its alignment with governing bodies and local authorities is both cordial and formidable. Given the continuing desire of Welsh men and women to achieve excellence, within teams or in individual events, and a general willingness to 'have a go', there exists a totality of potential which can urge sport in Wales confidently towards the next century.

And there is the prospect of ever increasing help from the private sector – in the best traditions of Thatcherism – whereby governing bodies, clubs and individuals are encouraged to look less to the public purse than to industry, commerce and the 'sponsors'. Patronage on the grand scale seems set to characterize a fourth major era in Welsh sport, though what its ultimate repercussions will be is hard to predict.

Here is a phenomenon which is already massively augmenting public funds from both central and local sources. Wales has its Schweppes

Sally McKenzie (née Hodge), first Welsh woman to win a world cycling title when she took the inaugural points race championship in Europe in 1988.

Cup, its Abacus League and its Whitbread Merit Table. But above and beyond these high-profile examples, an astonishing amount of cash from big business is now finding its way into the backing of champions, the supporting of clubs large and small, and the provision of basic trappings like boots, balls, jerseys, changing-rooms, team buses and even clubhouses.

Years ago the brewers led the way, fitting out bars and lounges (in which sportsmen slaked their thirst with the correct brand of beer); soon the commercial potential of advertising on hoardings around touch-lines and on grandstands was perceived; and, when television threw in the towel and conceded that permanent advertisements constituted a legitimate feature of sports stadia, the sudden vast increase in the size of audiences proved irresistible to firms with cash to spend – in greater or lesser quantities – that the Inland Revenue would otherwise have acquired.

Thus, to take examples at random, a substantial number of sports and participants have benefited. The World Track Cycling champion Sally Hodge was sponsored by her employers, Office Cleaning Services; ASW, the Cardiff-based steel firm, has ploughed £250,000 into the development of cricket at all levels in Wales; since 1972 Esso has regularly put more than £50,000 a year into youth sport. British Gas is now associated with Wales-England Rugby International matches to the tune of £500,000, with South Wales Electricity, Hoover and British Steel also jumping on to the Rugby bandwagon. Japanese companies have not been slow to join in: Kubota UK were among twelve sponsors of the European Golf Championship hosted by the Welsh Golf Union at the Royal Porthcawl links in the summer of 1989, and Aiwa give backing to Newbridge RFC.

Such largesse is part of a trend which saw an investment in sport all over Britain of nearly £250 million in 1989, a figure expected to reach £300 million in 1990. Sport is continuing to be the main sponsorship vehicle, its 73 per cent of the market share pushing the arts into a poor second place.

Many onlookers wonder what the big spenders hope to gain in return for their outlay. The answer has to do with the enhancing of company names and images. Marketing managers evidently feel that there is profit to be secured from the association – however sub-liminal – in the consumer's mind between their product or service and the excitement, vitality and virility of sporting competition.

What excites their interest, of course, is the intensity of the tele-vision coverage already mentioned. Viewers have become accus-tomed in the last decade or two to the sight of sports stadia festooned with hoardings, banners and lurid panelling proclaiming the virtues of everything from abdominal supports – jock-straps in the vernacu-lar – to domestic fuels, from brands of bitter beer to building societies. Some Welsh Rugby clubs whose fixtures are frequently televised sport jerseys supplied by Adidas with the three distinctive strips down the sleeve; players wear boots with identifying strips across the instep; athletes, golfers and tennis-players bear tell-tale logos on their breasts.

Such exposure appears to convince boards of directors that there will be a pay-off at counters and cash desks. Adults may pride them-selves on customer resistance to such unsubtle persuasion; but doubtless it works with the young – my own schoolboy contem-poraries in the 1940s all coveted a Gradidge cricket bat signed by Len Hutton (though I am not sure how many followed Denis Compton's example and smeared their hair with a certain brand of cream, or 'creem').

On the whole, this must be good for sport so long as the biggest proportion of the cash is channelled through a governing body which can be relied upon to make prudent decisions about its redeployment. Sponsorship has opened up major new avenues, the best example of which in Wales is the Welsh Brewers Cup involving Rugby football's 'minnows': this funding makes it possible for less affluent clubs like

Dolgellau, Bethesda, Heol-y-Cyw or Blaenavon Forgeside to meet the hotel and petrol bills that must be paid if they are to compete in a tournament that is genuinely nationwide. In other sports sponsorship puts payment for training, the purchase of sophisticated equipment, and the cost of travel for practice or to major events within the reach of indigent youngsters whose incomes would otherwise not permit indulgence on such a scale.

As Welsh sport moves into the 1990s, however, and towards the twenty-first century, it is to be hoped that it will exploit, rather than be exploited by, its new riches. Throughout history, beginning with gladiators and court wrestlers, men — and sometimes women — have taken money for competing in public against opponents, thus providing thrills or spectacle. Professional sport is as old as Greece and Rome. But even paid participants have usually striven for some one — a patron — or some ideal, just as the unpaid amateur has tended to represent a village, a town or a nation. This motivation has been especially firm in Wales, a small nation seeking to establish and underline its identity within the shadow cast by a giant neighbour. It is plain that Welsh athletes and Rugby players — even those who take part in the League code which occasionally throws up a Wales XIII — have been inspired to world-beating feats by the thought of the expectations of their three million compatriots: the putting on of a red Welsh jersey or vest has contributed to superhuman performances. Long may this special power persist; and long may the stars of Welsh games put the representative ideal before an amorphous concept of playing to oblige market forces.

Sponsorship can function at a less opportunist and cynical level. During the 1980s British Coal's Opencast Executive turned over a new leaf and sought to banish its gloomy image by putting a greener, cleaner stamp on the valleys and hillsides from which it had clawed mineral wealth. The result, to take two examples, has been admirable. The Brynbach Park initiative at the Heads of the Valleys has seen the creation of a marvellous water-sports facility on a spent site. Before long the Llanelli area will boast a superb eighteen-hole municipal golf course at Carwe where once bulldozers chewed the terrain in search of coal. This is low-profile sponsorship, a kind of smokeless fuel for sport.

The facilities, then, exist in Wales; so does the backing, from public and private sources. Evidently, too, the wish to take part is present in the population: the latest statistics show that 1,250,000 people participate in some kind of game or sport each year, over half the adult population. In addition to the 112,000 who play soccer and Rugby's

46,000 adherents, there are 630,000 walkers, 325,000 swimmers and 133,000 cyclists, not to mention 20,000 ice skaters and the several thousand who have taken to the new sport of American Football popularized by television.

There seems no doubt that Wales will continue to make a contribution to sport on a scale out of all proportion to its size. The winners and world-beaters will go on emerging, using the numerous launch-pads available. The great majority of middle-rank performers will go on practising their skills within clubs. The Sports Council for Wales and the local authorities will continue to dream up ideas like Operation Sport, which draws in and involves those who simply want to 'have a go'. All these things must – and need to – happen, given that leisure-time is destined to loom ever larger in people's lives.

Sport for All is with us. And as a result the Sports Council has been able to state: 'Sport has much to contribute to the enhancement of the quality of life and ... the Sports Council for Wales is confident of progress resulting in increased well-being and healthier living in Wales.'

MORE WORDS AND PICTURES IN THE AIR

DAVID SKILTON

THE media in Wales show a high level of vitality, and in the audio-visual media in particular there are signs of a very important cultural and economic future for the Principality. The effort and funding put into the provision of electronic mass communications in the medium of Welsh are not only performing their intended role of widening use of the language, but have provided the foundations for a film, video and television industry of international significance.

Network television has a strong cultural and economic presence in Wales. The BBC, HTV (Wales) and S4C between them have establishments which are of considerable size in relation to the population of the capital city in which they are based. Taken together the BBC and HTV (Wales) have five major production studios in Cardiff, which has been a significant centre for television for some time and has attracted a concomitant concentration of television expertise.

BBC Wales sees itself as having two functions: producing programmes for Wales both in English and Welsh, and reflecting Wales on the British networks (BBC 1 and 2). It is interesting that in a situation in which there are frequent complaints about the shortage of Welsh stories on national network television TV-AM is establishing a heavier presence in Cardiff to meet the growing need for regional newsgathering in an organization which has rejected the regional 'opt-out' in favour of the inclusion of more regional stories for all. BBC Wales specializes in drama and music, and on occasion the level of technical services and proficiency in Cardiff has made it attractive to London producers as well.

The start of the Welsh-language fourth channel (Sianel Pedwar Cymru or S4C) in 1982 stimulated unprecedented growth in all aspects of the industry. Thanks to S4C there are more independent television producers in Cardiff than anywhere else in Britain outside London, in which city the growth of the independents was also brought about by the fourth television channel. Throughout Britain in fact the independents are growing at the expense of the established duopoly. Following the government's acceptance of the Peacock Committee's principle of expanding the contribution of independent producers to network television, both BBC Wales and HTV Wales have shed staff. Nevertheless it is the opinion of those involved in projecting future needs in personnel that the overall size of the industry is increasing. Cardiff is in a strong position to establish itself firmly as the leader in the field outside London, unless, as some investigators claim, the independents remain too firmly shaped by S4C's requirements. While some people argue that the general effect of the strength of the television industry in Wales is to retain talent (including acting talent) which once automatically would have gone elsewhere, others suspect that employment opportunities are being artificially created for Welsh-speakers at the expense of monoglot English-speaking technical staff, actors, journalists and administrators.

Publication of the White Paper, 'Broadcasting in the 1990s: choice, competition and quality' (1988) has aroused understandable concern on the subject of the funding of the Welsh-medium channel, S4C. The predicted reduction in advertising revenue for land-based television as a result of the growth of satellite television might leave S4C with a serious shortfall. In fact S4C will in future be funded from the franchise bids for the Channel 3 regions, including those covering Scotland, despite emphatic Scottish preferences for more money to increase Gaelic-language programming. Over the ten years from 1993 to 2003, however, the funding derived from the franchise bids might well show a worrying decline in real terms and some sort of financial security has been urgently sought from the Home Office.

None the less, the prospect of a healthy income in the short term means that S4C is able to modernize to enter the 1990s. Its budget for 1990, increased to £52 million, made possible significant investment in new technology, in emulation of Channel 4 in London, which has been comparatively automated ever since it was launched in 1982. The announcement that S4C is building a new studio complex in Swansea underlines the size of the provision made for Welsh-language television, while the fact that the development is aimed at capturing new viewers from the second-language Welsh-speakers of the south indicates that the industry can no longer justify its level of funding on the basis of the number of first-language viewers. The strength of S4C is evidently important to the future of the film and video industry in Wales as a whole. In this context the investment of £2 million by Barcud in new studios in Caernarfon is an important sign of confidence in the industry. Its continuing prosperity depends in the long run on successfully competing with other parts of the UK in unsubsidized English-medium productions.

When the current ITV franchises run out in 1992 a crucial question for the future of commercial television in Wales will be whether the present ITV boundaries will be retained. If they are not, some argue that there could be a break up of a distinctively Welsh viewing public, with north and south Wales separately attached to neighbouring English franchise areas. Home Office promises that Wales will be left untouched in this respect are welcome.

One of the success stories of the Welsh media industry then has been the growth of the independent sector working in film, video and animation. With both production companies and suppliers of facilities and services represented in Wales, the industry is largely self-sufficient. Most independent companies are small, with 72 per cent reported in 1988 as having an annual turnover of less than £0.5 million. Independent television producers are represented by Teledwyr Annibynnol Cymru (TAC), which deals on their behalf with the unions and with S4C, and liaises at a policy level with BBC, HTV, S4C and the Welsh Office, as well as acting at the practical level as a public relations service for the independent sector.

S4C, of course, has been the catalyst in a great deal of the growth of the independent sector and is crucial to its survival. Consequently, S4C wields considerable influence over these smaller companies, an influence which some regard as rather too paternalistic. According to Cook and Gahan's *The Television Industry in Wales* independents were supplying around five hours of programmes a week to S4C for £11 million in 1987/8. However, with HTV's new contract with S4C obliging the company to supply fewer hours of programmes, approximately seventy extra hours per year will be supplied by independent companies. After a few years S4C's programme quality has generally improved to a fairly acceptable level.

The least developed area is film. In 1985 Wales was the only country not represented during British Film Year. Recent productions such as *Coming up Roses* and *Boy Soldier* have helped to raise the status of the industry in the Principality and 1989 saw the foundation of Ffilm Cymru, funded by S4C and BBC Wales. Described as the first real step in establishing a Welsh film industry, Ffilm Cymru already has a number of international projects lined up, beginning with *Whirligig*, a film based on the last days of Dylan Thomas.

Finally, in the commercial sector there is the Welsh animation industry, which is based largely, though not exclusively, in Cardiff. Once again S4C has been responsible for its development and although it is a young industry there were at least a hundred animators working for eight Welsh companies in 1989. S4C spends around £1 million a year commissioning animated programmes, and the total budget is effectively much larger because of the number of co-production agreements. Some of the most popular programmes have found valuable overseas markets, with *SuperTed*, for example, selling to fifty countries. Lack of staff and infrastructure threaten the further growth of the Welsh animation industry, and S4C has taken the initiative in encouraging awareness among school and college

Dafydd Hywel in the role of Trevor in Stephen Bayly's Coming up Roses. *The film was also produced in Welsh as* Rhosyn a Rhith. *It received a nomination in the category 'in certain regard' at the 1986 Cannes Film Festival and has since been screened at film festivals in Switzerland, London and Edinburgh.*

pupils of the possibilities the industry offers. With the biennial British Animation Awards initiated in Cardiff in 1988, and a feasibility study completed in 1989 into plans to transform the city's Old Library into a museum of animation, it is likely that Cardiff will confirm itself as a centre of excellence in animation.

Sociologically one of the most interesting developments within the independent media industry, although commercially the least significant, is the growth of community film and video workshops. Whereas

Richard Lynch in the title role in Karl Francis's Boy Soldier *which was also filmed in Welsh as* Y Milwr Bychan. *The film was judged best television film at Mannheim in 1985 and has been screened at film festivals in London, Edinburgh, New Delhi and Chicago.*

the commercial sector produces almost entirely for television, community workshops engage in a variety of activities, including production, exhibition, distribution and education. All are concerned to become an integral part of the social fabric of their communities, and are characterized by a wish to encourage people from within the community to determine for themselves how they want to be represented. These community projects include Valley and Vale Community Video in the Ogwr Valley, the Black Video Project in Butetown, Cardiff, and, in north Wales, Scrin at Caernarfon. Red Flannel of Pontypridd is a community workshop with a staff of six, run by and for women, and is unusual in being Wales's only Channel 4 franchised workshop. The franchise enables Red Flannel to work with and receive funding from Channel 4 UK, and in return the project produces programmes which are used by Channel 4, including the acclaimed *Mam*.

In the radio sector in Wales there are three components. BBC Wales acts as both a regional and local radio broadcasting authority, transmitting Radio Wales in English and Radio Cymru in Welsh. Further down the BBC structure there are two 'opt out' stations, Radio Gwent and Radio Clwyd. Finally, there are the three independent local radio stations, Red Dragon Radio at Cardiff, Marcher Sound at Wrexham and Swansea Sound. Although no independent listening figures are available for BBC radio services, their own figures suggest that Radio Wales is popular and second only to the British national pop station, Radio 1 in terms of listeners.

Opinions on the success of the Welsh-language service, Radio Cymru, vary considerably. It was launched in the late 1970s, when it became responsible for all Welsh-language radio broadcasting. Faced with a very limited budget and the need to cater for all tastes through the one service, it has been quite successful, covering science, pop music, light entertainment and comedy, as well as news, political debate and the inevitable sport. Cymdeithas yr Iaith Gymraeg (the Welsh Language Society), on the other hand, argues that much more should be done by the BBC to attract and retain the attention of young listeners.

The 'opt out' stations in Gwent and Clwyd are somewhat of an anomaly. Established in the mid 1980s, they were originally intended as the first step towards an all-Wales system of local radio stations. However, stations were not established in other parts of Wales. These two stations complement Radio Wales, offering local news and views during their few hours of transmission each morning. Moreover, they do not resemble English local radio, which occupies a different place in the BBC structure and whose stations aim at much larger audiences than do those of Gwent and Clwyd.

Independent Local Radio (ILR) in Wales is going through a profitable period. The profits of Marcher Sound, for example, Wales's newest commercial station, almost trebled in 1988. This is said to have been the highest growth rate in profit in independent radio anywhere in Britain. Swansea Sound, the oldest of the ILR stations, started broadcasting in 1974. Its listening figures have dropped off somewhat since, but in October 1989 it was still reported to be reaching 37 per cent of its potential audience of 470,000. Red Dragon

Radio, which was a new franchise covering the areas of the unsuccessful Cardiff and Newport Stations, CBC and Gwent Broadcasting, was reaching 31 per cent of its larger potential audience of 710,000 at the same time.

The most significant development foreseeable in radio is the government's planned 'deregulation of the airwaves', by which it is expected that hundreds of new third-tier 'community' radio stations will be established. There are already a number of such radio stations elsewhere in Britain, concentrated in the larger cities. Prospective third-tier radio services will have to meet a number of criteria. They must provide an alternative service to that being offered by ILR or the BBC, they must not be reliant upon public funds, and there must be sufficient room on the air-waves to accommodate them. It is not clear how many areas of Wales have a sufficient concentration of population to support such stations, but there has been considerable speculation in the press about when and where the first community radio station in Wales might be opened. However, according to the Independent Broadcasting Authority in Wales, at the time of writing no firm proposals have been drawn up for the establishment of any community stations in Wales. It might be, therefore, that this development, which is so significant in parts of England, will not affect radio in Wales, at least in the short term.

There is also a good level of activity in the realm of print journalism in Wales, though the financial prosperity of the Welsh-language sector seems less assured in this medium than in television. Various strands of the press in Wales must be identified, including the national and English regional dailies sold in Wales, the Welsh dailies, English-language and Welsh-language weekly newspapers, *papurau bro*, freesheets, and the most recent development, Wales's only Sunday newspaper, *Wales on Sunday*. In 1986 a report in *Welsh Nation* estimated that around 600,000 British national newspapers were read a day, 300,000 English-language newspapers from Wales, and a few thousand Welsh-language papers and journals of all sorts.

In the south, the *Western Mail* is the undoubted leader, and for all that it periodically comes under attack in Welsh-language and Plaid Cymru circles for voicing English concerns, it gives the most coherent impression of a Welsh cultural and political unity of any paper produced in the Principality. The *Western Mail* is the only morning daily produced in Wales, and it circulates primarily in industrial south Wales, mid Wales and Dyfed. Its claim to be 'the national newspaper of Wales' is, therefore, a trifle overstated. Nevertheless it gives the best coverage of Welsh affairs of any paper in the English language and it also carries a small number of articles in Welsh. Four English-language evening papers complete the daily scene: the *South Wales Echo* (Cardiff), the *South Wales Argus* (Newport, Gwent), the *South Wales Evening Post* (Swansea), and Wrexham's *Evening Leader*. Once again the concentration in the south is notable. The three southern titles have a combined circulation of over 200,000, compared with the Wrexham's paper's 27–28,000.

Welsh daily newspaper circulation January to June 1989
(*UK Press Gazette*, 25 September 1989)

South Wales Echo (Mon–Fri)	91,085	
(Sat)		90,642
Western Mail		77,830
South Wales Evening Post	68,908	
South Wales Argus (Mon–Fri)	41,461	
(Sat)		33,906
Evening Leader		27,893

Turning to readership figures, the strength of the English national newspapers becomes apparent, with the *Western Mail* holding its own in the list by virtue of its coverage of Welsh business, finance, law, etc.:

Daily newspaper readership in Wales, January to June 1989
(National Readership Survey Half-Year Study)

Daily Mirror	646,000
The Sun	553,000
Daily Express	217,000
Western Mail	212,000
Daily Mail	155,000
Daily Star	122,000
Daily Telegraph	69,000
Today	66,000
The Guardian	55,000
The Times	34,000
The Financial Times	20,000
The Independent	12,000

(Figures not available for the Daily Post.)

The *Western Mail* combination within its broadsheet format of the type of story usual in the tabloids with more usual broadsheet material may be the only way of creating a viable circulation in a market the size of Wales. The cement holding the public together is undoubtedly the fact that business people of all sorts in the south simply depend on the paper in order to know what is going on. Welsh news is not strikingly well covered in the English newspapers. In the mid 1980s *The Times*, the *Guardian* and the *Financial Times* all withdrew their Welsh correspondents from Wales. It is notable that with the challenge of *Wales on Sunday*, the *Sunday Times* made its Welsh news more visible for a while.

Wales on Sunday is the most recent addition to the press sector in Wales, and is Wales's first complete Sunday newspaper launch this century. It is impossible to speak confidently about its prospects at an early stage in its development, since few figures are being released. When it was launched, however, it was set a circulation target of 60,000 copies week, and had to be made viable with the same broad appeal that characterizes the *Western Mail*, without the advantage of the day-by-day business readership, but with, it was hoped, an avid sports following to compensate. Whether or not the challenge it represents is sufficient to persuade the national Sundays seriously to increase their coverage of Welsh news is open to dispute. It would certainly be to the advantage of the projection of Wales elsewhere in the United Kingdom, and in the centre of political power in particular, if the interest of the national newspapers in things Welsh were permanently enhanced.

There is no Welsh daily in North Wales. The *Daily Post* of Liverpool has the largest readership of a regional daily in the north, but it is confined largely to Gwynedd and Clwyd. Its Welsh news coverage is distinctly local to the area of its Welsh circulation, and it attempts less coverage of news concerning the whole of Wales than does the *Western Mail*. By contrast there is a significant presence of Welsh weeklies in the north, the *North Wales Chronicle* and the *Holyhead and Angelsey Mail* having circulations of 15,000 and 6,000 in 1986.

Of the weekly newspapers sold in Wales, only a few are published in the Welsh language. The monthly scene is quite different with the growth of *papurau bro* (or community newspapers) in Welsh. These newspapers started in the mid 1970s with the aim of increasing the number of people who regularly read Welsh, and thus helping the survival of the language. The pioneers claim that these papers have helped boost the proportion of Welsh-speakers who regularly read

Welsh from 10 or 20 per cent to around 90 per cent. These all-Welsh newspapers, which consist almost entirely of local news, are usually produced on a monthly basis, and invariably by teams of volunteers. Although they receive a certain amount of help from the Arts associations, they are financed primarily through cover price and fund-raising.

Naturally these publications are concentrated in those areas of Wales with large Welsh-speaking populations, although there are some in the more Anglicized areas. Estimates of their number vary. It is known that in 1988 there were twenty-nine groups in north Wales producing newspapers of this kind each month. Since the aim of these newspapers is to achieve as wide a readership as possible, they are popular in character, with a high proportion of human-interest stories and a large number of photographs. It is undoubtedly true that they are culturally far more significant than their modest journalistic ambitions would suggest, representing as they do one of the only places in which the major local variants of the Welsh language are written down. They provide therefore, a written alternative to standard Welsh, with its strong links with the great literary works of the past, Bishop Morgan's Bible and the pulpit. The *papurau bro* have been praised for just this feature, on the grounds that they have provided an alternative to the language of the literati and the clergy and returned it to the people.

Freesheets have proliferated. In 1989 there were at least fifty-two such weekly newspapers published in Wales, and the circulation figures can be considerable. Campaign Free Newspapers Limited of Caerphilly, for instance, had a circulation of 190,000 for its six titles in November 1989, while the *Cardiff Independent* boasted a weekly delivery of 110,000 in the same month. Whether freesheets are a positive development is as hotly argued in Wales as elsewhere. Their news content is of course normally secondary to their advertising role. On the other hand they do offer a valuable source of local information.

The magazine industry in Wales is one of the less developed sectors of the Welsh media. *Benn's Media Directory* for 1989 lists thirty-seven periodicals as diverse as the *Bulletin of the Board of Celtic Studies*, published annually, with a circulation of around 300 copies, to *Welsh Farmer (Y Tir)*, with a circulation of around 16,600 copies every other month. Bearing in mind the unstable character of the magazine sector, with titles often appearing for only a few issues before disappearing altogether, the actual number of titles at any given time is likely to be considerably more than thirty-seven. Given the modest circulation of Welsh magazines, funding is usually the major problem, and the Welsh Art Council plays a central role in ensuring the survival of a number of Welsh arts magazines, while the Welsh Books Council also helps magazine production in fields other than the arts.

Here are some examples of the Welsh Arts Council's subsidy per copy in 1987, *Planet*, £7.30; *Anglo-Welsh Review*, £4.44; *Y Faner*, £0.37. Subsidies for the financial year 1989/90 are:

Planet	57,100
Golwg	51,000
Barn	30,600
New Welsh Review	17,800
Poetry Wales	12,800
Taliesin	12,200
Barddas	6,600
Y Traethodydd	4,450
Y Casglwr	1,530
Others	500
Total	194,580

The importance of Welsh Arts Council funding was underlined when in 1988 it was withdrawn from the *Anglo-Welsh Review*, which was considered rather lacklustre and too irregular in its appearance. As a result of the withdrawal of subsidy, the journal folded. In 1988/89 one of the nine titles which the WAC supported was the *New Welsh Review*, a new English-language literary magazine, whose existence was thereby assured in the short term. The target circulation for the *Review* was just 1,400. In contrast, magazines which cannot attract subsidy, such as the investigative magazine *Rebecca* (named after the nineteenth-century Rebecca riots against toll charges) have to struggle if they are to survive at all. In fact *Rebecca* collapsed in 1982 despite claiming a circulation of more than five times the target for the *New Welsh Review*. The lack of a grant and unattractiveness to advertisers made the magazine unviable, indicating perhaps a limit to the possible Welsh outlets for radical Welsh magazine journalism.

In view of the precarious financial position of many Welsh magazines, EEC plans to add up to 9 per cent VAT to published material could jeopardize the survival of almost all the remaining Welsh magazines. The Welsh Arts Council is gravely concerned at this prospect, since the market might well not accept the increased cover price, and the Council would be unable to increase its subsidies to help offset the fall in revenue from a declining circulation.

In the rapidly changing field of high-technology media, precise employment statistics and trends are difficult to establish. Nevertheless there have recently been studies which give at least some indication of the growing importance of the media for employment in Wales. A study carried out by the Manpower Services Commission (now the Training Agency) in 1987 in Mid and South Glamorgan, whilst geographically restricted, does at least cover a wide range of media sectors. Unsurprisingly the study pinpoints Cardiff as a key centre of the industry in Wales, and indeed in Britain as a whole, with growth particularly apparent in the docklands area of the city. The MSC found that most media operations were small, 63 per cent having a work-force of fewer than ten employees. Estimates of the total media work-force were made difficult by the proliferation of freelance staff in this sector. At any rate employment appeared to be buoyant, with 44 per cent of employers forecasting an increase in their work-force within the following twelve months, and only one organization predicting a reduction. A wider survey would have met with optimistic predictions about growth in media employment in other towns such as Carmarthen and Llandeilo, where Welsh-language independents were establishing themselves, but it is not sure how viable these smaller centres will be in the medium or long term. More significant is the announcement of the £2 million studio development by S4C in Swansea, to service the considerable population of new Welsh-speakers centred in West Glamorgan and Dyfed. It is not clear whether this will lead to spare capacity in Cardiff, or how such spare capacity might be used.

There is a significant personnel shortage in the industry in Mid and South Glamorgan, and recruitment difficulties and training problems may be inhibiting growth. Media personnel are often required to possess industry-specific technical experience and/or to be bilingual, since even in south Wales a great deal of media output is carried out through the medium of Welsh. Employers surveyed found themselves forced to adopt such alternative job-filling measures as retraining existing staff, while headhunting is as accepted a feature of the industry in south Wales as in London. Recruitment and training difficulties in the independent sector lead to the shortages which are most severe in trained and experienced personnel in the Welsh-language sector. (At one time Saint David's University College, Lampeter boasted that its own minuscule audio-visual studio was the only one in the country able to operate entirely through the medium of Welsh!) To overcome this shortage a training company has been formed in Caernarfon by a consortium of the union ACTT, S4C and TAC (the Welsh Independent Producers), to produce Welsh-speaking technicians for the television industry. Cyfle mounts courses in direction and production skills, as well as short courses aimed at updating those already working in the industry. Meanwhile the dictionary of modern technical terms in Welsh is expanding rapidly.

A number of other training issues have presented themselves. An overall training strategy embracing the media industry was felt to be needed, covering not only technical skills, but also media management and finance. Some criticism was aimed at college courses, which were said often to fall behind important new trends in the media industry. Concern has also been expressed over the very small number of women in technical occupations. In the training of broadcast and print journalists, however, Cardiff is acknowledged to lead in Britain, having the most prestigious postgraduate training programme at the Centre for Journalism Studies in the University of Wales College of Cardiff. In addition it houses the Thomson Foundation, a unique organization devoted to the training of Third World journalists both in their home countries and in Cardiff.

Employment statistics for the media are difficult to ascertain, not least because of the extensive use of freelance workers within the industry and fluctuations occurring as productions within the visual media begin and cease. However, the Census of Employment for September 1987 does give some statistics which help build up a picture of media employment in Wales as a whole, and on a county basis:

	Wales	S.Glam	Gwynedd
Film (production/exhibition/ distribution)	4200	2600	500
Television and radio services	3220		
Printing and publishing	6600	1350	280

No reliable calculations are available of the effect on the Welsh economy as a whole of other employment created indirectly by the media industry. Measuring the 'multiplier effect' is notoriously difficult, but it has been estimated that the local Caernarfon economy, for instance, receives £6 million in this way from the television industry alone.

It seems unlikely that magazines and newspapers will grow in Wales in the foreseeable future, but the strength of the broadcast media is a result of the uniqueness of the Principality in the United Kingdom and the deliberate fostering of broadcasting has produced an expanding industry which should be ready to assume an important role in the world, beyond local and regional needs.

EDUCATION IN A NEW ERA

R. BRINLEY JONES

THE world of Wales is changing. As we enter the last decade of the twentieth century Wales will be faced with a new set of problems, challenges and opportunities. The threat of nuclear conflict, north/south polarization, the exhaustion of natural resources, the great advances in science, the challenges to law and order, the erosion of standards of personal morality, the rights of individuals, economic progress, cultural diversity – all these and many more colour the aspirations and fears of the Welsh as of men and women all over the world. Against the background of such aspirations and fears young minds are fed and trained to meet the challenges and chances ahead. Wales is part of a larger island; that island is part of Europe and Europe is aware of belonging to a larger world. No longer is a knowledge of that world confined to those who travel. To think, in context, means to think world-wide, but to do so in Welsh terms adds a diversity and a quality all of its own.

The Wales of pre-War years caricatured in rugby shorts, blue scars and voices in harmony has changed. Some boarded chapels, conifers on upland areas, a ski slope outside Merthyr, bilingual signs and marinas beckoning the sun are just some indications of a new Wales. Gone is the dependence on the old basic industries of coal and steel. The coal industry that once employed more than 250,000 now employs fewer than 5,000 and the pits now consist of six in the south and one in the north. In the 1920s Rhondda coal derived from the sixty-six pits there; now there is one. Tourism employs more than three times the combined total of those who work in coal and steel. And there are other changes, too, in the homes whose children and young people leave for education. Today more than one in five of Welsh manufacturing workers are employed by foreign-owned companies and the names of Aiwa, Hitachi, Sony, are now as much part of the scene as Powell Duffryn was. Companies proliferate from North America, Japan and Europe. In 1950 there were some eighteen foreign-owned manufacturing firms in Wales employing just over 14,000 people; by 1988 there were over 250 firms employing 45,000 people. Wales enjoys one of the largest concentrations of Japanese manufacturing investment in Europe. Recently Ford has announced a major programme for its engine plant at Bridgend and related components plant at Swansea. Toyota is building a large engine plant at Shotton, Bosch is building a sizeable plant at Cardiff and the capital city is already gaining a name in the field of finance and pensions. The face is the face of a new Wales and the brands of coal are replaced by disc production, optics, electro acoustics, stabilizers for the food industry, clothing fabrics, petrochemicals, automotive engineering, oil refining, whisky, and vodka. Nevertheless, there remain areas of high unemployment – 13.3 per cent in Aberdare, 10.9 per cent in Merthyr, 13.7 per cent in Pwllheli, for example.

The relevance of these factors for education is manifold. Can the diversification of the Welsh economy keep the Welsh at home rather than send them in search of seeking greener pastures elsewhere ... and are the training and culture-communication related to the demands of the new economy and new technologies ... and the new avenues of thought and behaviour? For those who remain at home or spread their wings abroad and beyond, is the education they receive fulfilling and purposeful? Education for the 1990s will call for expertise, managerial capability and communicative skills; it will call for training in the craft of living and leisure.

In addition to the world forces that contribute to the shape of education in Wales, there are the forces within Wales itself. There is a new awareness of national institutions with a Welsh Office, Wales Tourist Board, S4C, BBC Wales, HTV Wales, TUC, Welsh Development Agency, Welsh Water Authority, Welsh National Opera, Welsh Arts Council, for example, added to a National Library, a National Museum and a University of Wales which grants 'national' degrees. And despite the fact that only roughly one fifth of the population speak Welsh, the language is now not only a culture asset but a career one, too; actors, writers, television presenters and technicians, local government officers, teachers, for example, see its advantage. The most promising aspect is its growth among the young, and that in the Anglicized areas; there are sixty-seven designated primary bilingual schools and sixteen designated secondary bilingual schools in predominantly English-speaking areas. But there is a Welsh dimension to other disciplines, too, – music, art, geography, history, science (in the area of natural resources and local application) etc. and literature, not only in Welsh but in the vibrant writing of the so-called Anglo-Welsh school. All this colours Welsh education. And so it should.

Education is there, right in the centre of social and economic pressure and political concern. Now, as always, it aims at producing men and women fit and equipped to fulfil their potential and to serve their society but education, too, is subject to the winds of change. Wales has shared in the *explosion scolaire* of the second half of the twentieth century. In 1945, for example, there were seventeen universities in the United Kingdom compared with forty-seven now; in addition thirty polytechnics have been opened since 1967. These dramatic changes represent a major increase in the prospects for entering higher education; the opportunities and places offered by

*Japanese children at a
prize-giving ceremony and
open day at a Saturday school
held in Cardiff.*

other institutions in the public sector are further proof. The population explosion of the mid-sixties has been followed by a marked drop in the birth-rate; in the primary and secondary sector it has resulted in closures, mergers, redeployment. But the effect on the teaching profession of the decline in school numbers coupled with other significant contributory factors, such as conditions of service, has resulted in a marked drop in the number of new recruits. In 1972 in the United Kingdom there were more than 100,000 student teachers in training; by 1985 there were fewer than 30,000. In addition, by 1990, 60 per cent of teachers will be over forty years old. In Wales, the closure of rural schools, the early redundancy of teachers, the demise of some teacher-training departments and the closure of some institutions which specialized in teacher training have occurred at a time when the demand for bright, able minds is great and when competition is so marked in the world outside. The shortage of teachers in mathematics, physical science and craft, design and technology (CDT) remains acute; the provision of teachers to instruct such subjects through the medium of Welsh will be a major task ahead for the departments at Aberystwyth, Trinity College Carmarthen, and Bangor.

As has been said, educational practice is conditioned by economic and social change, by cultural awareness and by political dictate normally precipitated by public concern. In the years since James

Callaghan's Ruskin speech of 1976, education in some form or other has been on centre stage. In 1985 the policies of the Conservative Government were outlined in a crucial White Paper *Better Schools* (Cmnd 9469) which was followed by three pieces of educational legislation all of which significantly affect education in Wales as they do the rest of the United Kingdom. The 1986 Acts aimed at raising standards by improving the management of schools, by promoting teaching quality, by granting parents a greater say in the running of schools. Corporal punishment was abolished, and safeguards were to be provided in the teaching of sex education and political issues. More effective in-service training would be provided for teachers and there would be an appraisal of their performance.

The Education Reform Act of 1988 included major and wide-ranging measures affecting both schools and post-school education. The Act gave all secondary, in addition to the larger primary schools, responsibility for managing the greater part of their budgets including costs of staffing and the option, if the parents so wish, to withdraw from local authority control and be directly financed by central government. (The first ballot, however, on opting-out to be held at a Welsh school, John Beddoes School in Presteigne, Powys, resulted in a sizeable majority – with 70 per cent in favour of remaining with the local education authority.) As a result of a rigorous examination of the content of school work, a National Curriculum was proposed with core subjects and foundation subjects. The core subjects will be mathematics, English and science with Welsh in Welsh-speaking areas; as well as foundation subjects of history, geography, technology, music, art, physical education, a modern foreign language and Welsh in non-Welsh-speaking areas. The subjects would have attainment targets and assessments at the ages of 7, 11, 14 and 16. Religious education, which had been made compulsory by the 1944 Education Act, remains a requirement for all pupils although parents will have the right to withdraw children from religious education classes. Such is the theory of the National Curriculum but already there are concerns about the overloading of the timetable ... and about the implication of the inclusion of Welsh as an 'extra': whether, for example, this will be reflected in the attainment targets. And will the language be given its rightful place?

During the last few years a variety of educational jargon has entered our vocabulary; its abbreviations proliferate – TVEI (Technical and Vocational Education Initiative, a national scheme providing for 14–18 year olds of all abilities, within a framework of general education to give teenagers a curriculum more relevant to adult life and work), CPVE (Certificate of Pre-Vocational Education, a one-year full-time or two-years part-time course for a wide variety of ability range at 16+); CATE (Council for the Accreditation of Teacher Education); CDT (Craft, Design and Technology); YTS (Youth Training Scheme giving 16-year-old school-leavers two years and 17-year-olds one year of training and planned work experience). The GCE and CSE examinations have been replaced by the GCSE (General Certificate in Secondary Education) with its 'criteria referenced testing', each of the seven grades (A–G) representing not merely a numerical mark out of 100 but rather an indication of exactly what candidates are capable of doing. (The emphasis is less on rote-learning, more on understanding, using knowledge and practical and oral skills such as designing and setting up experiments, making observations, recording information and drawing conclusions; the 'new' demands on the teacher in approach and preparation are considerable.) Then there is A/S (Advanced Supplementary level) with the intention of broadening the curriculum for A-level students without diluting academic standards; it was intended as a corrective to over-specialization. At present the A-level remains though there are those who regard its organization as anachronistic and believe that the curriculum on offer to the 16–19 year olds will have to be substantially revised if a larger proportion of youngsters is to remain in full-time education and training. And there are those who believe that the best interests of this age group will be served by tertiary colleges (first proposed in the late 1960s) where the range of academic and vocational abilities can be educated together. Despite considerable reorganization of examining boards, the WJEC (Welsh Joint Education Committee) is the sole one for Wales.

These are the contexts and proscriptions governing the practice of nursery, primary and secondary education in Wales. Compulsory education is the order of the day between the ages of five and sixteen. Responsibility for it lies with the Secretary of State for Wales as do all non-university institutions of higher and further education, the youth and community services and adult education. Schools and other educational establishments, apart from universities, are inspected by Her Majesty's Inspectors – fifty-four of them in Wales. The local education authorities employ the teachers, provide and maintain the buildings, supply equipment and materials, and award grants for further and higher education. *Mudiad Ysgolion Meithrin* – the Welsh Nursery Schools Movement founded in 1971 – goes from strength to strength catering for first and second-language groups of youngsters; in 1971 there were sixty such nursery schools, now there are over 800.

Welsh-language playgroup at Felin-fach, Dyfed.

According to a recent survey of the maintained schools in Wales there were fifty-eight nursery schools with 1,297 full-time pupils and 127 full-time teachers; 1,753 primary schools with 245,300 full-time pupils and 11,078 full-time teachers (20 per cent of primary schools have classes where Welsh is the sole or main medium of instruction): 233 secondary schools with a population of 199,279 pupils and 12,639 teachers (of the pupils presented for GCSE, 3.2 per cent entered through the medium of Welsh, 2.8 per cent of all those at A-level). There are sixty-five special schools catering for learning difficulties arising from emotional or behavioural disorders as well as physical or mental handicaps. There are independent schools, too, sixty-seven of them with a total population of 11,703 pupils and 954 full-time teachers.

Already, computers are commonplace in primary schools. Soon, 16-bit micros with vast memory capacities will be the standard for secondary schools. And before long, too, all pupils will be issued with a written record of their school achievement and performance when they leave school, noting achievement right across the educational programme. It is all a far cry from the rote-learning and school-leaving certificates of a few decades ago.

The National Youth Orchestra of Wales in performance at St David's Hall, Cardiff.

Schooldays over, what are the opportunities for young Welshmen and Welshwomen for continuing their education and training? Of course the world of education is open to them but within Wales itself there is a wide variety of provision, from vocational training to higher degree level; each local authority provides a breadth of further education in its colleges – full-time, part-time, day-release and evening classes devoted in the main to work-related studies. There is, in Wales, provision for the education and training of teachers, clergy, librarians, farmers, artists, journalists, musicians, actors and almost all the other acknowledged professions. The opportunities are limitless.

In the field of higher education, apart from the University , Wales has its Polytechnic at Treforest (on the site of the former School of Mines), now catering for a wide spectrum of applied disciplines, its six local authority institutions and one voluntary institution (the North-East Wales, South Glamorgan and West Glamorgan Institutes, the Gwent College of Higher Education, Bangor Normal College, the Welsh College of Music and Drama and Trinity College Carmarthen respectively). These, between them, have some 12,500 full-time and 7,500 part-time students compared with 22,000+ full-time students in the University. A recent government White Paper indicated that these colleges constituted a small enough sector to remain within the brief of the Wales Advisory Board for Local Authority Higher Education (WAB); WAB would be in a position to offer advice based on national rather than on local considerations to the Secretary of State for Wales. All the Welsh Institutes and Colleges during the last few years have expanded dramatically their provision for various spheres of higher education; many of them have valuable and advantageous contacts in countries overseas. They continue to attract a greater proportion of students from within Wales than does the University.

The University of Wales, the University Funding Council (with its Welsh sub-committee) and WAB between them control the destiny of higher education in Wales; as such there is a grand opportunity for developing a coherent system of higher education across the binary line and to the mutual advantage of all parts. Already the seven colleges and institutes of higher education have chosen the University of Wales to be the validating body for nearly all of their rapidly expanding range of courses; some 4,500 students in these institutions take these validated courses. The possibility of movement between various parts of the higher education sector may well give Wales, eventually, a unique national system.

Higher education is entering upon a period of fierce competition. Cost-effectiveness and the relevance of courses to the demands of modern life together with the demographic changes resulting in a substantial reduction over the decade 1985–95 in Britain from which the University of Wales in 1988–89 drew 88 per cent of its students (27 per cent from Wales, 61 per cent from the rest of the United Kingdom; 12 per cent from overseas countries) – all these factors contribute to the challenge facing higher education. The University of Wales and places of higher education in Wales are in competition with each other and with similar institutions in the rest of the United Kingdom and elsewhere. In addition, there are business companies and organizations seeking accreditation of academic courses relevant to their needs. Despite the size of the overall University of Wales, most of its colleges are relatively small and there are difficulties in such colleges covering a wide range of subjects and maximizing research potential. Rationalization was called for, resulting, occasionally, in the closure or transference of departments which had earned considerable distinction over the years. Such pruning can encourage the ablest academics to seek possibilities elsewhere, and Wales like the rest of the United Kingdom has suffered a measure of brain-drain.

It is in response to the challenging threats that the University of Wales has accepted, recently, the recommendations of the Powers and Functions Group chaired by Sir Goronwy Daniel that the federal university should take concerted and federal action to maximize the potential of a university with a staff of some 1,800 (second in size to the University of London) and make it an institution in the forefront of teaching and research. In consequence there would be a University planning system with Boards of Studies and a Joint Planning and Resources Committee which will collate and, where possible, harmonize the short-term plans of the University's institutions and prepare long-term plans, too.

The federal University of Wales was established in 1893 when the three existing institutions were incorporated – Aberystwyth, Cardiff and Bangor. By today there are six constituent colleges offering a breadth of academic disciplines, resources and diversity; each has its own particular location (rural, sea-resort, ancient or modern town, large or small), its own atmosphere and cultural experience. It is an experience which Wales offers to its own and to the world.

There are eighteen different initial degrees, with a variety of subject combinations, directed towards honours or joint honours lasting three years normally. With the exception of such vocational courses as medicine, dentistry, nursing and engineering, students pursue a broad first-year course followed by a more specialized course in the second and third years. The language of the University's courses, in the main, is English though some specific courses are also offered to students who wish to study through the medium of Welsh – a natural follow-up for those who have had their secondary education in Welsh.

The Vice-Chancellor of the University is one of the College Principals who serves a two-year term, in rotation. The central administration of matters relating to the University as a whole is at the University Registry in Cathays Park, Cardiff. Otherwise, the colleges enjoy a great deal of autonomy, and they offer a wide range of courses.

The University College of Wales, Aberystwyth was founded in 1872; it has some 3,662 students, combines the old college buildings and a fine modern campus overlooking Cardigan Bay, and is close to the National Library of Wales, a copyright library. The college's strengths lie in agriculture, biological and earth sciences, international politics, political science, law, bilingual education and Celtic studies.

The University College of North Wales, Bangor, founded in 1884 has 3,301 students; the college is set in the National Park of Snowdonia, an area of outstanding beauty with magnificent mountain ranges and spectacular coastline waters. Bangor is to the fore in agriculture, forestry and marine science.

The University of Wales College of Cardiff of 1988 (the combined 'new' college of University College, 1883 and the University of Wales Institute of Science and Technology, 1967) has 8,432 students. It is right in the heart of the capital city with its 300,000 inhabitants. Many of its degree schemes are vocational, orientated towards the requirements of the professions and of industry. Individual departments are quite large and offer a wide range of courses in arts, business and law, applied science, engineering, health and life sciences and environmental design.

The College of Medicine, 1931, is also in Cardiff with 849 students pursuing courses for medical, dental and nursing degrees together with higher degrees and diplomas.

The University College of Swansea, 1920, enjoys a magnificent campus in Singleton Park facing the wide sweep of Swansea Bay, on the edge of the Gower Peninsula which acts as a natural field laboratory for students reading natural sciences. There are 5,207 students in five faculties – arts, economic and social studies, educational studies, engineering and science.

Saint David's University College Lampeter, established in 1822, opened in 1827 originally for those destined for holy orders; by 1852 it was empowered to grant the BD degree and by 1865 the BA degree – the first university degrees to come out of Wales. It became part of the University of Wales in 1971 and offers languages, divinity and the more traditional arts subjects. It has 873 students.

These are the constituent parts of the University but the other institutes and colleges of higher learning have charms, specialisms and distinctions of their own whether they be at Wrexham, Swansea, Cardiff, Caerleon or Trinity Carmarthen or Bangor Normal (the last two ante-dating the university colleges in foundation, Lampeter excepted).

For those who missed an opportunity earlier, apart from mature entry to places of higher education there is the impressive provision of the Open University with its combination of correspondence courses, TV and radio, audio and video cassettes and summer schools and study centres. It currently has 4,600 students enrolled at its regional office in Cardiff, opened in 1969. Already over three and a half thousand have graduated. There is also Coleg Harlech, opened in 1927 and founded by idealists who were inspired by Welsh radicalism, the Independent Labour Party and the Workers' Educational Association (whose first branch was opened in Barry in 1906 and which continues to operate all over Wales). And the leisure and professional continuing interests of people are further supported by extra-mural classes organized by the university colleges. Continuing

Multi-cultural group of pupils at the United World College (Atlantic College), St Donat's South Glamorgan.

education for those in employment to enable them to keep apace with technological change has offered a new challenge and opportunity for sectors within the educational system.

In September 1962 a new and major experiment in international education was launched when the first United World College, known as Atlantic College, was established in a medieval castle at St Donat's, in the Vale of Glamorgan; it stands only a short distance away from Llantwit Major, that site of a seminary of distinction in the sixth century which educated and trained missionaries to evangelize Wales and Europe. In many respects, the richest periods in the cultural history of Wales were those when it was most in contact with Europe. Now, politically, Wales with the rest of the United Kingdom has a new allegiance to Europe. It may be that, in time, the education of our children will be the education of the *homo europaeus* whose service to Wales – and the world – will be greater because they will have come into contact with that ground which gave them root long, long ago.

A TIME OF PARADOXES AMONG THE FAITHS

D. P. DAVIES

S EVEN miles to the north of Carmarthen in the rural calm of the upper Gwili Valley lies the village of Llanpumsaint. The parish church stands at the centre of the village on a site commonly associated with the enclosed community (*llan*) founded well over a thousand years ago by the five saints from whom the village takes its name. Tradition has it that the five were Gwyn, Gwynoro, Gwynno, Celynin and Ceitho, but the association of the same five with Pumsaint in the Cothi Valley in north Carmarthenshire should put us on our guard against relying too much on this particular tradition. None the less, there can be no dispute that there has been an unbroken Christian presence in Llanpumsaint for over a thousand years. Through the Middle Ages this presence reflected the catholic tradition of western Christianity, which at the Reformation became the catholic but reformed Church of England in Wales. Recent centuries, however, have witnessed the introduction of other forms of Protestant Christianity to challenge the monopoly of the Established Church. For example, at the beginning of the nineteenth century the effect on Llanpumsaint of the Calvinistic Methodist revival took physical shape in the form of Bethel chapel, built defiantly alongside the parish church.

Like many rural Welsh communities Llanpumsaint has for most of its history been relatively isolated from the outside world, an isolation now broken by the huge expansion of private transport and mass communication in the post-Second World War period. Yet even today some of the religious traditions of the eighteenth and nineteenth centuries, such as the annual *Cymanfa Bwnc* (an oral examination of the whole congregation on a set passage of Scripture), are still preserved more or less intact. Again this largely Welsh-speaking community has faithfully fulfilled its outward Christian duty to an extent not experienced in urban areas for some considerable time. Over the latter part of the last century and most of this, church or chapel membership has been almost universal, and church or chapel attendance high. Sunday has traditionally been a day of secular inactivity — no travelling, no trade, no newspapers and no Sunday opening of the local tavern. For much of this century the kind of puritanism associated with the so-called traditional Welsh way of life reigned supreme in Llanpumsaint, as in much of the rest of rural Welsh Wales.

But if a latter-day George Borrow were to pass through Llanpumsaint on a summer Sunday today, he would see that things have changed almost beyond recognition. Today the village, like other parts of rural Wales, has its share of immigrants, who know little or nothing of this Welsh way of life, but more significantly even the natives have changed their habits. True, the parish church still has a vicar, but with the care of two other churches he now spends much of Sunday in transit from one to another, while many of his parishioners are bent on travelling way beyond his pastoral reach on a range of secular pursuits. The present-day resident of Llanpumsaint is as likely to be engaged on odd jobs like washing the car or in some leisure activity like playing cricket or watching television as in attending one or other of the Christian places of worship. Even the tavern is open to all who care to walk through its front door in search of spiritual uplift of an alcoholic kind – no more do the Welsh sneak surreptitiously in by the back door. Gone too is that particular hypocrisy of days gone by.

So this typically Welsh village with its church and three chapels, seemingly remote from the 'pernicious' influence of the outside secular world, is by now hardly recognizable in terms of the stereotype of puritanism normally associated with the traditional Welsh way of life. Many of its inhabitants have no formal religious affiliation. To some extent this is due to the immigration typical of our modern mobile society, but even among the indigenous population religious observance is in decline, as is the influence of organized religion, if by that we mean the mainline Christian denominations.

And yet Llanpumsaint is still a popular place of pilgrimage. Sunday afternoons can see groups of pilgrims in the village, though none of them has been born in Llanpumsaint; indeed, few if any of them have been born in Wales or even in Europe. For the focal point of the modern pilgrim is not one of the ancient sites of Celtic Christianity, but the Temple of the Many Names of God, otherwise known as Skanda Vale, a syncretistic Buddhist/Hindu Temple established in a renovated barn on a farm just outside the village. Right here in the heart of rural Welsh Wales, in the most unlikely of locations, the exclusively Christian history of Llanpumsaint now has to accommodate a new religion with its temple, complete with sacred elephant (rescued, so it is said, from the indignities of life in a travelling circus).

Of course, this sea change in the religious life of Llanpumsaint is hardly typical of rural Wales as a whole, though it is symptomatic of the not inconsiderable changes that have affected the religious life of the country over the decades following the high tide of Welsh Nonconformity in the early years of the present century. Particularly significant changes such as the decline in the influence of organized Christianity, the corresponding secularization of Welsh society with the virtual disappearance of the traditional Welsh Sunday, accompanied by the weakening of the place of the Welsh language in some of its traditional strongholds and the immigration of families of non-Welsh and sometimes of non-European origin, who have, in some instances, brought with them a non-Christian religion and a foreign culture.

Again it would be quite misleading to suggest that any of these non-Christian religions as yet represents a significant presence in Wales. Wales has yet to become the kind of multi-faith society found in some of the major conurbations of England. None the less, other non-Christian religions cannot be ignored in a survey of the religious life of Wales as we approach the twenty-first century.

The major faiths of the world have assumed a far greater significance for those of us who live in Wales today than for our forebears fifty and certainly a hundred years ago. For this reason it is instructive to ask where and how the presence of non-Christian religious groups affects the life of Wales today. It is, in other words, incumbent upon us to recognize that Wales is no longer an exclusively Christian country, not simply as a consequence of widespread secularization, with its rejection of Christianity or indeed any religion, but also because of the gradual importation of other faiths over the past hundred years.

The colourful, creative and controversial contribution of Leo Abse and his brother Dannie to politics and poetry in recent years is both characteristically Jewish and typically Welsh. The Welsh Jewish community has also given us the contemporary novelist Bernice Rubens (winner of the Booker Prize in 1970), and in Dr Norman Solomon one of Britain's leading rabbis, even if neither of them now lives in Wales. The Jewish community has deep roots in parts of Wales, particularly in the urban centres, and many Jews, like the Abses, are thoroughly integrated into Welsh society. This, of course, spells danger for Judaism as a faith, and indeed the evidence suggests that religious observance among Jews in Wales is in serious decline. Cardiff still has several synagogues, representing both the orthodox and the reformed traditions, as well as being the home of Wales's only rabbi. There are also synagogues in Newport and Swansea, but once flourishing synagogues in Llandudno, Llanelli and some of the valley communities are no longer active.

By contrast, the Muslim community in Wales is growing apace. Muslims first came to Cardiff over a century ago, when Yemeni seamen settled in Butetown. However, in recent years the Muslim community in Wales has grown in numbers and in the kind of self-confidence characteristic of contemporary Islam the world over. True, Wales has not seen Muslims taking to the streets over *The Satanic Verses*, but Muslims are making their presence felt. There are

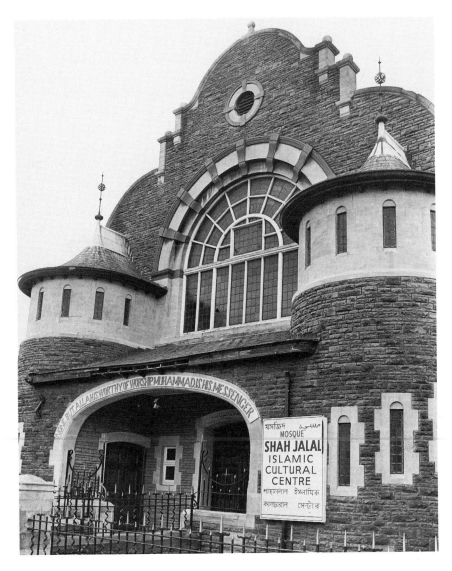

Capel y Crwys, the former Welsh Presbyterian Chapel now the Shah Jalal Mosque.

now five mosques in Cardiff, one in Newport and two in Swansea, as well as prayer rooms/mosques in Bangor, Chepstow and Lampeter. The drive to attract overseas students to the colleges of the University of Wales has brought a number of Muslims into the University, and endowments from the Middle East have supported the successful introduction of Islamic Studies as a degree course at Lampeter, the erstwhile stronghold of Welsh Anglicanism.

The other major religions of the world are less prominent in Wales. Small communities of Hindus and Sikhs are to be found in Cardiff, and the odd family in Newport and Swansea. The Sikh community in Cardiff has recently opened a new temple, again reflecting the growing self-confidence of ethnic minority groups in contemporary British society and their determination to preserve their own identity. The only major non-Christian religion which has attracted native Welsh people to its ranks, though not in large numbers, is Buddhism, particularly in parts of rural Wales. The casual visitor to tea and coffee shops run by health-food enthusiasts in places like Aberystwyth, Machynlleth or Llanidloes will come across posters inviting those interested to attend a meeting of a local Buddhist group. Similarly, various forms of nature religion have their adherents in rural Wales, while the capital city can boast its Rastafarians as well as a Hari Krishna centre.

Numerically non-Christian religions are hardly significant in Wales – the Muslims claim around 80,000 adherents and are by far the largest single group. None the less, the social, cultural and political significance of these religious communities as well as their philosophical and theological interest and importance is now acknowledged by educationists and others in Wales. Recent years have seen the total revision of syllabuses in Religious Studies (no longer Religious Instruction) for A-level and GCSE students in schools and the establishment of departments of religious (no long biblical) studies in the University as a response to the major impact of non-Christian faiths on society in Britain, if not so dramatically in Wales. The same is true of the broadcasting media, where the radio and television channels frequently find room in their religious magazine programmes for items on the activities and beliefs of non-Christian religious communities. This is as true of BBC Radio Cymru and S4C as it is of the other channels. Nor have the native Welsh entirely ignored the presence of adherents of other faiths in the streets and villages of Wales, as is attested by the growing instances of intermarriage and indeed the heightened awareness and tolerance of different habits of eating and styles of dress.

So where does the faith preserved and delivered to the people of Wales by the Celtic saints down the ages stand as we approach the dawn of the third millennium of the Christian era? More particularly, does institutional Christianity in the form of the mainline Churches have a significantly weaker hold on the hearts and minds of the people of Wales today than it has enjoyed in previous centuries?

If this question were to be considered in terms of the numerical strength of the Churches today compared with, say, their strength at the turn of the century, the answer would be clear. By any estimate – for example, a comparison of the statistics produced by the Royal

Commission set up to consider the strength of the religious bodies in Wales in the context of the disestablishment debate in 1906 and the results of the MARC Europe Survey *Prospects for Wales* undertaken in 1982 – the percentage of the people of Wales claiming membership of one or other of the mainline Churches as well as the number of those attending a Christian place of worship on a typical Sunday is far lower at the end than it was at the beginning of the century. This is true not only of the percentage (around 40 per cent of the adult population were church members in 1905, compared with 23 per cent in 1982); the same is true of absolute numbers, even though the total population of Wales has increased in the intervening years. In 1905 the total membership of 'Protestant' (i.e. excluding Roman Catholic) Churches was 743,361. The corresponding number in 1982 was 393,500. Interestingly, Roman Catholic membership, which was some 64,800 in 1905, had risen by 1982 to 129,600, i.e. it has doubled over the course of the century. So if we are considering numbers, there is no question but that organized Christianity is considerably weaker in Wales today than it was at the turn of the century. In other words, statistics confirm the subjective judgement advanced in our anecdotal account of Llanpumsaint.

Having said all that, however, Christianity is far and away the main religion of Wales even today. One in four of the adult population is still formally affiliated to one or other of the mainline Christian Churches. Well over half the children born in Wales are 'christened'; over half the 'first' marriages are solemnized in a Christian place of worship and in excess of 95 per cent of the Welsh dead are laid to rest in a Christian burial ceremony. Christianity is still the official religion of state and civic occasions, notwithstanding the disestablishment of the Church in Wales earlier in the century. One could easily multiply examples. Furthermore, at a deeper and personal level the influence of the revivals and of puritanical Nonconformity still has a residual hold on the Welsh subconscious and results in the odd pang of guilt in a son of Wales who finds himself playing cricket on Sunday or enjoying a pint of beer. However, the truth is that secularism has had its impact, as the statistics for church membership and church attendance as well as the enormous changes in public and private morality and social mores ruthlessly reveal.

And yet, paradoxically, alongside all this, there is an enormous interest in religion in Wales. The departments of philosophy of the University of Wales are stiff with philosophers of religion. Ecclesiastical history is one of the favourite preoccupations of professional and amateur historians alike. Many schoolchildren opt of their own free will to study religion, as do a significant number of students both in the University and in other institutions of higher education. Nor are all these students of religion committed adherents of the Christian faith. Now, as never before, secular educational principles with their deliberate rejection of religious tests reign supreme. Again the prominent place given to religion, predominantly Christianity, by the broadcasting media in Wales is a commercial response to public demand. As many, if not more, people listen to or watch an act of worship on radio or television on a Sunday as attend a place of worship, while religious 'entertainment' programmes such as *Highway* (ITV), *Songs of Praise* (BBC) or *Dechrau Canu Dechrau Canmol* (S4C) have an enormous following. Furthermore, 'hymns and arias', to quote Max Boyce, are still the staple diet of spontaneous choirs at Welsh rugby internationals.

The paradox of Wales at the end of the twentieth century, therefore, seems to be that religion as a phenomenon, and indeed Christianity in particular, arouses widespread public interest at all levels in society, from philosophy seminars to community singing on the terraces, and yet there is a serious decline in the numbers of those committed to one or other of the main Christian denominations, with the exception of the Roman Catholic Church and some of the evangelical Protestant Churches.

Indeed, it is interesting to look briefly at the relative standing of the Churches in Wales today, both in relation to one another and in

Welsh Presbyterian Chapel – Capel y Groes, Wrexham, Clwyd.

relation to their own past performance. If we take the statistics for membership for 1905 provided by the Royal Commission and the evidence of membership in 1982 collected by MARC Europe the following picture emerges:

	1905	1982*
Church in Wales	193,081	137,600
Welsh Independents	175,147	65,200
Presbyterians (Calvinistic Methodists)	170,617	79,900
Baptists	143,835	50,200
(Wesleyan) Methodists	40,811	25,300
Other Protestant	19,870	35,300
Roman Catholic	64,800	129,600
Total all Churches	808,161	523,100

* MARC's figures are to the nearest hundred.

The strict accuracy of the 1982 figures has been challenged and cannot be guaranteed since, as the Report itself acknowledges, many of the figures are based on self-estimates by various Churches. Furthermore, their definitions of membership are not consistent and we may not be comparing like with like in each case. None the less, the statistics provide us with a useful rough guide and permit a number of general observations.

The more spectacular losses seem to have been sustained by the Welsh-speaking, 'reformed' Protestant denominations, particularly the Presbyterian Church of Wales (the old Calvinistic Methodists), the Union of Welsh Independents and the Welsh Baptist Union. Wesleyan Methodism was never in the same league as the others, but as a denomination the Methodists must look to the next century with alarm. Ironically, the disestablished Church in Wales, whose allegedly English and aristocratic orientation and position of financial privilege lay at the root of the Nonconformist discontent that fuelled the fires of the disestablishment campaign, has suffered less than its former rivals. Indeed, it is probably fair to conclude that the Church in Wales has in the event benefited from disestablishment. It has become more Welsh in its social and cultural, if not in its linguistic orientation, and considerably less elitist in its social and intellectual attitudes.

The 'new' Church in Wales is aptly personified in its present primate, Archbishop George Noakes, on his own admission hardly an intellectual (an Archbishop lacking the traditional Oxbridge pedigree) and the typical product of a modest Welsh-speaking home in rural Cardiganshire. The contrast between George Noakes and Wales's first Archbishop, Alfred George Edwards (Bishop of St Asaph, and elected Archbishop of the newly disestablished Church in Wales in 1920) is perhaps replicated in the very different personalities of Lord Crickhowell (formerly Nicholas Edwards, Secretary of State for Wales and a nephew of A. G. Edwards) and his fellow parliamentarian, Geraint Howells, that worthy son of the soil of Ceredigion.

Two points may perhaps be added about the decline in Welsh Nonconformity: first, that its rise owed so much to the emotionalism of the various revivals that in the end it lacked staying power and, secondly, that the inevitable consequence of the interdependence of the Welsh chapels and the Welsh language has been that any weakening in the influence of the one has precipitated the decline of the other.

The growth points of Christianity in the new Wales are to be identified at the two ends of the spectrum, in the urban rather than the rural areas and in the Anglicized parts of Wales. The Roman Catholic Church is now the spiritual home of a number of Welsh intelligentsia, following the lead of Saunders Lewis, and no longer exclusively dependent on families of Irish descent and other immigrant communities, such as the Polish community in Ceredigion. At the other end of the spectrum evangelical and charismatic forms of Christianity are attracting an increasing number of Welsh people disaffected with the apparent lifelessness of the main denominations. Again, the new United Reformed Church, created in 1972, now seems to be growing. Nor should we forget those who have deserted the institutional Churches to form house Churches of varying degrees of orthodoxy.

Perhaps the most significant response of the mainline denominations to their numerical decline has been their growing willingness to work together and the genuine and sincere desire of many of their leaders to look for a greater degree of unity and even union between them. The cynic might say that their numerical and financial weakness has driven the Churches to seek to recover some degree of strength in unity, but few could have predicted that within half a century of the end of the disestablishment campaign, with its sad legacy of bitterness and distrust, we would have a Council of Churches for Wales, followed a few years later by a Covenant on the part of some of the major protagonists to move towards full organic union.

The Council of Churches for Wales was formed in 1956 as an institutional Welsh expression of the influence of the world-wide ecumenical movement that brought the World Council of Churches into being in 1948 (the British Council of Churches, of which the Churches of Wales are members, also preceded the formation of the Council of Churches for Wales). In recent years the work of the Council of Churches has yielded two concrete results – the first exclusive to Wales and the second part of a British and Irish process of establishing new and more appropriate ecumenical instruments.

The commitment of the Church in Wales, the Methodist Church, the Presbyterian Church of Wales and the United Reformed Church to enter into a covenant to seek and eventually to arrive at organic union in 1975 had its origin in a recommendation of the British Council of Churches' Faith and Order Conference at Nottingham in 1964 that member Churches should covenant together to work and pray for union in appropriate groupings such as nations. The ten-year period of discussion between 1964 and January 1975 involved the Union of Welsh Independents and the Baptist Union as well as those Churches that eventually committed themselves to the Covenant, but apart from eleven individual Baptist congregations those Churches with a congregationalist order felt unable to enter into the Covenant. In 1975 the Covenanted Churches in Wales could boast that ecumenical co-operation had achieved a measure of success that had eluded their sister Churches in the other nations of the British Isles.

Unfortunately, the 1980s have seen little substantial progress despite the efforts of the Covenanting Commission and its dedicated Secretary, Noel Davies (also Secretary of the Council of Churches for Wales). A scheme for bringing the Covenanted Churches into a more formal union by reconciling Churches and ultimately ministries is now floundering and likely to be rejected. The Covenant seems to be a matter of sublime indifference to the ordinary churchgoer, and it has not been difficult for reactionary forces within the Covenanted Churches to stifle any serious attempt to make it work.

More promising have been the moves to extend the scope of the Council of Churches to include the Roman Catholic Church that can be traced to the visit of Pope John Paul II to Wales (and the rest of Britain) in 1982. These discussions have, in the main, concentrated on restructuring and ultimately replacing the British Council of Churches, and in its wake the Council of Churches for Wales, with a new ecumenical instrument. The year 1990 therefore brings the inauguration of *Cytun*, a new body incorporating not only the present member Churches of the Council, but the Roman Catholic Church as well. This is a highly significant development. Indeed, it is gratifying that as the twentieth century draws to a close the mainline Churches

in Wales are, for a variety of motives, some positive and some negative, achieving a greater degree of co-operation leading possibly to
union, when at the turn of the century Christians in Wales were
engaged in the bitter internecine warfare of the disestablishment
campaign. At the same time we should not forget that there are other
groups of Christians in Wales on the fringes of the mainline denominations, particularly in the conservative evangelical and Pentecos-
talist traditions, who will have no truck with ecumenism, and that
these fringe groups exhibit a vitality and growth not always found in
the older denominations.

Wales may no longer be a Christian country, but Christianity is
still the dominant religion, in so far as any religion is dominant. There
are in excess of 5,500 Christian places of worship in Wales, many of
them financial millstones around the necks of today's faithful,
whereas the growing Muslim community has as yet no more than
some ten to fifteen mosques. Many Christian congregations are now
small, and in the Welsh-speaking Churches getting smaller. However,
there is evidence of numerical growth and certainly a deeper commitment in the younger congregations in the Anglicized areas, particularly in the Roman Catholic Church, the Church in Wales and the
Baptist Churches. This may reflect a trend that is identifiable in other
areas of life in Wales today, namely that erstwhile differences in
attitude, custom and practice between Wales and England are now
becoming blurred. There is a distinct danger that the celebration of
the Quatricentenary of Bishop Morgan's Welsh translation of the
Bible, which did more than all else to preserve the Welsh language,
and the publication of *Y Beibl Cymraeg Newydd* (the New Welsh
Bible) in 1988 may yet prove to have been the last gasp of a distinctively Welsh form of Protestant Christianity. The decline of the Welsh
language and the trend towards uniformity encouraged by the mass
media have taken their toll on Welsh Christianity. Party strife and the
agonizing over making a decision on admitting women to the priest-
hood are threatening the unity of the Church in Wales in a manner
reminiscent of the internal wranglings of the Church of England. This
would be a shame since the Church in Wales, forcibly separated from
the Church of England in 1920, has achieved a remarkable degree of
coherence and self-confidence over the second part of this century.

In drawing this survey to a close we have to conclude that to all
outward appearances organized Christianity plays a far less significant part in the social, cultural and political life of Wales today than
it did at the turn of the century. Education and the media now fulfil
the cultural role of the chapel literary society. Many of the familiar

faces on Welsh television are children of the manse, whose fathers escaped from the drudgery of the coalface, the quarry and the farm into the respectability of the pulpit. For the next generation, however, this seems only to have been a temporary stepping-stone along the path of progress from the bosom of the rural and valley working class (*y werin*) to a place in the Welsh bourgeoisie of Cardiff suburbia. Similarly, the local and parliamentary politicians of Wales are now the products of the Polytechnic and the Trade Union rather than of the chapel Sunday school. No Bishop David Jenkins ruffles the feathers of the Welsh political establishment. In effect, the Christian Churches in Wales are in danger of becoming as marginalized in their native land as the immigrant religious communities that are now a feature of our pluralist society. More and more Wales is becoming a secularized

St David's Cathedral, Dyfed. The cathedral is named after David (Dewi), the patron saint of Wales, who lived in the sixth century. Work began on the cathedral late in the twelfth century and was not completed until 1522. The present cathedral is at least the third to be built at this location.

and rootless society. This, of course, presents an opportunity and a challenge to those who believe that they have a message that can bring meaning to the lives of those around them, but will that challenge be taken up?

Note
Statistics for Church membership in 1905 are derived from the *Report of the Royal Commission on the Church of England and other religious bodies in Wales and Monmouthshire*, 8 volumes, 1910, and for Church membership in 1982 from Peter Brierley and Byron Evans, *Prospects for Wales*, Bible Society and MARC Europe, 1983.

CHANGING
SOCIAL
CONDITIONS

C. C. HARRIS

THE author of this chapter is an Englishman, who 'came down' to Wales from London in 1959. He experienced, as many visitors to Wales did at this time, what can only be described as 'cultural shock'. The 'shock' – that is non-fulfilment of cultural expectations – had both an 'upside' and a 'downside'. We make sense of what we do not know by employing what we do know. Industrial Wales was thought of as a predominantly working-class area with employment chiefly in the traditional industries of steel-making and coal-mining. The expectation, therefore, was that south Wales would approximate to the East End of London with the docks being replaced by coal-mines and steelworks: drab, poverty-stricken, squalid and hidden by a perpetual pall of smoke. Instead my first reaction was that it was breathtakingly beautiful, despite the all too obvious scars inflicted on the landscape by the Industrial Revolution. The (relatively) low density of population and the magnificence of the terrain which it inhabited gave a sense of light and space far removed from the crowded and often severe image of traditional industrial areas.

That was the upside. The downside was that in terms of buildings and communications Wales still appeared to be in the nineteenth century, with works, factories and roads presenting vistas that would have been familiar to George Borrow. The overall impression was of a remote peripheral region, lacking modern amenities, with a low standard of living and poorly connected with the outside world.

The impression was misleading even then. It is true none the less to say that Wales has been transformed in the past thirty years, more especially in the last fifteen, so that it now presents an image which is far more consistent with that presented by other regions of Great Britain. Great strides have been made in repairing the ravages which industry had wrought on the environment of which the total transformation of the lower Swansea Valley, once the largest area of industrial dereliction in Britain, is perhaps the most notable example. The gaunt, grim, derelict works of the past have long gone to be replaced either by large modern plants or areas of light industry. The spoil heaps on the hillsides have been landscaped and grassed. The number of working mines has shrunk to a handful. Road construction of east–west routes, in both north and south, has reduced the distance by road between Wales and England, and rail journey times have fallen by two-fifths. Even the length of that most difficult of journeys, from south Wales to north Wales, has been reduced by a third as a result of a continuous improvement of trunk roads in mid Wales over a quarter of a century. The net result has been to create an area for which it can genuinely be claimed both that it is accessible and that its quality of life is greater than that experienced by those living and working in the south-east of Britain.

Up until the 1980s it was possible to present the history of post-War Wales as one of steady progress, with the gap between Welsh and British prosperity steadily narrowing. Unfortunately, Wales, and especially industrial Wales, was hit exceptionally hard by the recession of the 1980s. Because of the concentration of its employment among traditional industries most affected by the recession, it experienced high rates of unemployment (though these have fallen sharply since 1986), a loose labour market and a replacement of high wage jobs in traditional industries by lower paid jobs in service industries. The result has been a decline in average earnings from 97.2 per cent of the average weekly earnings for Great Britain in 1976 to 91.8 per cent in 1986. However the shift of emphasis from heavy industry to tourism has resulted in the continuation and even acceleration of the improvement in the lived environment in areas of traditional industry.

In terms of average male earnings the most prosperous areas of Wales are east Clwyd and South Glamorgan. West south Wales (chiefly West Glamorgan) is only just above the Welsh average. This pattern is substantially the same as that in 1976. In the last ten years, however, Gwent has fallen from just above to just below the Welsh average while South Glamorgan has substantially increased its relative advantage over the rest of Wales. Women's wages were 92.2 per cent of the British average in 1986 and showed little variation between the sub-regions.

Because in the past Wales has been an economically peripheral area, British national economic fluctuations have been magnified in Wales, leading to net outward migration to more prosperous areas in times of recession, classically in the 1930s. Until 1970 Wales was a net exporter of population. During the 1970s and 1980s both Gwent and West Glamorgan experienced substantial net loss of population through outmigration, as has Mid Glamorgan during the latter part of the period. South Glamorgan, however, which had suffered a small loss through migration in the 1970s became a small net importer of population in the 1980s. Wales as a whole, however, was a net importer of population in the 1970s, but its net gains from migration disappeared almost completely during the 1980s. This is not to say that inmigration ceased. On the contrary the gains made by continued inmigration were balanced in the 1980s by recession-induced outmigration. Continued inmigration is associated with areas outside industrial south Wales and appears to be connected with Wales's increasing attraction as a retirement area.

The importance of migration as a determinant of population change makes the prediction of population extremely hazardous. Current forecasts assume no net migration effect, which is certainly wrong but wise since accurate predictions require foresight as to the performance of the British economy and the relative position of Wales *vis-à-vis* other regions in the next twenty-five years. A 2 per cent growth in the Welsh population by 2001 is foreseen, with little change in the proportions of the population below and above working age. But Wales, as elsewhere, will experience a very significant increase in the number of the 'old' (as opposed to 'young') elderly, i.e. in the numbers aged over seventy-five.

The relative stability envisaged of both the population and the proportion formed by the employed masks wide divergences between the sub-regions. The populations of the sub-regions constituting rural Wales are forecast to grow by between 3 and 6 per cent. In industrial south Wales the population is likely to remain static, growth in South Glamorgan and Gwent masking a minor fall in Mid Glamorgan and substantial loss in West Glamorgan. Mid Glamorgan, Gwent and South Glamorgan experienced natural growth in the 1980s and this is likely to be reinforced by some migration growth in the last two areas, although in Mid Glamorgan growth will be cancelled by migration loss. In West Glamorgan migration loss will be added to natural loss. In all other areas migration gain will offset natural loss. The working population is forecast to form a high proportion of total population in Mid Glamorgan, Dyfed and South Glamorgan; Gwynedd's working population will fall below the Welsh average and remaining areas will approximate that average.

The population in 1986 comprised 1,035,300 households. The average size was 2.7, fractionally larger than the figure for Great Britain (2.6). A fifth of all households comprised only one person and a third two persons. The proportion of households of five or more people was under 10 per cent. Over time Wales, like Great Britain as a whole, has experienced a decline in the number of households of three or more and a rise in the number of small households. Particularly striking in recent years has been the rise in single-person households, which rose in Wales from 5 per cent in 1931 to 9 per cent in 1951 and by 1986 stood at 21 per cent. The rise in single-person households resulted from three circumstances: first the increase in the number of elderly in the population, a large proportion of which are widowed; second the increase in rising divorce rates; and lastly, the increasing tendency of young people on maturity to live independently of their parents.

As a result more than a quarter of all households are single-person households, or households comprising unrelated persons; nearly two-thirds are households of married couples with or without children and 8 per cent are lone-parent households. It is notable that only 0.8 per cent of all households include two or more families. In terms of household composition, the extended family, once thought to be a traditional Welsh arrangement, has almost disappeared. More generally, the distribution of household over type approximates to that for Great Britain as a whole.

In 1986, 57 per cent of all households had an economically active head. Of these 36 per cent were in skilled manual occupations, 21 per cent in semi- or unskilled occupations and 43 per cent in non-manual occupations. There is marked variation between sub-regions in the social status of households as measured by the occupation of the household head. Powys and South Glamorgan have the highest status household heads, followed by Gwynedd and Dyfed. Mid and West Glamorgan households have the lowest status household heads, while the most easterly counties of Clwyd and Gwent are characterized by a higher than average proportion of households with heads in skilled occupations. The low status of household heads in Mid and West Glamorgan is clearly related to selective outmigration and the high status of South Glamorgan heads is related to its ability to retain better qualified people and the number of white collar jobs available. The high or relatively high status of the rural counties of Powys, Gwynedd and Dyfed is due to the absence of job opportunities for unskilled workers and the size of the service sector. Both Gwent and Clwyd have above average proportions in manufacturing industry, which accounts for their having higher than average proportions of households with skilled heads.

Comparing not households but the average household, we find that household *income* in Wales is 10 per cent lower than in Great Britain. That is rather lower than one would expect from the earnings figures and is due to the higher rates of unemployment experienced by the Principality. The proportion of households headed by someone in full-time work in Wales was 6 per cent below that of the United Kingdom in the mid 1970s. By the mid 1980s it had fallen more sharply than the United Kingdom figure to only 37 per cent. The comparable UK figure was 45 per cent. The effect of the recession on Welsh household income sources is reflected in two ways. First the proportion of the income of the average household contributed by social security benefits rose to 18 per cent, a third higher than the proportion for the UK as a whole. On the other hand the 1980s witnessed an expansion of self-employment in Wales, self-employment contributing 8.2 per cent of the average household income, a proportion higher than that for the United Kingdom as a whole.

Household expenditure patterns are similar to those of the UK as a whole, with a slightly smaller proportion being spent on housing and services and fractionally more on other items. Possession of consumer durables also follows the UK pattern, though there are slightly fewer two-car households and 7 per cent fewer households have telephones.

A not unreasonable expectation after the Second World War was that Wales would have a very poor housing stock and one of the major tasks would be the clearance of unfit dwellings. Some slum clearance had already been undertaken by the Luftwaffe, especially in Swansea, but though Wales had a housing problem it was not, chiefly, that of slum clearance. Because of the availability of stone many Welsh houses were solidly constructed and durable. However, a great proportion had been constructed in the nineteenth century and in 1962, 52 per cent dated from before the First World War. So the problem was not of unfit dwellings but of large numbers lacking basic modern amenities. Though great strides have been made in improvement of the housing stock over the last forty years, it is still the case that 9 per cent of Welsh dwellings lack either a bath, inside WC or both. Such substandard properties are to be found most frequently in Mid and South Glamorgan and Dyfed. The two most easterly counties, Gwent and Clwyd, together with Gwynedd and West Glamorgan, have fewer substandard properties than the Welsh average, while Powys approximates it.

One of the causes of the improvement of the housing stock has been the increase in owner occupation, which has risen from 49 per cent in 1961 to 69 per cent in 1988. The incidence of owner occupation shows little variation between Welsh sub-regions. What does vary is the balance of remaining tenures between the public and private rented sectors. The proportion in the public sector is highest in West Glamorgan and Gwent, and lowest in rural Wales and, curiously, South Glamorgan. Mid Glamorgan approximates the Welsh average of 26 per cent. Substandard housing is concentrated in the private rented sector, with 30 per cent of furnished and 16 per cent of unfurnished properties being classified as substandard compared with only 3 per cent of owner occupied properties and 1 per cent of publicly owned dwellings. All categories of tenure showed improvement between 1981 and 1986 with the notable exception of the private rented sector.

Between 1950 and 1980 the average number of houses built per

annum went up by about 40 per cent, the proportion being built by
the private sector increasing from just over a quarter in the 1950s to
just under two-thirds in the 1970s. The private sector further increased its share of house building between 1981 and 1986 from 60 to
70 per cent. The average number of houses completed per annum in
this period fell sharply, however, by more than 50 per cent. In this,
Wales has followed the British national pattern, though in the Principality the fall in building activity as measured by the number of
houses per thousand population has been slightly more marked.

After the Second World War there was an absolute shortage of
housing as measured by the average number of people per dwelling.
The high rate of house building in the 1950s and 1960s abolished that
shortage, but two new problems immediately emerged. First, the rate
of household formation changed due to earlier marriage, increased
longevity and the rise in divorce rates and the resultant increase in the
number of lone-parent households. As a result of these changes the
number of dwellings required to house a population of any given size
increased. Secondly, because of the changing distribution of population, housing shortage was experienced in some areas where population growth outstripped building, while there was an excess of
housing in areas with declining populations. This second problem
exacerbated the first.

There was, however, a third problem. The increase in earnings in
prosperous core regions of Britain, combined with the declining quality of life associated with high population density, created a demand
for second homes in the periphery where population pressure on the
housing stock was less great, house prices lower, and the quality of
life better. The result was a classic example of the social disutilities
which can be produced by the free play of market forces. Price
differentials in housing did not lead to a beneficial redistribution of
population to the cheaper areas of Britain, since jobs were concentrated in the core areas. It led instead to an inflation of house prices in
peripheral areas as a result of the demand for properties from people
normally resident in core areas. Because of the difference in pur-
chasing power between second-home owners and the local population the result in some areas has been an increase in prices beyond
the capacity of local people, who have found themselves unable to
buy first homes in the area of their employment. The mismatch
between housing costs and earnings in these peripheral areas consti-
tutes an incentive to outmigration of native inhabitants, while the
purchase of second homes in such areas is an incentive to the inmigration of non-natives on retirement. The net result of price different-

Typical rows of terraced houses, Stanleytown, Rhondda, Mid Glamorgan.

ials between regions (when combined with earnings differentials) has been to increase yet further global demand for housing.

The number of households in Wales is expected to increase by 9 per cent between 1985 and 2001. South Glamorgan's households are expected to increase by 12 per cent. All other areas with above average predicted increases are in rural Wales. Gwent and Mid Glamorgan show only small expected increases and West Glamorgan none at all. It follows that increases in local demand for housing are likely to be highest in the very areas where there is competition from second-home owners and retirement-home purchasers, especially in Dyfed and Gwynedd.

The second-home problem is not peculiar to Wales. What is, however, is that Wales has a distinctive language and culture and its inhabitants have a strong sense of their identity as a separate people within the United Kingdom. Historically the most important sign of this identity has been the Welsh language, the only Celtic tongue to survive as a majority language well into the twentieth century. This century has seen a dramatic decline in the number of Welsh-speakers, due, at first, to the coming of universal education conducted through the medium of English and, later, to the associated influence of the mass media. By 1931 the proportion of the population aged three and over speaking Welsh had fallen to 37 per cent, by 1961 to 26 per cent and by 1981 to 19 per cent. The language is most spoken in western counties (Gwynedd, 61 per cent; Dyfed, 46 per cent) and least in Gwent, once Monmouthshire (2.5 per cent) and in eastern industrial south Wales (South Glamorgan, 6 per cent; Mid Glamorgan, 8 per cent), other areas approximating the Welsh national average.

In general the counties with the lowest proportion of Welsh-speakers are those which are most densely populated (between three and nine persons per hectare), while the counties with the highest proportion are those with the lowest densities (around 0.5 persons per hectare). There are two exceptions to this generalization. Powys (0.2 persons per hectare) has an average proportion of Welsh-speakers as does West Glamorgan (4.4 persons per hectare).

The south Wales linguistic distribution points up a very important circumstance. There are two quite distinct areas in industrial south Wales. Cardiff and the Vale of Glamorgan are historically areas of greatest penetration by non-Welsh *people*. The mining valleys (part of Mid Glamorgan) and the industrial areas of West Glamorgan and Llanelli area of Dyfed were the areas of the greatest penetration of foreign *capital*, which nevertheless employed a local labour force. These northern and western areas have retained a strong Welsh cultural identification marking them off from those parts of industrial south Wales to the south and east. The mid Wales situation reflects English penetration into rural areas, which was particularly marked in the (now) sparsely populated district of Radnor.

The relation between the distribution of population over language and density produces paradoxical consequences. The high Welsh-speaking area, though large in extent, contributes only 55 per cent of the half million of Welsh-speakers, while as many as 17 per cent reside in areas where the proportion speaking Welsh is 10 per cent or less. One key to the retention of the language is the provision of Welsh-medium education for children living in predominantly English-speaking areas. The other, of course, is preventing the out-flow of native Welsh-speakers from the Welsh heartlands of Gwynedd and Dyfed and their replacement (not merely by non-Welsh-speaking) but by non-*Welsh* second-home owners and retirees. The concern over this second issue is widely misunderstood both within and outside Wales. The Welsh have been, traditionally, an extremely hospitable people, and English settlers have contributed greatly to both Welsh prosperity and culture. The increasing hostility to non-Welsh residents in some parts of rural Wales is the result of a particular form of inmigration which does not add to a stable Welsh way of life but threatens its very basis.

Welsh culture, however central the language is, extends beyond it. In the last two hundred years it has come to be associated with a particular form of religious expression (discussed elsewhere in this volume). One of the emphases of this tradition has been upon the special character of Sunday and has been manifested in special legal provisions which provide for local option, on the basis of a ballot, as to whether the pubs should stay open on Sunday. When the provision was first introduced in 1959 the ballot resulted in the division of Wales into 'wet' and 'dry' areas. Since then the 'wet' has steadily expanded at the expense of the 'dry', to the delight of the tourist industry and the Licensed Victuallers Association and the chagrin of Welsh Nonconformist ministers. In truth there have always been two Wales: the beery, bawdy world of industrial south Wales of which Dylan Thomas is the best-known exponent, and the chapel-going, abstaining world which originated in the countryside but which for a hundred years preserved its distinctive attitudes and values in an industrial setting.

This polarization is confirmed by the statistics on Welsh drinking habits. Among its men, Wales has more heavy drinkers than Great Britain (29 per cent as opposed to 20 per cent) but also more abstainers and occasional drinkers (20 per cent as opposed to 16 per cent). Great Britain has more light and moderate drinkers (64 per cent compared with Wales's 51 per cent). Welsh women on the other hand are like British women only more so. In both populations there are only tiny proportions of moderate to heavy drinkers among women, but fewer Welsh women are frequent drinkers and more abstain altogether.

Welsh culture is also alleged to have resulted in greater emphasis being placed on education in Wales than elsewhere in Britain. Two quite distinct factors are of importance here. First is the significance of religion in emphasizing literacy because it afforded access to the Word of God written in God's own tongue, for as everyone knows, 'Welsh is the language of heaven'. The second concerns opportunities for social mobility. The failure of Wales to develop large towns meant a lack of occupations of the middling sort, somewhere between the landowner and entrepreneur on the one hand and the skilled manual worker on the other. The only avenues of social advancement out of the working class were provided by the liberal professions, particularly 'teaching and preaching'. Economic and social mobility thus came to be identified with educational mobility. This emphasis on education became, however, the culture's undoing. Wales could not absorb the teachers and preachers it produced, so that it exported its best people. Moreover, after 1901, the medium of education was English. To the loss of a proportion of each generation by outmigration was added, therefore, the Anglicization of those that remained.

The cultural stress on education earned Wales a reputation for educational achievement superior to that of England. This reputation is not warranted by current figures. A slightly smaller percentage of all Welsh school-leavers obtain three or more A-levels, and whereas those in England who leave with no qualifications number only 10 per cent, the Welsh percentage is 16.

There are wide variations between counties in these measures, but they are not in the expected direction. The most Welsh counties, Dyfed and Gwynedd, approximate the Welsh average in respect of the proportion with no qualifications, but have above average proportions obtaining A-levels, a distinction they share with their cultural opposite, South Glamorgan. Mid Glamorgan has a staggering 27 per cent leaving school without qualifications. No other area approaches this figure, the nearest being that of, of all counties, South Glamorgan with 19 per cent. All other areas, except Clwyd, approximate the (high) Welsh average proportion of leavers without qualifications. The Clwyd figure of 8 per cent betters the English average.

Educational success at both the top and bottom of the achievement range is not the result of cultural factors alone, but also of the hierarchy of social and economic advantage and disadvantage or what is popularly called social class. This explains the poor showing of Mid Glamorgan, which includes some of the worst areas of disadvantage in Wales. It likewise explains the A-level successes in South Glamorgan. The failure to achieve a lower rate of leavers without qualifications by the counties of the Welsh heartland, in spite of A-level success, reflects the distinctive Welsh division between the abstemious, ambitious 'people of the chapel', and the happy-go-lucky 'people of the pub'. This distinction, though strongly related to material advantage and disadvantage, is not identical with it. It is a distinction that operated, and still operates to some extent, within the working class, and among 'the people', rather than being a distinction between a lower class and a higher one.

Another image associated with the Welsh is that of the adult student, slaking his thirst for knowledge while earning his living. This is really a nineteenth-century rather than a distinctly Welsh image. Nevertheless there is a strong cultural tradition in Wales which regards higher education as proper to the people, rather than being the privilege of the élite. This was the sentiment that underlay the establishment of the University of Wales. The rate of university students per

100,000 population for Wales was 63 in 1986, the higher rates being provided in South Glamorgan (96), Gwynedd (78) and Dyfed and West Glamorgan (65 and 68). Predictably Mid Glamorgan had the lowest participation rate (43). Approximately two-fifths of Welsh university students studied at an institution in Wales. The choice of subject of Welsh students varied little from the British average, but at the postgraduate level they exhibited a distinct preference for education, languages and literature, a culturally predictable result.

The demise of the sixth form in Wales complicates the statistics for students in further and higher education, since many sixteen to eighteen year olds now study in these institutions. If we ignore the under eighteen, for the 18–20 age group, which corresponds approximately to that of university students, the participation rate in 1986 was 188 per thousand for men and 141 per thousand for women. Adult education rates were 18 per thousand for both sexes. Participation on both sides of the boundary line has increased in the last ten years and it is probable that that increase will continue into the 1990s.

In the popular imagination, if a Welshman is not praying, drinking or learning then he is thought likely to be playing or watching Rugby football. A quarter of all men over fifteen regularly participate in outdoor games, compared with only 7 per cent of women. Other outdoor pursuits attracted a similar proportion of men and 13 per cent of women, a quarter of both sexes participating in indoor games. Mid Glamorgan is best provided with swimming-pools and with sports halls without pools although Gwent and Gwynedd head the table in the category of sports halls without pools. West Glamorgan, however, is the county with the best provision of outdoor sports facilities, the number having doubled between 1982–3 and 1986–7. The distinctiveness of West Glamorgan in this respect is no accident. Of all the Welsh counties it has been the one most challenged by the restructuring of industry in the 1980s and is in the process of transforming itself into a tourist area.

In Wales, as in Britain, the rise in the educational level of the population, the increase in the quality and choice provided by the mass media, greater geographical mobility and decline in household size have all resulted in a more privatized life style centred on the family household with the resultant decline in attendance at public entertainments. In 1988 only 4 per cent had attended a pop concert in the preceding month, only 5 per cent a theatre and 9 per cent a cinema or participated in indoor sports. However, 11 per cent had attended a musical event and 22 per cent some outside sport. While these figures

An enthusiastic crowd watch the Schweppes Cup semi-final between Neath and Swansea at the National Stadium.

give some support to the traditional 'choirs and rugby' image of the Welsh their chief significance lies elsewhere. Pop concerts, cinemas and indoor sports are more favoured by young people; 'other musical events' are more popular among those over thirty-five, while outdoor sport attracts a high percentage of supporters at all ages up until fifty-five. The Welsh musical tradition is strongest among older generations, but the sporting tradition remains strong. Indeed it has been argued that Rugby is the one true Welsh national religion, a form of piety inexplicably omitted by the author on the chapter on religion.

It is salutary to compare the figures for public entertainment, struggling up from 4 per cent to the mid twenties, with that for home entertainment. The proportion of households having video recorders is a staggering 66 per cent while even the proportion with home computing (24 per cent) rivals that of people attending outdoor sports.

It is sometimes said that Britain despite its small size encompasses greater variety of terrain than any other country in the world. The physical terrain of Wales is also remarkably varied, the grandeur of Snowdonia, the Berwyns and the Brecon Beacons contrasting with the rocky coasts of south-west Wales and the rolling hills of Carmarthenshire and mid Wales with the almost 'English' pastoral landscapes of the Vale of Glamorgan and Gwent. More remarkable still, however, is its social and cultural diversity. This makes it impossible both for the sociologist, fond of generalizations, and for the poet, seeking to snare reality in a phrase, to capture the essence of a quite unique place and people. Dylan Thomas, no more myopic than most people, but no less so, writes of wild Wales full of choirs and rugby teams and steeple hats which lay beyond the little piece of the Welsh kaleidoscope which he knew and loved. It is, of course, nonsense. The rest of Wales can no more be summed up in this way than the whole of England north of Watford Gap. Each part of the Principality has its own peculiar combination of distinctively Welsh factors which drive statisticians to despair and challenge the imaginative powers and cultural sympathies of the sociologist.

Dylan wrote of Swansea that it 'had as many layers as an onion and each one could reduce you to tears'. Had he known his native land better he would have extended this insight to the whole of Wales – and recognized that it was precisely this quality which made Swansea Welsh. What do tears signify? Are they tears of joy or of sorrow? In this post-modern age, both. Joy that Wales has put the deprivations and sufferings of the past behind her; sorrow that they are to be rediscovered amidst its late twentieth-century prosperity. Joy that the dirt and the sweat and the danger of coal-mining have all but gone; sorrow at the passing of a way of life built round mining, and the failure to find substitute sources of employment. Joy that the decline of the language has been halted among native inhabitants; sorrow that new forms of English settlement are language unfriendly. Joy that basic industries like steel have recovered from the recession; sorrow that this recovery has meant fewer not more job opportunities. Gratitude that European membership has attracted badly needed funds to Wales; fear that Britain's peripherality will mean that Wales will become the periphery of the periphery.

Wales, like the rest of Britain, participates in the ambiguity of the post-modern age as symbolized by the clean modern high-tech but now environmentally unfriendly and threatening nuclear plants at Wylfa and Trawsfynydd, and by the sleek new works of the British Steel Corporation at Shotton (demolished), Velindre (closed) and Margam and Llanwern once the symbols of employment but now associated firmly with redundancy. Yet Wales remains, in spite of the changes and chances of this fleeting world peculiarly itself, in the post-modern world but not of it. It would be a brave person who attempted to define wherein the distinctiveness lies. But it is not unconnected with a deep and abiding sense of the particularity of places, so that paradoxically the Welsh are united in the profound recognition of their differences.

THE INCOMER'S VIEW

DAVID WATERSTONE

MY feelings about Wales have suffered something of a roller-coaster ride. On arrival, a shock of pleasant surprise took me to the top of the first crest from where, for a brief moment, the view seemed to be superb. Then came the stomach-churning crash down the succeeding slope as one bad impression followed another and the temptation to get off the ride and go home became almost overwhelming. Then, with greater knowledge and understanding, came the realization that these depressing characteristics represented only one face of a complex character which, when viewed in different aspects or different lights, developed attractive strengths. So life since then has been a long climb up another incline to brighter things. Am I again at a crest where a new discovery or a twist in circumstances can throw me down a long slope?

Of course, when I came to Wales six years ago, I had all the prejudices of an ignorant non-Welshman. Years in the steel industry, with the occasional dash up and down to a steel mill or to a steel fabricating plant in the Valleys (which I had to close in very depressing circumstances), should have taught me better, but it did not. The mind's eye is a poor observer and retains its pictures often in spite of all the evidence. In my mind's eye, the Valleys were all of Wales and the Valleys were full of short, dark men standing between the black spoil heaps, singing bravely in spite of the drizzle. But the job seemed interesting and, for various reasons, I needed a change, so I packed my bags.

My London friends did nothing to provide encouragement: the usual reaction on hearing news of the decision was one of sympathy, as if they had heard I had lost a relative or caught some dreadful disease. It was not difficult therefore for the experience of arrival to produce a sharp change of mood. The train was on time, the sun shone, and it took only a few days to discover that Cardiff was a very pleasant city with all the amenities of a capital without the discomforts caused by the inhuman scale of larger cities. It took me several days to find a coal-mine, let alone a spoil heap: people seemed much as they were elsewhere. Even if my first business lunch took an unscheduled three hours and involved sitting through several speeches, well that was only a charming confirmation that the spirit of Dylan Thomas still lived and that in Wales there were values that we had lost in the mindless rush of London.

I knew before I arrived that the organization which I was joining was in a mess and that the economy with which it was supposed to be dealing was in an even more distressing state. So confirmation that both these things were true was no reason in itself for the slide down the slope of the roller-coaster. However, what was almost over-whelming was the mood that was prevalent in Wales. I am a Scot, and I suppose I share something of the arrogance of my countrymen in believing that we are equal to circumstances and better than most people, in particular better than the English. This belief is probably nonsense but it accounts for most of the successes and a good many of the failures that happen in Scotland. Anyway, I found it difficult to adjust to an attitude towards circumstances which could only be described as defeatist and an attitude towards England which could only be described as subservient. The two things went hand in hand. If times were bad, they were only likely to get worse unless 'they' did something about it and what could a poor Welshman do but mourn the passing of a much-loved way of life? The only satisfaction seemed to be in totting up the disasters and in choosing ever-darker hues with which to paint the scene. Everyone seemed to be at it, whether private citizens, politicians or newspaper and television practitioners. I had never met a people so apparently intent on talking themselves down into terminal disaster.

From where did this attitude come? From a long history of unequal union with England, said my new friends. From the centuries of exploitation of the Welsh people and the riches of the Welsh earth by incoming English entrepreneurs. It was said that the Welsh them-selves had a poor head for business and disliked taking risks. The Welsh had a Celtic ease with music, poetry and learning, and a Celtic inability to work with one another. It stood to reason that in a crisis the leadership had to come from outside, that 'they' would have to supply the resources which the Welsh needed to survive out of the vast store that they had stolen from Wales in the past.

How much of this self-image was true and how much illusion? The union with England is, of course, a fact and, compared with the relationship between Scotland and England, it is far more all-absorbing, with Scotland still having distinctively separate institutions. Perhaps this is because of the greater disparity between the size of the two units involved or perhaps it is simply because the unity in Wales and England happened far sooner. England is certainly the dominant partner. But not too much should be made of this point. After all, since Tudor times at least, Welshmen have been prominent in British politics and it could be argued that Wales has as much ruled as been ruled. If at times the Welsh Office governing apparatus seems less of an expression of national individuality, on the lines of the Scottish Office, than an expression of vice-regal rule transmitting power from elsewhere, then that is as much a reflection on the people of Wales as it is on the intentions of the central government – a nation is to a large extent defined by its institutions.

For a non-Welshman at least, the concept of Wales is surprisingly difficult to grasp. It is no accident that one of the most readable books of Welsh history is entitled *When Was Wales*. In it Professor Gwyn Alf Williams describes at length the constantly shifting patterns of loyalties which coalesced and dissolved to shape and reshape Wales up to relatively recent times. And yet, it is unquestionably there. The story, shocking to a newcomer, that even in this century children were punished for speaking Welsh, speaks volumes for the power of the feelings involved: the surviving power of Welshness shown by people's bothering to repress it and the power of the sense of inferiority to the English culture in that it was felt necessary to suppress Welshness in order to get on.

In Wales's historical patterns of shifting loyalties, one can trace elements of a tribal culture which can still be discerned today. As the roller-coaster of my feelings about Wales went down into the gloom, I could only see the small-mindedness and the inability to strive together for a wider good, which can make working in public life such a dispiriting and fruitless endeavour. But, and here my roller-coaster started to rise up into the sunlight again, it has its strong and positive sides as well.

I was truly amazed when for the first time I heard a grown man talk about himself as a 'Neath boy'. He was a very fully-grown man, too, probably the wrong side of eighty, and rubbed in the point by reckoning up by name the alumni of his primary school, recalling their fates and gleefully calculating that another hard winter would kill the last two off and leave him as the sole survivor! I have lived all my life amongst people who wandered all over the world, being born in one place, working in several others and dying in yet another. This attachment to place, the *bro*, and to the sense of life that emanates from it struck me powerfully and I now know it to be very characteristic of the Welsh. If it has the bad effects that I have indicated, it also provides a strong foundation for a particular and deeply-felt patriotism. With such a driving force behind it, a nation can achieve much.

Institutions to harness this drive are not easy to devise because, if they are to be successful, they cannot impose but must be flexible enough to allow the proper expression of this attachment to place. Perhaps the recently formed Institute of Welsh Affairs, with its emphasis on canalizing the voluntary efforts of people of all kinds towards the consideration of national issues, points a way forward.

Another aspect of this original tribal society which can be still discerned today is the exceptional part which persuasion has to play in leadership in Wales. Ancient Welsh history is full of stories of how the tribes would listen to and debate problems and the views of their leaders before agreement was reached on a decision. I do not think it is altogether fanciful to see traces of the same sort of thing in modern industrial society. Anyone with a background in steel knows what an appalling reputation the Welsh plants used to have. It was only when the managers realized that by bringing the units down to a small enough size where managers could seriously communicate with the men and could discuss the needs and problems of the business with them, did this reputation change and the excellent results now being achieved by the steel industry emerge. I believe that the stunning success being achieved by Japanese companies in Wales is to a large extent dependent on the fact that the communicative, consensus style of management comes naturally to the Japanese and to the Welsh work-force alike. The results are undeniable and magnificent.

What, then, of the Welsh self-view that they are not entrepreneurs? Given that the kind of people who first sold me this line were mostly very prosperous middle-class Cardiff professional businessmen whose families had dragged themselves out of obscure poverty in the mines in the short space of a generation or possibly two, the proposition that the Welsh do not succeed in business seemed inherently unlikely. A walk across the hills round Nant-y-glo and Bryn-mawr with Trevor Rowson demonstrated unequivocally that such a proposition could not have been true and, incidentally, underscored one of the other underlying likeable strengths in Welsh life.

Trevor is the Ebbw Vale local historian. He is a former steelworker, unemployed in all the long years since the major part of the Ebbw Vale plant closed down. If Trevor bothers to read this, I am sure he will not mind my saying that if your picture of the historian is of the tall, slim aesthetic, then he does not measure up. Stocky and wild-maned as a mountain pony, he likes a pint of beer as most Welshmen do, but also has in full measure the Welshman's respect for culture and learning which is such an attractive, positive force. Without the benefit of formal education, of which his luck gave him but little, he knows as much about the archaeology and industrial political history of the region, and of its national and international ramifications, as any other man and more than most.

In a fascinating Saturday ramble over the hills, we seemed to have run the gamut of Welsh history from the fossilized collapsed sand dunes of the prehistoric sea-shore, through biblical texts carved into the rocks by a born-again upholsterer driven to recall God's word in his rare spare time, through massive evidence of the early industrial development of Wales in the shape of old lime kilns, padstones, tramways, inclines, furnaces, and the fortified iron tower house of the ironmaster, whose idea of labour relations was to discharge a musket through a loophole in his front door at the workers outside. Through Trevor's great learning I was able to glimpse something of the turmoil, energy, cruelty, and sheer magnitude of achievement of the early industrial times. It is true that a good number of the industrial chieftains were English, or Scots, or something else other than Welsh – this whole region was, after all, a seething Klondike, attracting people from all over Europe at least. But if many names were not Welsh, it is quite inconceivable that the Welsh themselves were simply bystanders, and not participators, in this enormous outburst of energy. It is also true that for a relatively short period from the beginning of this century the Welsh seemed to have directed themselves towards secure lives in things like teaching and the gentler professions. But this was possibly in reaction to the gross insecurities and dangers of the foregoing period, and there seems to me no evidence that the Welsh are any less inclined or able than any other group of people to strive for success in business and, indeed, there is plenty of evidence to the contrary.

Over the last six years, it has been a privilege to witness and, in a small way to participate in, an enormous change in Welsh affairs. It is true that a great deal remains to be done. If there is ever an acceptable level of unemployment, the level in Wales is clearly quite unacceptable. The level of disposable personal income per head is nearly the lowest in the United Kingdom and it cannot be said that we have a truly prosperous and successful society until this has been altered. Looking ahead, it may be that another problem is emerging in that the dynamics of modern industry are tending to create more jobs for women than they do for men and steps will have to be taken to ensure that male employment is also resilient. But the great change is that we now seem to have the means for dealing with the problems because the spirit of determination and risk-taking that drove the industrial expansion of the last century seems to have returned.

The Welsh tendency to talk down their own achievements can still be seen but whereas, six years ago, no self-respecting reporter would spend time on good news when bad was available, it seems now that the preference is reversed. The impact on public morale is palpable. Almost anything can be proved with economic statistics, often by using the very simple device of changing the start date of a series. But a combination of statistics and one's own observation of what is happening provide convincing evidence that something has changed.

It is important to emphasize that the cause has not been the arrival of the Japanese or any other foreign group in Wales. Inward investment is important and provides jobs and often introduces new processes and management techniques. This is welcome and often politically eye-catching but the effect must be kept in perspective. Less than 7 per cent of the work-force is employed in foreign-owned firms in Wales. The engine of recovery in the Welsh economy in fact lies in the resurgence and diversification of the Welsh small and medium business sector. From a somewhat low position in the tables, Wales has now become one of the high scorers in the formation of new companies, and one of the highest also in the levels of self-employment. Entrepreneurship is alive and well in Wales and, with it, prosperity and the good things of life can be won. The population of Wales is beginning to grow again, not least because people are being attracted back to Wales by the prospect of success.

But if a few years back we were suffering from an illusion of failure and despair, are we about to replace it with another illusion of success? Is the roller-coaster about to go crashing downhill again? I do not think so, but care and effort will be required to make sure it does not. On the wall of my office hangs an original Gren cartoon. It shows an archetypal south Wales mam, leaning on a broom and directing a visiting motorist. The caption reads, 'Straight on to the proposed helicopter pad, right at the proposed monorail terminal, left at the proposed six-star hotel, and the Bracchi's on your left'. The cartoon bites home: it is easy to plan and more difficult to achieve. The strengths inherent in Wales and the Welsh character will be tested to the full in the coming years and it is, perhaps, now time to reconsider the framework within which these strengths and energies can be brought to bear. It does seem to me that the necessary self-confidence is beginning to emerge in Wales and certainly the sense of nationhood is struggling for expression. Surely it is better to regard this as a source of energy from which we can draw strength rather than a threat?

A nation is defined by its institutions, and language is one of these. Whether one is a Welsh-speaker or not, we ought to be able to see the Welsh language not merely as a source of cultural enrichment, though it is that, but also as a source of vigour and cultural individuality. I have the impression that at the level of schools at least, the language is beginning to experience a very welcome revival. Anyone who has been to the Royal National Eisteddfod must be impressed by ordinary people's sheer enjoyment of the event and of the creativeness that it represents. It seems to be, and one hopes will always remain, a great distance from the dead end of the cottage burnings and letter bombings.

Elsewhere, the Welsh National Opera is a magnificent success. The Welsh press and television are full of vigour. Do we need to think again about Welsh government institutions? What seems to be a new energy in Wales is matched in the United Kingdom as a whole as a growing realization that, in terms of politics and economics, the nation is over-centralized on the south-east and that this represents a major danger to future political, social and economic development. Undoubtedly there will be reconsideration of the question of a Welsh Assembly. The advocates will argue that it would be a proper expression of a new and growing self-confidence and creative self-provision.

I do not know whether the roller-coaster will continue to go up or whether it will crash down again. But I do know that I do not want to move and am happy if my gypsy days end right here.

CONTRIBUTORS

David Cole was editor of the *Western Mail*, editorial director of Thomson Regional Newspapers then chief executive and chairman of that group, chairman of the Press Association, a director of Reuters, chairman of Thomson Books, chairman and chief executive of Thomson Information Services, and deputy managing director of International Thomson plc. He is currently chairman of Western Mail and Echo Ltd, the Civic Trust for Wales and The Thomson Foundation, and a trustee of Reuters.

Allen Williams was educated at Abersychan Grammar Technical School and University College of Wales, Aberystwyth where he graduated in economics in 1971. Following a career in sales and marketing with a number of companies, he joined the Welsh Development Agency in 1978. In 1988 he was appointed regional director for the Valleys, managing the WDA's contribution to the 'Valleys Programme'. He has recently been appointed chief executive of the Mid Glamorgan Training and Enterprise Council.

Roland Brooks has been agricultural editor of the *Western Mail* for thirty years and has written extensively about farming in Wales, Britain and Europe. He is a fellow and past chairman of the Guild of Agricultural Journalists.

Gwynfor O. Davies was development director and later director of corporate and external affairs with the Wales Tourist Board from 1979 to 1988. He is now a consultant and has recently set up CELTS – Communications, Enterprise, Leisure, Tourism Specialists – a company which aims to carry out promotional and development activities associated particularly with Wales and Scotland.

Geoffrey Inkin was educated at Dean Close School, RMA Sandhurst, Staff College Camberley and the Royal Agricultural College Cirencester. From 1983 to 1986 he was chairman of the Cwmbran Development Corporation. He has been chairman of the Land Authority of Wales since 1986 and of Cardiff Bay Development Corporation since 1987.

Gwyn Griffiths is a chartered civil engineer. He was educated at Brecon Boys' Grammar School and University College, Swansea. In

1977 he joined the Welsh Development Agency and has been director of Land Reclamation Wales since 1984.

Dale Owen is an architect and planner. He studied at the Welsh School of Architecture, Cardiff, the School of Planning, London and as a Smith-Mundt and Fulbright scholar at M.I.T. and Harvard. He worked with Walter Gropius in the USA, with Sir William Holford in London and on the new towns of Crawley and Cwmbran before joining Sir Percy Thomas at Cardiff in 1958, becoming a partner in the practice in 1964. He has been responsible for the design of a number of award-winning buildings, several relating to his planning and urban design work.

He has been president of the Society of Architects in Wales, a Council member of the RIBA and serves on several Institute committees as well as national and local organizations concerned to improve the quality of our built environment. Recently retired as the senior Welsh partner of Percy Thomas Partnership he continues in practice as a private consultant.

David Parry-Jones was educated at Cardiff High School and Merton College Oxford where he read Greats, played Rugby for the University and gained an Authentic at cricket. Before becoming a television director with the BBC he worked for the *Western Mail* and *The Sunday Times*. He has also worked as principal presenter on programmes including Wales Today, Sports Line Up and Weekend Rugby Union. From 1967 to 1974 David Parry-Jones was Welsh Rugby correspondent for *The Times* and is currently a correspondent for the *Sunday Mirror*. He has published eleven books on Rugby football.

John Petts has been described as the doyen of creative artists in Wales today, and also the most versatile designer-craftsman in Britain. For over forty years he has worked in the varied fields of painting, sculpture, engraving mosaic and stained glass. Founding the Caseg Press in the 1930s he established a reputation as a wood-engraver; he has also illustrated books for the Golden Cockerel Press. In recent years he has concentrated on commissions for stained glass, enriching buildings on both sides of the Atlantic. His interest in the use of words has made him known as a lucid speaker and broadcaster.

Mike Baker is a graduate of the University of Wales. He worked in the professional theatre and in drama in education before joining the

Welsh Arts Council in 1979. As drama officer he was responsible for the policy unique to Wales which has established a full-time professional company in every Welsh county to service schools and smaller communities. He has recently been appointed to the post of drama director of the Welsh Arts Council.

Geraint Lewis was a junior scholar at the Welsh College of Music and Drama, subsequently reading music at St John's College, Cambridge. He lectured at the University College of North Wales under Professor William Mathias, before joining the music staff of BBC Wales where he continues to work frequently on radio and television. In 1988 he was appointed to the music department of Nimbus Records. In 1983–5 he was invited to edit an eightieth birthday celebration for Sir Michael Tippett. He is currently writing the authorized biography and study of Alun Hoddinott.

Deborah Cole has worked as a journalist for the *Illustrated London News*, the *South Wales Evening Post* and the *South Wales Echo* – writing a pop music column in both Welsh newspapers – and the *Western Mail*. She is now press information and public relations officer at the National Museum of Wales.

R. Gerallt Jones is currently warden of the University of Wales, Gregynog, Powys. He read English at the University College of North Wales and has since worked as a lecturer in English and in education, principal of a college of education in Jamaica, warden of Llandovery College, a full-time writer, and a senior tutor at University College of Wales, Aberystwyth. One of the most prolific of contemporary Welsh writers, R. Gerallt Jones has published poetry, novels and works of criticism. In 1982 he was elected chairman of the Welsh-language section of The Welsh Academy.

David Skilton was educated at King's College, Cambridge. He lectured at the University of Glasgow prior to his appointment as professor and head of the department of English at the University College of St David's Lampeter, and later at the University of Wales Institute of Science and Technology. He is now head of the School of English Studies, Journalism and Philosophy at the University of Wales College of Cardiff. He is general editor of the Trollope Society/ Folio Society edition of the writer's novels, and author of *Anthony Trollope and His Contemporaries* and *Defoe to the Victorians: two centuries of the English novel.*

R. Brinley Jones was educated at University College Cardiff and Jesus College Oxford. He has been, successively, an RAF education officer, a schoolmaster, a university lecturer, director of the University of Wales Press and warden of Llandovery College. Currently, he is a member of the Board of the British Council and a member of the Broadcasting Standards Council. His main research interests have been in the history of education and in the history of the language and literature of Wales.

David Protheroe Davies is deputy principal and dean of theology at St David's University College, Lampeter. He is the author of several books and numerous articles on the New Testament, the theology of liberation and the interaction of church and society. He has served on a number of bodies within the Church in Wales, the Council of Churches for Wales and the British Council of Churches. He is also a frequent contributor to radio and television, as well as being a member of the panel of Religious Advisers of the IBA and of the Central Religious Advisory Committee of the BBC and IBA.

C.C. Harris is professor of sociology at University College of Swansea. His publications include *The Family and Social Change* and *Redundancy and Recession in South Wales*.

David Waterstone was educated at Tonbridge and St Catharine's College Cambridge. Following a career in the diplomatic service, he joined the British Steel Corporation in 1971 and was executive chairman of BSC chemicals from 1977 to 1981. He has been chief executive of the Welsh Development Agency since 1983.

ACKNOWLEDGEMENTS

The publishers gratefully acknowledge the permission of Western Mail and Echo Ltd. to use many of the illustrations reproduced in this book. Acknowledgement is also due to the following:

Terance Soames (23, 72, colour section 2 (bottom left)); Celtic Picture Agency (29, 44, 50, 51); Nicholas Lampkin (32); Wales Tourist Board (35, 36, 37, 38 (top), 39, 42, 45, 47, 54, 55, 58, 226, colour section 3 (bottom), 4 (top and bottom)); Cardiff City Council (60); Welsh Development Agency (64, 65); Dale Owen (71, 73, 85, colour section 2 (top right and left)); Development Board for Rural Wales (74); Brian Middlehurst and Percy Thomas Partnership (75); Ken Kirkwood and Richard Rogers Architects (78); WHCSA (80); UMT Architects (84); South Glamorgan County Council (87); Kyffin Williams and the Board of Trustees of the NMGM (97); Estate of Ceri Richards and Welsh Arts Council (99); Sara John (100); the Trustees of the Estate of David Jones and the Tate Gallery (102); Will Roberts, private collection (104); Arthur Giardelli and the Tate Gallery (105); Michael Flynn (106); Jack Crabtree (107); Peter Prendergast and the Tate Gallery (108); Ivor Roberts-Jones, Welsh Arts Council collection and Chris Ridley (110); Friedemann Simon (113); HTV Wales (114 (top), 139, 142, 143); S4C (114 (bottom), 146, 183, 184); Gerallt Llewellyn (118); Phil Cutts (120); Tony Standley (121); BBC (128, 130 (bottom)); John Ross (136); Ken Smith (137); Phillip Hall (145); Jeffrey F. Morgan (149); Welsh Arts Council (151 (top and bottom), 152, 156); Welsh Books Council (152); Susan Butler (158); Mudiad Ysgolion Meithrin (199); National Youth Orchestra (200); United World College, St Donat's (204); Bowen Dann Davies (212); Royal Commission on Ancient and Historical Monuments in Wales (217); John Elwyn (colour section 1 (top)); John Petts (colour section 1 (bottom left)); William Powell Wilkins (colour section 1 (bottom right)); Gwynedd County Council (colour section 2 (bottom right)); Royal Welsh Agricultural Show and Tecgwyn Jones (colour section 3 (top)).

Every attempt has been made to contact copyright holders. Any queries should be referred to the publishers.